The Romagnolis'

Italian Fish Cookbook

The Romagnolis'
Italian Fish Cookbook

A LARGE EMBRACE AND A LIGHT TOUCH

Margaret and G. Franco
Romagnoli

HENRY HOLT AND COMPANY   NEW YORK

Henry Holt and Company, Inc.
Publishers since 1866
115 West 18th Street
New York, New York 10011

Henry Holt ® is a registered
trademark of Henry Holt and Company, Inc.

Published in Canada by Fitzhenry & Whiteside Ltd.,
195 Allstate Parkway, Markham, Ontario L3R 4T8.

Library of Congress Cataloging-in-Publication Data

Romagnoli, Margaret.
The Romagnolis' Italian Fish Cookbook : a large embrace and a light touch /
Margaret and G. Franco Romagnoli.—1st ed.
p.   cm.
Includes index.
1. Cookery (Fish).   2. Cookery, Italian.   I. Romagnoli, G. Franco.
II. Title.
TX747.R66   1994
641.6′92—dc20   93-21633
                                                                CIP

ISBN 0-8050-2526-X

Henry Holt books are available for special promotions and
premiums. For details contact: Director, Special Markets.

First Edition—1994

BOOK DESIGN BY CLAIRE NAYLON VACCARO

Printed in the United States of America
All first editions are printed on acid-free paper. ∞

1 3 5 7 9 10 8 6 4 2

Acknowledgments

It would be hard to mention all the helpful hands across the ocean involved in this book. However, not to name a half dozen friends on each side would not be fair. Here is a brief list of those who spent a nice bit of time and thought to guide us in the right direction.

Alfredo Bernardi, owner of Filippino Restaurant, Lipari, Italy;

William P. Castelli, M.D., director of the Framingham Heart Study, Framingham, Massachusetts;

Stephen H. Connolly, chairman of Steve Connolly Seafood Company, Boston, Massachusetts;

Caterina Conti, owner of Hotel Giardino sul Mare, Lipari, Italy;

Kenelm W. Coons, executive director of the New England Fisheries Development Association, Boston, Massachusetts;

Giorgio Luzzietti, Rome, Italy;

Ralph Musto, fish buyer for Star Markets, Boston, Massachusetts;

Gail Perrin, former food editor of the *Boston Globe*, Boston, Massachusetts;

Fred Stavis, Stavis Seafood, Boston, Massachusetts;

Nancy Stuzman, School of Agriculture, Extension Division, University of Massachusetts, Waltham, Massachusetts;

Allison Wheeler, associate director of communications, National Fisheries Institute, Arlington, Virginia;

Dottore Aldo Volpi, Milano, Italy.

Contents

Introduction

As a couple, we have lived, raised four children, and worked in both America and Italy. Franco, a cinematographer, and I met in Rome where I was on assignment as a Marshall Plan information officer. After learning the language, I delved deep into the cuisine, never to resurface fully again. The first dish of those days that comes to mind instantly is *baccalà fritto*: salt cod fillets touched with the miracle of a great batter, deep-fried, and served with a nondemanding white wine from the Roman Hills. Franco wisely had proposed them as an alternative to the "cosmopolitan embassy circuit fare" to which I was accustomed, and that was all that particular little eatery we frequented ever had on its unprinted menu. More intensive dining followed, but he never made a big deal of the fact that local cuisine was not only more interesting but also more attuned to his postwar finances. I became a convert to Italian food, especially to fish as prepared by fine Italian hands.

As an American bride, I learned the Italian way to cook from Rina, a devoted cook who stayed with me for five years, from Franco's mother, and from a large circle of Italian friends.

We moved to Massachusetts from Rome in 1955 with our two older sons. It was an eye-opener of a change for our household: American produce (year-round everything), my adjusting to doing all the cooking and housekeeping, Franco's discovery of America. Franco, led by the memory of Mediterranean feasts, searched for Atlantic ocean fish that could work well with Italian recipes and gave me hands-on demonstrations of how to cook them. Eventually we became rather attached to cooking together, and friends expected us to serve all things Italian. After two more long residences in Italy, we returned to the Boston area and were asked to do Italian cookery on PBS television.

We did two television series and wrote four cookbooks. As the third book went to press, we opened a restaurant, The Romagnolis' Table, in Boston's Faneuil Hall Marketplace in 1979. That was almost as much of a challenge as coming to America. It was fun and hard work. Our son Marco joined us from the very beginning and trained a host of help and worked with us for about four years. Our daughter Anna started with us as a sous chef about 1983 and ended as a manager in 1988. Finally we felt that, challenging as it was, it was time to move on.

We sold the restaurant in 1989 and traveled across the United States—twelve thousand miles, thirty-six states—with this book in mind. We saw America, big, beautiful, complicated America. We went to as many markets where they sell fish as we could manage: open markets, supermarkets, and just plain little fish markets. We ate fish about once a day, usually at dinnertime, usually in a different city every night. And, usually, we enjoyed the dish. When we didn't, it was not because of the fish but because of poor handling or cooking. We read, as well, and talked to a host of knowledgeable people about all kinds of fish. It was an amazing inland voyage of discovery.

That U.S. tour was followed by four trips to Italy for both business and pleasure. And then came an extensive trip in the spring and summer of 1992 to Italy's southern islands: Sicily, where we had been before a number of times, and the Aeolian Islands, the Aegadian Islands, where fishing for tuna with a small flotilla of fishing boats using a series of ever narrowing nets still happens once a year. We also went to the volcanic island of Pantelleria where fishing is the backbone of local culture. The waters down there are so clear, so clean, and the fish so delicious, our enthusiasm was underscored again. We stayed in the islands a great while and were reluctant to leave their tables.

However, these trips are only the most recent of a series of lifelong encounters with grand food. This book is the result of forty years of traveling and living in our two countries, discovering new food and new ways to cook it.

It is part nostalgia, a remembrance of things past, a recalling of wonderful happenings. It also represents a renewed admiration for Italian cooks' handling of fish, whether a fillet of sole smothered with caper sauce or a *zuppa di pesce*—a soup, a fish ragout rich enough to serve as the principal dish of the meal.

When we first started talking about putting some of our favorite fish recipes together, our shared enthusiasm underscored the luck we'd had exploring the Italian markets. We have been more than fortunate to idle around most of Italy's port cities and their attendant sparkle. Come with us to the island of Sicily, to the noisy fish market in Palermo or the one in Trapani, a city where fish couscous, the city's specialty, has flavors and aromas reminiscent of nearby Africa. Travel to Venice and begin at the fabulous market, where the fish is unloaded from gondolas, an extraordinary display: lit by dawn's light, it looks like a painting from a master, a modern-day Canaletto. End your day in a small, neat, no-stars restaurant beside a canal, eating a shrimp risotto so carefully composed you'd think a master chef was involved. And then go down to San Benedetto del Tronto, the largest fish market of the Adriatic; out of a crate, a fishmonger will choose for you the right combination of shrimp and fish for an unforgettable *brodetto*.

This is to name but a few places. . . . There are hundreds, each with its own spectacular sights, each offering different fish as well as different ways of treating them.

The average Italian consumer, who eats nearly twice as much fish annually as the average American consumer, won't be satisfied without fish, and meeting this requirement is increasingly facilitated by ease of transport to markets as well as knowledgeable suppliers who can select suitable quantities for their clientele. The clever fish supplier everywhere aims at bringing to market only that which will be sold before it is too late. This is easily reflected in the United States today by the dating system, which tells the customer the refrigeration life of his purchase. None of this ease and knowledge has been obscured by the passage of time and the arrival of new food fads. If nothing else, the good maintenance of fish from catch to kitchen has increased, as have the types of fish coming from whatever part of the seas the men must go to for a clean catch.

So we began this book, putting pages together that carry the message of

enjoyable dishes, most of them quick and easy to make: the road from fish market to the table, as they say in Italy, should be the shortest possible.

Italy's history, geographical diversity, regionality, and love of good food determine the condiments that surround our choices; we have chosen them to fit the American table as closely as possible. We have tried to be faithful to tradition, but also to give good consideration to those recipes that fit today's life-style of small families with little in-house help, most with a healthy concern for nutrition.

We hope you will find that cooking with olive oil and also with wine, in the Mediterranean fashion, will open new paths of enjoyment of the meal. The recipes are for everyday and Sunday too, or simply for a snack or a pizza. We hope that our readers will relish this collection of fish dishes as much as we have. Whatever pleasure you get from this book multiplies ours.

Franco adds: "This is Margaret's book. It is only for Margaret's gracious generosity that my name appears, undeservedly, on its frontispiece. After years of dedicated cooperation, of equal sharing of duties in all of our endeavors, my appearance on this project arrived at the tail end of Margaret's many years of work and research. Moreover, my participation has been at best marginal, mostly as an amanuensis, buying and cleaning fish for her productions. And, happily, taste-testing them all. I would have considered that reward enough for my minor contributions."

Fish

Our Global Resource

In most markets today, fish are coming increasingly from around the globe, although they may not necessarily be marked with a point-of-origin tag. Perhaps this is because the distances are so unbelievably great and some of the geographical names are so exotic. But the point of origin is known and being mentioned more and more. It is an increasingly global market with contributions coming from practically every country with a coastline.

In the last five years, immense innovations in transportation, packaging, and communications have been the major influences in globalizing the market. Swordfish, from the clean waters off the coast of Chile, hooked on a Thursday, can be in your store on Monday morning. From June to November, the swordfish may come from the North Atlantic; from December to April, it is shipped from the Gulf of Mexico and the Pacific Ocean. King crabs come from the North Pacific and the Bering Sea, and haddock comes from Canada, Iceland, and Norway. Canned tuna used to be shipped from Sicily, and now it is from the Pacific as well as the Persian Gulf. During the course of a year, the yellowfin tuna consumed in the New England area comes from Hawaii, the Gulf of Mexico, and the eastern coast of the U.S., from Florida on up.

We may now buy Argentinian whiting, frogs' legs from Bangladesh, Chilean octopus, French cuttlefish, Japanese scallops, New Zealand orange roughy, Taiwanese red snapper, Norwegian salmon, Indonesian blue shrimp, and sole from all over the world.

The wild catch, worldwide, is a mind-boggling 100 million metric tons, and

most of the fish and shellfish we eat are from the wild. The rest of our fishery intake, 15 percent, comes from controlled production, which means fish farming, ocean ranching, hatchery stocking, all of which offer better ways of standardizing than the wild catch.

Marine biologists think that future growth in seafood supplies will come from fish farming as the wild supply is depleted. Such "farming" is an ancient technology, practiced centuries ago by the Romans to raise oysters and by the Chinese to raise fish such as carp.

Today's methods vary from simple ponds used for raising shrimp and catfish to raceways in which a large supply of water is circulated past fish such as trout and hybrid striped bass. Virtually all Atlantic salmon is from farmed sources in which semi-submerged cages are used to hold the baby fish, which are then released into the wild ocean environment to feed and grow before returning to their place of birth to be harvested.

Shellfish such as mussels, clams, and oysters are taken up from one area and sent to another location to be raised on ropes and in trays where a combination of available nutrients and high-quality growing water speeds their growth and assures their wholesomeness. A good example of this is the farming of littleneck clams, which are raised by a Cape Cod lab in the sea and can reach the size of seven-year-old wild clams in a mere two years. Escargot, the beloved snail or mollusk of French cuisine, are now French-born and exported to be raised on farms in California.

Fish care gets very fancy when it comes to serving the Asian communities in the U.S.: closed systems, using recirculated water, are built near major markets to provide live fish for the local consumers. This system is a mix, a polyculture, of finfish and shellfish flourishing in the same growing water.

Along with the increased production in fish farming come significant problems of waste removal and prevention of disease, which require constant advances in technology.

Recent developments in aquatic farming have focused on shrimp, salmon, trout, catfish, crayfish, tilapía, sturgeon, turbot, oysters, mussels, clams, and various forms of seaweed and sea vegetables. Shrimp is the second most popular

seafood in the United States, and, according to Kenelm W. Coons of the New England Fisheries Development Association, Inc., some 30 percent of the shrimp purchased here comes from shrimp farms.

Experimental farming for halibut, mahimahi, cod, bluefin tuna, and lobster is continuing in an effort to develop commercially practical production techniques. All of this activity is reflected in the rising sales of farm-raised fish, from 18 percent of total U.S. fish consumption during 1992 to an estimated 25 percent by the year 2000.

By this point, one might ask where all this farming is taking place. Good question. The answer is: all around the world. At the International Boston Seafood Show in March 1993, over a thousand exhibits from more than twenty-five countries featured fish, farm-raised fish, and fascinating fish-related equipment such as transport refrigeration equipment, live seafood display tanks, holding systems, marine salt, activated carbon and poly filter pads for live seafood tanks, and weighing equipment. Fish farms whirl the globe: Bellevue, Washington, has Dory Seafoods, Inc., trading in farmed pan-size coho salmon, Atlantic salmon, king salmon, and Alaskan halibut. In Indianola, Mississippi, Delta Pride has farm-raised catfish, while Cargill Fishery Products in Minneapolis deals in aquacultured shrimp as well as farm-raised catfish. Fly to Peru and in Lima you will find Backustrading, a primary producer of farm-raised shellfish, finfish, and mollusks. The same firm, operating out of Miami, deals in wild-caught and farm-raised shrimp, scallops, squid, flounder, octopus, whiting, and sea bass. In Bangkok, ICC Cosmos Company has cultivated black tiger shrimp, cuttlefish, and squid. In the U.S., Atlantic Salmon in Fairfield, Maine, farms Atlantic salmon while Southern Star Shrimp Farm, Inc., in San Benito, Texas, produces and processes fresh farm-raised shrimp. Rain Forest Aquaculture Products, Inc., of Newcastle, Maine, produces tilapía, the fillets of which have made their way successfully to the markets in the Boston area. And finally, in this handful of hundreds, there is Jordan Lobster Farms, Inc., located in Island Park, New York, which claims to be the largest wholesale distributor of live lobster in New York, maintaining an inventory of forty thousand pounds.

A Safe Protein

According to the Centers for Disease Control data, fish is less likely than chicken to make one ill from disease-producing organisms, poisonous compounds, or contaminants.

There have been a number of stories in the press about fish contamination, but there is a wider perspective to be considered than that which was reported. Kenelm W. Coons has been deeply involved in work on shellfish toxins and contaminants and seafood-quality programs. He reports that "more than 3.5 billion pounds of edible seafood are processed or imported and distributed annually in the U.S., creating approximately 13 billion meals every year in which seafood is served." Coons adds: "Statistically, we are more likely to be struck by lightning than to become sick from eating seafood." Fishermen, major buyers, state and local inspectors at fishing ports as well as federal agencies (the U.S. Food and Drug Administration, the U.S. Department of Agriculture, the U.S. Department of Commerce, the Centers for Disease Control to name a few) are continually at work to ensure that the fish coming to market is fresh and uncontaminated.

As of this writing, the formal announcement of the adoption of a mandatory food-safety plan, following the recommendations of the National Academy for Sciences, is expected daily. The plan is entitled Hazardous Analysis Critical Control Point system of food safety assurance (HACCP for short). It was developed in the 101st Congress in 1990 to meet the demands of consumer advocates and the seafood industry. Further, it is the result of three legislative approaches: 1) that of the Department of Agriculture sponsored by Senator George Mitchell, majority leader, and Senator Patrick J. Leahy, chairman of the Agriculture Committee, and, in the House of Representatives, Representative Kika de la Garza, chairman of the House Agricultural Committee; 2) the Studds-Young bill, focusing on shellfish food safety hazards, and fish toxins drawn up by Representative Gerry Studds, chairman of the House Fisheries Subcommittee, and Representative Donald Young, the ranking minority member of the subcommittee; 3) that of the Department of Commerce, a combination of the two bills by Representative John

D. Dingell, chairman of the House Energy Committee and the Commerce Committee, which has FDA oversight authority.

Before the HACCP on fish per se was developed, it was used for many years in the low-acid canned food (i.e., mushrooms) industry. Unlike meat and poultry inspections, which observe the finished products about to go to market, the HACCP system concentrates surveillance and control wherever there is a potential food-safety hazard all the way from the harvest (or water, in the case of fish) to the table.

In 1992, the Department of Commerce, through its USDC seafood inspection program, offered the industry the opportunity to convert from end-product inspection to an HACCP-based program while maintaining the Grade A or "Packed under Federal Inspection" designations. Firms that have already undertaken their own HACCP-based program under the USDC will be eligible to adopt the joint FDA-USDC program which will carry a special HACCP shield complete with the registration number of the boat or processing facility.

When reviewing the various backgrounds that were built into HACCP, it became obvious that there was a whole lot of alphabet—government alphabet— involved. And the EPA, which does have clout, also has an enormous burden to carry since the environment is such a large part of seafood protection. However, on the overall worldly aspects of fish safety, the United Nations has already laid down the guidelines, Codex Alimentarius, that set worldwide food safety standards.

Earlier, in the spring of 1991, the National Academy of Sciences completed a two-year study on the type of seafood inspection program that was needed. Its nine overall conclusions included the following: most seafood-related health risks originate in the environment; the sources of most acute seafood-related illnesses are known; chronic illness is a result of environmental contaminants and requires better knowledge; contaminated products should be excluded from the market; action is needed to control added pollution of waters; and an improved national surveillance and reporting system is needed to establish a data base and to aid risk assessment. All these elements plus a host more, too many to list here, went into

the 1992 Senate Bill (HACCP) sponsored by the Commerce Committee chairman Senator Ernest Hollings, with an impressive list of sponsors, among them the FDA, the USDA, and the National Marine Fisheries Service of the U.S. Department of Commerce.

The HACCP system is also used to assure seafood safety in neighboring Canada and has been endorsed by the National Academy of Sciences. And, finally, exporters of seafood are eager to adopt HACCP so their surveillance system will be in harmony with Codex, which determines the requirements of the European Economic Community.

The FDA, in the meantime, has established a special Office of Seafood and has more than doubled the resources devoted to assuring the safety of the U.S. seafood supply, including stepped-up screening of imported fishery products, which provide about two-thirds of the U.S. supply.

None of these rules, inspections, and regulations, however, govern the sport fisherman's stream or lake, which may be contaminated but is not listed by authorities. Many who keep up with fishing news around the United States know, for example, that the Great Lakes are contaminated mostly by PCBs, which pollute the fish. But the news may not be out on your own local lake or stream, and thus the sportsman carries the burden of being extra vigilant over the waters from which his catch comes.

Health Food for the Future

Fish may easily be the health food of today, tomorrow, and the near and distant future. Professor William Lands, of the University of Illinois, has been involved in ongoing research that shows real evidence that increased fish consumption may help save us from such chronic illnesses as heart disease and strokes.

About a decade ago, Danish researchers found that only three in a group of 1,800 Eskimos had suffered heart attacks over a twenty-five-year period. The American rate was thirty times that. The suspected reason: Eskimos' high consumption of seafood gave them about thirty times more fish oil in their diet than

that consumed in the typical American diet. Extensive research since then, including Professor Lands's work, has confirmed that fish oil alters conditions that promote heart disease: it may help prevent blood clots that can lead to heart attacks and strokes. It may hamper inflammatory damage to artery walls and help control dangerous heartbeat irregularities. Fish oil also may lower a type of blood fat that is linked to heart disease. However, fish oil does not consistently depress levels of cholesterol in the blood.

Professor Lands's research points out that it is the ratio of omega-3s to omega-6s in the diet that makes the difference. Says Lands, "It is no longer enough to just say 'Eat more fish and omega-3s.' What is critical is the proper balance of omega-3s and omega 6s." That means, he says, cutting back on the vegetable oils as well as increasing consumption of fish oils.

Dr. William Castelli, the medical director of the Framingham Heart Study, carries the philosophy farther: he gives a cooking demonstration along with his lectures from time to time to show how one can eat a lot less saturated fat and have the food taste good at the same time. (The Framingham, Massachusetts, study is in its forty-fifth year; it started with an initial group of 5,100 residents, of whom 1,500 are still participating while 4,000 new names have been added.)

Dr. Castelli points out that heart disease is largely a Western phenomenon, limited to North Americans and Europeans, who eat many more fatty foods than do the people in other parts of the world. "Every man and woman in America ought to be on this diet [one low in saturated fat] because, let's face it, of the 5.3 billion people who live on this earth, 4 billion don't get this [heart] disease."

Recognizing the fact that most of us are stuck in our diet patterns, Dr. Castelli still keeps up what he calls an uphill battle. It does have a couple of great landmarks, however: breakthroughs from the Framingham Study have produced major advances in public health. The first was the proven link between smoking and heart attacks in the sixties. It led to some thirty million smokers giving up cigarettes. In the 1970s the doctor's second landmark was a persistent call for treating high blood pressure more aggressively. Dr. Castelli says the death rate from stokes has been cut by 54 percent. His current big effort is for better cholesterol testing and cuts in saturated-fat intake (meat, eggs, and dairy prod-

ucts, full of omega-6s). He adds: "The real heroes of the Framingham Study are the people who come in and let us see them every two or four years. They realize that what we find will probably not help them but may help their children." The doctor's goal is to prevent the preventable diseases. Heart and vascular disease currently cause twice as many deaths as all forms of cancer. "Maybe we can get the average [life expectancy] up to seventy-seven or eighty."

If you listen to and believe the experts, fish in the diet will help keep you healthy. And the Italian diet throws in something else to keep you even healthier: pasta. When the U.S. Department of Agriculture and the Food and Drug Administration brought forth their Food Guide Pyramid as the logo of the U.S. dietary guidelines in the spring of 1992 to show what is good for us and how much of it is necessary for a proper diet, Italy welcomed it like a long-lost cousin because pasta plays a major role in the pyramid. Italy's National Institute of Nutrition pointed out that the American principles of a sane diet as represented by the pyramid were the same as those of the traditional Italian diet, in which pasta plays a major role. Good nutrition means good use of carbohydrates. The benefits of the proper carbohydrates and fish's omega-3s is a super combination for healthy living.

We submit these few paragraphs in the hope of clarifying your thoughts on where your fish may come from, to help you get a better idea of the safety of fish in today's market, and to aid and abet in making tomorrow's meals above and beyond yesterday's. We also realize that there may be a stereotype parent or grandparent in the background who once said "You don't have to like it, you just have to eat it." That sort of parental advice shouldn't apply to meals in the twentieth and twenty-first centuries.

So, with your global knowledge, your safe wild and farmed seafood, plus some late words from specialists in nutrition, you have a passport to tomorrow, gastronomically speaking. Use it.

Fish Basics

Shopping List

When it comes to choosing fish and shellfish, the Italian buyer has a list of favorites, mostly Mediterranean, the majority of them easily found in American markets:

Anchovies (canned), bass (both salt- and fresh-water species), bonito, clams, cod, eel, haddock (member of the cod family), halibut (member of the flounder family), herring (smoked), lobsters, mackerel, mullet, mussels, oysters, perch, pollock (another member of the cod family), porgy, red snapper, salmon, salmon trout (also known as brown trout), shrimp, skate (occasionally), smelts, sole, squid, trout, turbot, fresh tuna, and whiting (which is the market name for hake, another member of the cod family).

The American shopper's list on the East, West, and Gulf Coasts could be about the same, by and large. Increasingly, other areas in the country are expanding their fish inventory where and when their customers ask for it. Several of the most popular new fish in our area include tilapía (farmed in Costa Rica and Maine), New Zealand orange roughy, and catfish (farmed stateside). The fish stores in the Italian neighborhood in our area (as in various cities around the country) provide fresh eel at Christmastime to maintain an old tradition. But when we queried the buyer about the availability of bluefish, we were told that its fast-spoiling trait, similar to that of other predatory fish, means it has to be gutted and iced almost right out of the water. This inhibits marketing it away from the coast, more or less. At seaside eateries and restaurants, one can find freshly gutted, iced, newly caught bluefish.

Stores in all parts of the country, however, carry canned fish. "Canned tuna is the most commonly consumed fishery product by far, representing over 20 percent of the per capita consumption (by weight) of fish and shellfish in the U.S.," says Kenelm W. Coons in his recently (1992) published book *Fish, The Truth*. Shrimp represents about 14 percent of the seafood coming to the American table.

The third group of most-consumed fish (15 percent) is that of the cod family—cod, hake, haddock, and pollock. The Alaskan pollock is the largest edible fish resource in the world and is the main fish ingredient in fish sticks and surimi in the American market.

Salmon makes up the fourth most popular species, accounting for 5 percent of domestic consumption. Salmon is increasingly farm-raised, not only in the United States but in Canada, Chile, Norway, and Scotland, for use as smoked salmon as well as fresh steaks and fillets. The fifth-favorite fish is the American fresh or farm-raised catfish. It is grown in forty of the fifty states and sold both fresh and frozen practically everywhere.

These five best-selling fish account for about 60 percent of all fish consumption in the U.S. "And all are extraordinarily safe foods," says Ken Coons.

Of course, there are lots more fish to be considered. In order to lengthen the shopping list and vary the challenge to the palate, one must remember that the availability of any sort of fish is ultimately up to the customer: it is the awareness and the demands of the customer combined with a reliable vendor that makes fresh and frozen fish (imported, local, farm-raised, or from the sea) show up in the stores.

Once you know what you want and it becomes available, there are only a few guidelines to consider:

1) Choose fish with firm flesh—if you can touch it and it bounces back, leaving no finger mark, it is fresh;
2) if the fish still has its head on, check the eyes—they should be bright, clear, and bulging;
3) check the smell—it should not be fishy or unpleasant;

4) buy the right amount—about ¾ pound undressed, whole fish per person; ¼ to ½ pound if buying dressed fish, fillets, steaks with no bones, scallops, and shrimp. This, of course, is only an indication—let your table partners lead the rest of the way.

How to Clean Fish and Shellfish

Now comes the moment of truth—you have the menu in mind, the fish in hand, and it is time to start.

If you skipped all the above checkpoints because the fish available to you is cleaned, cut, ready to cook, or canned, you can skip this section also. But if faced with a whole fish you bought or received from a fisherman friend, here are a few more simple guidelines:

1) Gut it as soon as you can to rid it of the parts that deteriorate quickly and which you do not eat: the intestines, liver, heart, and gills. Make an incision into the belly from the tail to the head. This allows for the quick removal of all the above-mentioned innards. Scrape away the membrane that covers the backbone where the innards were and then wash the fish thoroughly so that no blood remains. You now have what the experts call a "drawn" fish.

2) Scale the fish with a fish scaler (available in kitchen equipment stores) or scrape the scales away with a knife. Hold the fish securely by the tail and work toward the head, being careful to keep the flying scales from traveling too far. Most experienced scalers say a wet fish scales more easily than a semi-dry one, while some experts say scale control can be achieved by scaling fish immersed in water. Others who scale a lot of fish do so in a deep sink, the sides of which contain most of the separated scales. It all depends on you—some fish lovers we know attach their fish to a good-sized clipboard with a very efficient clip, immerse the whole thing in water and scale away.

3) You may leave the fins on a fish to be baked; they come off quite easily once the flesh is cooked. But if you are not baking, cut carefully around the pelvic fins (those on the underside, toward the head) and pull them off. A quick jerk after

knife-point-cutting does the trick. The same with the pectoral fins (those just behind the gills). As for the fin on the back, the dorsal fin, cut along each side of it and jerk the fin forward, toward the head. The reason for the jerk is to pull the fin with its root bones so that those little ones do not remain to surprise the eater. There are now only the fins at the back of the underside (the ventral fins) to be removed . . . in the same manner. Don't cut the fins; cutting gets rid of the fins but leaves in the flesh the little bones at their base.

4) Wash the fish again and, depending on size, cut it in steaks (at right angles to the backbone) or in fillets.

5) To separate the fillets from the backbone: Score the fish along the backbone. Insert the point of the filleting knife well into the flesh just behind the head, close to the backbone, and cut away the flesh in one piece, separating it from the bone. Continue to separate until the fillet thins at the tail and is easily removed.

6) If you are working with a big fish, such as a filleted monkfish, you may want to cut that thick fillet into rounds or medallions, 1½ to 2 inches thick. This is easily done at a 45-degree angle and produces a medallion with an increased amount of cooking surface. The completely ready-to-cook fish, whether fillet or steak or whole but clean, is a "dressed" fish.

To clean squid: Cut the tentacles from the head just below the eyes. Save the tentacles, but discard the mouth, which is hidden at their center. Hold the body of the squid under running water, and peel off the thin outer skin. Squeeze out the insides as you would a tube of paste, pulling the head off at the final squeeze. Discard both head and insides. Pull out the transparent center bone, and wash the body, which is like an empty sack. Slice the body into little rings or squares. If the tentacles are bigger than a mouthful, cut them in half or quarters accordingly.

To clean mussels: Scrub the mussels with a stiff brush, pull off any bits of hemp or algae that may remain, and squeeze them to make sure they are lightly closed and alive and well. If opened slightly, the live ones will fight back and close; if they are open and won't shut, throw them away. Rinse carefully under cold running water.

Clams usually carry a bit more sand than mussels do, so we usually soak them

in water for several hours before opening them. Razor clams with their long, partially open shells are easy to open with an ordinary knife.

The big hardshell clams (quahogs) are seldom used in Italian cookery and really call for a lesson or two from someone who has shucked a lot of them, or buy them already shucked.

There is really nothing that can replace fresh Italian *vongole* or *vongole veraci,* baby clams, but we suggest you buy the smallest littlenecks or cherrystone clams, as big as, or barely larger than, a quarter. Or buy canned *vongole* or whole baby clams: they are small, tasty, tender . . . and above all available. When the fancy strikes for a "clam sauce," in a storm every port will do: and so will the canned "babies." Do not use fresh or canned "chopped clams" for an Italian sauce: they are way too hard and chewy, and better suited for a chowder.

In most American stores dried salt cod comes skinned, boned, filleted, all folded into a small wooden box. It needs about twelve hours of soaking, changing the water from time to time.

In Italian markets in the U.S., salt cod may be found dried, beheaded, opened flat, and stiff as a board. This version takes a longer time than the boxed version to become plump again and to lose most of its saltiness—up to twenty-four hours, changing the water frequently. This cod must then be skinned and boned, neither of which is difficult after all that drying and soaking and waiting.

Methods of Fish Cookery

There is nothing particularly difficult about the methods used by Italians to cook fish. The main point to remember is timing. Recipes often say a fish is done when it flakes, but frequently by the time the fish flakes easily it is overdone. Big fish, especially, keep on cooking for a time after they have been removed from the heat. "Barely flakes" or "just beginning to flake" or "turning opaque" are better descriptions. We use the Canadian method to calculate cooking times by measuring the thickness of the fish and cooking it approximately ten minutes per

inch. Or we rely on a thermometer as well as our eye and fork, depending on the fish itself.

Large fish to be poached, grilled, or baked really need the Canadian method. Measure the fish at its thickest and cook it almost ten minutes per inch: if a fish is two inches thick, cook it for eighteen to nineteen minutes, remove it from the heat, and it will continue cooking for a minute or so as it rests. In the case of fillets, which are fatter in the center than at either end, we find that turning the ends under a bit gives an even thickness to the fish and hence an even cooking based on thickness.

However, don't just go by the multiplication. Before the cooking time has elapsed, insert a fork gently into the flesh. The flesh should part easily, just barely flake, have turned opaque, not seem translucent close to the bone (if it has a bone) and still appear moist. Remember that a fish that flakes too easily can be overdone. If you don't wish to measure and multiply, you can rely on the use of an instant-read thermometer for a large fish. When the thermometer registers just under 140 degrees Fahrenheit on insertion, the fish is so close to being done that it is time to take it from the heat and let it rest and continue cooking with its own heat.

The Canadian method also works for rolled fillets: measure the total width of the roll and multiply by ten. Flat fillets usually aren't an inch thick, so you must reduce the timing on your own decision. Tuck the ends under, as mentioned earlier, if indeed they are very thin, and figure about six or seven minutes under the broiler or over the grill for a filet just under one inch at its thickest. Fish steaks are usually cut about an inch thick and take about ten minutes in a preheated broiler or five minutes per side on the grill.

Shellfish, on the other hand, should be cooked with a bit more dispatch than other fish. Lobsters, crab, and shrimp are perfect candidates for poaching. Bring water to a boil in a large pot and add the shellfish. When the water returns to the boil, lower the heat slightly and start timing. A 1-pound "chicken" lobster cooks in ten minutes. A 1¼ pounder should go for twelve minutes, a 1½-pound lobster needs fourteen minutes and from there on up to 5 pounds, add approximately two minutes per pound. The flesh should be snow white when cooked. See page 219 for more detail on poaching a lobster.

Crab is so perishable, it is usually sold whole, freshly cooked, or canned. To poach fresh crabs, right from the sea, bring sea water or salted water (1 teaspoon per quart) to a boil and drop in the crabs. Allow eight minutes per pound of crab and remove them from the water to cool before shelling them.

Shrimp cook in about one to three minutes depending on size and should be removed from their poaching water as soon as they turn red. For best results, cook the shrimp with their shells on; the timing is the same, but the shells add to their flavor and final texture.

If cooking shrimp in olive oil, remove the shells and sauté them first in the oil and then discard them before you add the shrimp. The final flavor of the dish will be enriched.

As for clams and mussels, they should be placed in a sauté pan over high heat with just a trace of water, wine, or oil, with or without a bit of herb for flavor. Cover the pan and keep over the heat until the shells open, about three to five minutes, depending on the size of the shellfish. The natural juices from the shellfish slide right into the pan and may be strained for use in serving.

Following are a few simple techniques for the round or flat fish.

PAN-COOKED FISH

When cooking a fillet or small fish, cooking in a wide, shallow pan with a little olive oil or butter (or a mix of the two) may be the nicest technique in the list. Pieces weighing up to half a pound should be dusted with flour and/or breadcrumbs and placed in a sauté pan with fairly hot butter and/or oil. Three to five minutes cooking on each side and your fish is done. A dash or two of lemon juice and a bit of salt and pepper in the cavity of a small fish add to its flavor.

GRILLED AND BROILED FISH

The verb "to grill" is constantly being interchanged with the words "to broil," with the first meaning to cook over the heat of hot coals and the other to cook

under a hot flame or coil. Either way, these techniques are both pretty superlative for some fish steaks: bluefish, halibut, monkfish, shark, swordfish, and tuna. All are firm fleshed and work wonderfully, especially if marinated. Nonoily fish steaks should be brushed with olive oil before grilling. The more oily fish, such as mackerel and eel, are particularly good when grilled or broiled as their flesh gives up some of its oil during the cooking.

When grilling a whole fish, the use of a grilling basket is a grand help. Generally shaped like a fish, and hinged to enclose one, the basket has two sets of adjustable supports, one for each side, to hold the fish the proper distance from the coals and to allow you to turn the fish easily when the first side is done. The rectangular or square grilling basket can do the same for steaks and skewered fish; although there are no supports, the basket may be either held or placed right on a grill.

BAKED FISH

Baking layered fillets, large fish fillets, or roasting large fish that have been stuffed are two favorite methods for oven cooking. The oven must be piping hot (400 to 425 degrees Fahrenheit) and the cooking time is easily calculated by the Canadian method: measure the stuffed fish at its thickest point and multiply that number of inches by ten, and that indicates the approximate time when the fish will be done. Remove the fish from the heat just under the total calculated time. Or you may use an instant-read thermometer—it is just as accurate if not more so: when it registers 138 degrees Fahrenheit, the fish is ready to come out and finish cooking by its own heat to reach 140 degrees Fahrenheit.

FISH IN PARCHMENT

Fish fillets, small fish, shrimp, scallops, and other shellfish are wrapped in parchment paper or aluminum foil and baked for five minutes. The packets are for

individual servings. The natural aromas and moisture of a sauce or filling create a steam that cooks the fish in five minutes and ensures a fish with good taste, texture, and a superb aroma when the packet is opened at table.

Cut pieces of parchment paper or foil twice as big as each serving (either heart-shaped or moon-shaped). If making hearts, fold the parchment paper in half, figure a half a heart twice as wide as your fish filet. Cut through the folded paper, open up the heart, butter it lightly, and when the fish and its sauce are partially cooked, place them on one half of the heart; fold the other half over the fish and crimp the edges to seal. Or you may cut a complete circle, which may be folded in half and close the fish in. Any way you cut the paper is fine as long as it has just room to hold the fish, the sauce or herbs, a dab of butter or dash of wine, and the steam. Preheat your oven to 450 degrees Fahrenheit, place the packets on a cookie sheet, and bake for about five minutes and until the steam on the inside of the packet has puffed up the parchment and the fish is done. You may even place partially cooked pasta in parchment with a partially cooked sauce and flavorings. The parchment packets may be prepared and sealed ahead of time, and then baked just before serving.

Boned, whole, small, raw fish may be placed in parchment with flavorings, put in an oven at 375 degrees Fahrenheit, and baked for about twelve minutes. In Italy one finds this technique used with mullet, porgy, and trout. Salmon steaks may also be cooked in parchment.

POACHED FISH

We most often think of salmon when we think of poaching fish, but bass, haddock, perch, pike, porgy, and trout may also be poached successfully. You may use salted water, water with lemon juice or white wine or wine vinegar, or Basic Fish Stock I with aromatic vegetables and herbs (page 166).

Start big fish in cold water or broth and heat slowly to a low boil; place smaller fish in water that is just barely boiling. In either case, the fish should be wrapped in cheesecloth with a good handy knot at each end of the fish for easy removal from

pan to platter. If the fish has a head and tail when you buy it, leave them on during the poaching as they add flavor. When done, skin the fish and bone it while hot.

Equipment

Having talked about the methods, we list here pieces of kitchen equipment you may find helpful for the actual cookery, from sauces to the final dish. Of course, you don't have to start out with all of them. We certainly didn't. But when you decide which type of cooking and which type of fish suit you best, then is the time to start adding to your equipment. Here is a baker's dozen of useful things:

1) A fish poacher with a rack to hold the fish away from the pan bottom as well as to remove the fish easily from the pan;
2) a grilling basket, to hold and protect the fish while grilling, either fish-shaped or the rectangular folding holder used to turn steaks or skewers easily;
3) an instant-read thermometer to check the inner temperature of a poached or baked fish;
4) a snub-nose pliers for pulling off the skin and a needle-nose pliers for removing recalcitrant bones.
5) a filleting knife with a most flexible blade;
6) an electric deep fryer that provides good temperature control;
7) a food mill for gentle processing of fish and other ingredients;
8) a food processor for more serious processing;
9) a pasta cooker, a large pot with a colander insert that is handy for pasta and some fish soups;
10) a sieve and cheesecloth to line it for straining broth;
11) a blender for making mayonnaise and working with some of the sauces;
12) a pizza-baking stone or heavy iron baking sheet;
13) a kitchen scale.

Notes on Freezing

Following is a partial listing of storage guides put out by the National Fisheries Institute, covering some of the fish in this book.

SEAFOOD STORAGE GUIDE

Product	Purchased Frozen Commercially for Freezer Storage	Purchased Fresh & Home Frozen	Thawed; Never or Previously Frozen & Home Refrigerated
FISH FILLETS/STEAKS			
Lean:			
Cod, Flounder	10–12 months	6–8 months	36 hours
Haddock, Halibut	10–12 months	6–8 months	36 hours
Pollock, Ocean Perch	8–9 months	4 months	36 hours
Sea Trout, Rockfish	8–9 months	4 months	36 hours
Pacific Ocean Perch	8–9 months	4 months	36 hours
Fat:			
Mullet, smelt	6–7 months	N/A	36 hours
Salmon (cleaned)	7–9 months	N/A	36 hours
SHELLFISH			
Dungeness Crab	6 months	6 months	5 days
Snow Crab	6 months	6 months	5 days
Blue Crabmeat (fresh)	N/A	4 months	5–7 days
Cocktail Claws	N/A	4 months	5 days
King Crab	12 months	9 months	7 days
Shrimp	9 months	5 months	4 days
Oysters, shucked	N/A	N/A	4–7 days
Clams, shucked	N/A	N/A	5 days
Lobster, live	N/A	N/A	1–2 days
Lobster, tail meat	8 months	6 months	4–5 days

Although clams and oysters are listed, they, as well as mussels, are not available frozen. When buying them fresh, or freshly shucked, they should carry a "sell by" date.

Fresh farm-raised mussels will keep alive, if well refrigerated, for five days after the date of shipment to the market. There are 3 rules to follow: 1) keep them cool, spread out on lots of ice at a temperature close to thirty degrees Fahrenheit; 2) let them breathe by keeping them in packages with air holes; 3) don't wrap mussels in plastic.

Lobsters, cooked, canned, and frozen, may be treated like the lobster tail meat listing. Freezing smoked fish is not applicable; herring may be refrigerated for three to four days, while smoked salmon and whitefish are good for five to eight days.

The Enhancers

ANCHOVIES

BATTERS

Baking Powder Batter

Yeast Batter

Egg Batter

BUTTERS

Anchovy Butter

Caper Butter

Parsley Butter

Herb Butter

MARINADES

Garlic and Herb Marinade

Marinade with Mint

Peppery Lemon Marinade

OILS

ROASTED PEPPERS

SAUCES

Anchovy-Garlic Salad Dressing

Egg-Lemon-Cream Sauce

Garlic, Olive Oil, and Hot Red Pepper Sauce

Green Sauce

Green Sauce, Piemontese Style

Blender Mayonnaise

Mayonnaise with Fresh Basil

Parsley Mayonnaise

Olive and Caper Sauce

Basic Tomato Sauce

Tomato and Basil Sauce

Hot Tomato Sauce

Pesto

Red Pesto

Walnut Sauce

White Sauce

Fish White Sauce

Mornay Sauce

HERBS AND FLAVORING PLANTS

GARNISHES

WINE

It occurred to us that this chapter is like the old-fashioned kitchen pantry, without which one could not cook. It holds the ingredients that round off the recipes: the special flavorings, the final touches, the framework for sauces, the background for the main dishes. Welcome to batters and butters and marinades and basic sauces, the enhancers, if you wish. We are placing it up front, before you start cooking your main choice of the day.

A few comments on ingredients that are basic to our cooking: we buy hearty Italian- or French-style breads because they have fine flavor, firm texture, and behave well in many procedures. Italian bread comes in large rounds, French bread in 3-inch-wide, 18-inch-long baguettes. We always buy sardines and tuna canned in olive oil because we think the taste is top quality and a tablespoon of olive oil is worth its weight in gold. In a recipe like Mussels with Sardine Butter in Aspic (page 86), however, the oil would inhibit the jelling process, so it should be drained off before using the sardines. This oil is never wasted in our house; Franco usually scoops it onto a nice piece of bread and has a quick snack. A 3¾-ounce can of sardines contains about four teaspoons of olive oil.

Anchovies

Anchovies are mostly known and used in their preserved state. Salt-cured and packed in oil, they are sold either as flat fillets or rolled (around a caper) fillets. In Italy, and in some Italo-American markets, they can still be found in

barrels simply salted and sold by weight. Purists insist on these salted anchovies, which need to be washed before use. We prefer the canned, flat anchovies as they are ready to use and have a milder taste. Taste is where the anchovy shines. In Italian cookery, anchovies show up in hundreds of sauces and entrées, never obtrusively strong but as an enhancer of other flavors. This use goes back to Roman times when the product of fermented anchovies and other fish, "garum" or "liquamen," was widely employed as a spicy condiment. Many prefer to cut the salty taste of anchovies by blending them with butter for use on toast and in sauces.

Batters (pastelle)

For frying fish, a batter is a flavorful shield against the high heat and delivers tender moist fish with a slightly crackling crust. Italy is not unique, of course, in using batters, but it's hard to beat the yeast or baking powder batter when it comes to *baccalà*—dried, soaked, dipped, and deep-fried. A third commonly used batter is made with eggs. Try them all and let your palate decide.

Baking Powder Batter

pastella svelta

1 cup unbleached all-purpose flour
¼ teaspoon salt
1½ teaspoons baking powder
1¼ cups water, approximately

This is also perfect for use with vegetables.

Put the flour and salt in a shallow, wide bowl. Add the baking powder and stir once. Pour in the water, whisking as you pour, and work until smooth. Let stand a few minutes until puffy and bubbly.

Dip fish pieces into the batter a few at a time and then fry them.

Yield: 2½ cups, approximately, or enough for 4 portions (1½ pounds fish)

Yeast Batter

pastella al lievito

Dissolve the yeast in the warm water and stir to make sure it has all dissolved. Slowly sprinkle in the flour, beating with a whisk until it is all absorbed and the batter is smooth. Let rise in a warm place for about an hour, or until it has doubled in bulk and become light and full of bubbles. Stir in the salt and use immediately to batter fish for deep frying.

Yield: about 3 cups, enough to prepare 4 to 6 portions

1 packet active dry or "rapid rise" yeast or 1 square compressed fresh yeast
1¼ cups warm (115 degrees Fahrenheit for active yeast, 120–130 degrees for "rapid rise" yeast)
1½ cups unbleached all-purpose flour
½ teaspoon salt

Egg Batter

pastella all'uovo

This is a batter with an egg base, lighter than the yeast batter, and is suited for delicate fish and vegetables. It is easily cut in half for a small batch for two or doubled for a larger group.

2 large eggs
1½ tablespoons olive oil
⅔ cup warm water
½ teaspoon salt
¾ cup unbleached all-purpose flour

With a whisk, beat the eggs, oil, water, and salt until smooth and well mixed. Sprinkle the flour slowly into the egg mixture, whisking as you do so. Continue with the

whisk for 2 to 3 minutes, or until the mixture is the consistency of pancake batter.

Let stand 30 minutes before using. Or let the batter stay in the refrigerator up to 3 hours. Reconstitute it with a good whisking before using.

Yield: 1½ cups, or enough for 1 pound fish or vegetables or 2 portions, approximately

Butters (burri)

While Italy, by and large, uses olive oil in many of the ways America might use butter, Italian cuisine does indeed use butter, especially as flavored butter to melt on a freshly grilled piece of fish. Here are three favorites, which may be portioned out according to your taste: ¼ teaspoon for a small portion, ½ teaspoon for a large portion, and 1 teaspoon for a nice big fillet.

As for the butter itself, Italy, like France, uses unsalted butters. Thus, all the butter called for in this book is unsalted. However, if butter is off your list, it is quite acceptable to try some of these recipes using butter substitutes. You may find your choice very nice indeed. Furthermore, where possible, many cooks substitute olive oil for butter for the flavor alone.

Anchovy Butter

burro di acciuga

4 tablespoons unsalted butter, at
    room temperature
4 flat anchovy fillets, minced
½ teaspoon chopped fresh flat-leaf
    parsley

Cream the butter with the minced anchovies. Add the chopped parsley and form the butter back into stick shape. Chill and then cut according to amount desired for use over freshly grilled or broiled steaks, still warm, or poached fish.

Yield: enough for 4 portions grilled or broiled fish steaks, approximately

Caper Butter

burro ai capperi

Clarify the butter by melting it over low heat and skimming off the froth. Heat already clarified butter or olive oil over low flame.

Add capers, lemon juice, salt, and pepper to the butter. When the fish is done, pour melted butter over the entire fish.

Yield: enough for 4 portions poached or broiled fish

* NOTE: Commercially prepared clarified butter is now available in specialty stores.

4 tablespoons unsalted butter or 3 tablespoons clarified butter* or 4 tablespoons olive oil
2 tablespoons capers, rinsed, drained, and chopped
Juice of ½ lemon
¼ teaspoon salt, or to taste
Freshly ground white pepper to taste

Parsley Butter

burro verde

Proceed exactly as with caper butter.

Yield: enough for 4 portions

6 tablespoons unsalted butter
3 tablespoons coarsely chopped fresh flat-leaf parsley
Juice of ½ lemon
¼ teaspoon salt, or to taste
Freshly ground white pepper to taste

Herb Butter

burro all'erbette

2 tablespoons unsalted butter, at
   room temperature
¼ teaspoon chopped fresh rosemary
   leaves
¼ teaspoon dried tarragon
1 sprig of fresh flat-leaf parsley
¼ teaspoon Dijon-style mustard
½ teaspoon lemon juice
Dash of salt
Abundant freshly ground black
   pepper

Mash the butter with a fork. Mince together the herbs and mustard, and mash them into the butter. Sprinkle with lemon juice, salt, and pepper, and mix well. Spread half the mixture on the upper part of the fish fillet before broiling. When you turn the fish, spread with the remaining butter and continue cooking.

Yield: sufficient for 2 to 3 servings of fish, 1 large steak or fillet, weighing approximately 2 pounds; multiply according to the number of servings needed

Marinades (marinate)

A good number of recipes for the larger, shall we say more serious, fish call for a marinade before grilling, broiling, or roasting. These same marinades may be used during cooking or as an additional flavoring after cooking.

One of the more efficient ways of marinating a fish is to put the marinade in a plastic bag, slip in the fish, and seal the bag well. Turn the bag around two or three times during the waiting period to keep the fish nicely dampened.

Garlic and Herb Marinade

marinata all'aglio

Whip all the ingredients together and pour over 2 portions of fish to be grilled or broiled. Let rest for 30 minutes, turning at least once. When grilling fish, brush both sides before they are positioned on the grill and brush the tops as the bottoms grill.

Yield: ⅓ cup, approximately, or enough for 2 portions or 8 to 10 ounces of fish

1 garlic clove, minced
2 tablespoons olive oil
2 tablespoons white-wine vinegar
Pinch of salt
Pinch of freshly ground white
    pepper
½ teaspoon minced fresh flat-leaf
    parsley
½ teaspoon dried thyme
1 bay leaf

Marinade with Mint

marinata alla mentuccia

Mix all the ingredients together well and pour over fish to be grilled. Let stand at least 30 minutes, turning the fish at least twice.

Yield: 1½ cups approximately, or enough for 2 pounds or 4 portions, approximately

Leaves of 3 to 4 sprigs fresh mint,
    chopped (1 rounded tablespoon)
Leaves of 3 to 4 sprigs fresh basil,
    chopped (1 rounded tablespoon)
½ teaspoon freshly ground white
    pepper
½ teaspoon salt
¾ cup lemon juice
¾ cup flavored olive oil (page 37)

Peppery Lemon Marinade

marinata piccante al limone

Dash of Tabasco
Juice of 3 lemons
⅓ cup olive oil
3 tablespoons white wine
    Worcestershire sauce
2 anchovies
2 tablespoons minced fresh flat-leaf
    parsley
1 teaspoon celery salt

Place all the ingredients in a food processor with the cutting blade. Process until all the ingredients are minced and mixed.

Place fish in a deep platter and pour the marinade over it, or place it in a plastic bag and pour in the marinade. Let stand at least 30 minutes, turning the fish at least once.

Lift the fish from the marinade and broil in a pre-heated broiler. Heat the remaining marinade and when the fish is done, pour a splash of marinade on each plate, place the fish over the marinade, and serve.

Yield: 1½ cups, or enough for 2 to 3 pounds fish or 6 portions

Oils

For Italian cookery, the preferred oil is olive oil. Like many of the ingredients in the Mediterranean diet, it is good for you. Practically speaking it is a bit like saffron, in that it takes a great amount, eleven pounds, of the original product, olives, to make the final product—approximately one quart of olive oil. It is a lengthy process and the various classifications (extra-virgin, virgin, 100 percent pure, and plain olive oil) depend on the acidity of the final product. In extra-virgin olive oil, the acidity is less than 1 percent.

Italian olive oil is monounsaturated, believed to lower cholesterol, and full of vitamins A, D, and E.

Personally we love the extra-virgin olive oil with salads and vegetables, but we do not fry with it; and when making mayonnaise, we use pure olive oil but do not disdain the use of vegetable oil.

If making a very herbed mayonnaise, we usually use vegetable oil. It is not a sin, just a choice.

If you are not really familiar with the various brands and types, we suggest you try as many as you can (buying in small amounts if possible), and then choose the type that suits your palate.

Roasted Peppers

The appearance of sweet bell peppers in Italian cuisine is honored and carried to wonderful gastronomic extremes when they are roasted and peeled. They will delight the palate both as an antipasto and as a flavoring. We recommend that you roast at least six peppers at one time so you will have some on hand; they keep well in the refrigerator for a day or two.

Using a gas stove, turn the grates of the top burners upside down to cradle the peppers on the grates. Position the peppers and turn on the flame. As soon as one side of a pepper is blackened, use tongs to turn it a bit to the next uncharred portion. Keep turning until all the outer skin is blackened and blistered.

Using an electric stove, put the peppers in the broiler, as close to the heating element as possible, and keep turning them as they blacken. Use really fresh, plump peppers for the best results, especially when using the broiler. Roast until the outer skin of the peppers is completely charred.

Put the charred peppers under a cold stream of water and peel off the black with your fingers. This makes a great mess in the sink, but the taste of the peppers will repay you for the cleanup.

Cut off the top stems, take out the inner seeds, and slice the peppers lengthwise into ¼- to ½-inch-wide strips. Drain briefly and add to your fish soup. Use any remaining pepper strips, dressed with olive oil and lemon juice or red wine vinegar, as an antipasto.

Sauces (salse)

Following is a collection of Italian sauces of which some, such as the Garlic, Olive Oil, and Hot Red Pepper Sauce, are used to begin soups as well as more complicated sauces. Some are basic to the entire cuisine, such as White Sauce (to hold layered lasagne and wrap around fillings for patty shells) and Basic Tomato Sauce. Finally there are the heavily accented sauces for myriads of poached fish: Mayonnaise, Red Pesto, Egg-Lemon-Cream Sauce, and Olive and Caper Sauce to name just four.

Anchovy-Garlic Salad Dressing

salsina all'acciuga

¼ cup egg substitute (equivalent of
  1 egg)
1½ cups olive oil
½ cup red-wine vinegar
1¼ teaspoons garlic powder
4 anchovy fillets
1 teaspoon salt
¼ teaspoon freshly ground black
  pepper
1 tablespoon chopped fresh flat-leaf
  parsley

Place the egg substitute in a blender. Blend for a second or two, and begin to add the oil slowly.

When the mixture is very thick, slowly add the vinegar, garlic powder, anchovies, salt, pepper, and parsley.

To serve: toss 1 to 2 tablespoons of dressing per portion of salad.

Yield: 2 cups, approximately, or enough for 12 portions Shrimp and Pasta Salad (page 100)

Egg-Lemon-Cream Sauce

salsa al limone

Place the vinegar, salt, and pepper in the top of a double boiler and put the pan over the bottom and begin to heat. Add the egg substitute to the vinegar solution and whip gently until the sauce begins to thicken. Melt butter and add it very slowly to the sauce. Finally whip in ¼ teaspoon of lemon juice. Fold in the cream. Taste for flavor and adjust as you wish.

Yield: enough for 4 portions of poached fish

1 tablespoon white-wine vinegar
Salt to taste
Pinch of freshly ground white pepper
1½ tablespoons egg substitute
10 tablespoons (1¼ sticks) unsalted butter
Juice of ½ lemon
½ cup heavy cream, whipped

Garlic, Olive Oil, and Hot Red Pepper Sauce

aglio, olio, e peperoncino

This is a classic simple sauce which is the basis of any number of sauté dishes, soups, and more complicated dishes, many of which include fish. It can be made in larger quantities and stored in the refrigerator.

This may be doubled or tripled, and of course it can be hotter: this is middle-of-the-road hot.

3 dried cayenne pepper pods, seeded, or ¼ teaspoon ground cayenne pepper
3 garlic cloves
⅓ cup olive oil

If using the pepper pods, sauté with the garlic in the olive oil over medium heat. When the garlic is golden and the pepper dark brown, remove them from the oil and turn off the heat.

If using the ground cayenne pepper, brown the garlic and when browned, remove the garlic and add the cayenne. Stir, cook a moment or two, and remove from heat.

Yield: enough for 6 portions of fish or as the beginning of many soups and sauces

Green Sauce

salsa verde

2 cups flat-leaf parsley leaves
2 tablespoons capers
1 garlic clove, optional
Juice of 1½ lemons
⅛ teaspoon salt, or to taste
½ cup olive oil

Chop the parsley, capers, and garlic coarsely. Put them in a blender with the lemon juice and the salt. Add half the olive oil and blend at low speed for 10 seconds or until the parsley looks minced. Add the rest of the oil and blend for a few seconds. Pour into a suitable bowl, stir, taste for salt, and adjust seasonings if necessary.

Yield: 1 cup, approximately, enough for 6 portions of poached or broiled fish

Green Sauce, Piemontese Style

salsa verde alla piemontese

Chop together thoroughly the anchovies, parsley, and garlic. Trim and discard the crusts of the bread, and soak the rest 3 to 4 minutes in the vinegar. Squeeze out the vinegar, and shred the bread into a small mixing bowl. Add the parsley mixture, and mix with a wooden spoon, mashing everything against the side of the bowl until well amalgamated. Add 2 tablespoons of olive oil and mix again. Finally, add up to 4 more tablespoons of olive oil to achieve a pourable sauce. Taste for salt and pepper. Add if necessary.

Yield: enough for 6 portions poached fish

2 anchovy fillets

3 cups loosely packed fresh flat-leaf parsley

2 garlic cloves

2 thick slices (2 ounces) day-old Italian bread

⅓ cup red-wine vinegar

6 tablespoons olive oil

Salt to taste

Freshly ground black pepper

Blender Mayonnaise

Mayonnaise may be stored in the refrigerator for use within five days. It also may be cut in half for a smaller batch. When you do store it, place a piece of plastic wrap right down on the surface to prevent a "skin" from forming.

Place the egg substitute in the blender. Add the lemon juice, salt, pepper, and mustard, and 3 tablespoons of the oil. Blend until the mixture is thick. Keep the blender

¼ cup egg substitute (or equivalent of 1 whole large egg), at room temperature

Juice of ½ lemon

¼ teaspoon salt

⅛ teaspoon freshly ground white pepper

¼ teaspoon dry mustard

¾ cup olive oil

going, and add the remaining oil in a slow, steady stream. If a small bubble of oil forms on the top of the mayonnaise, stop adding oil but keep blending until the bubble disappears. Continue pouring in the remaining oil, and blend a moment more.

Yield: approximately 1 cup; refrigerate until use or up to 5 days

NOTE: Raw egg yolks are no longer recommended due to the prevalence of salmonella in the yolk itself. While many have not heard of this warning or have ignored it, the U.S. Department of Agriculture reports that using raw egg yolks may be harmful especially to the very young or the very old and therefore we recommend using egg substitute in those recipes that call for raw eggs until the crisis passes.

Mayonnaise with Fresh Basil

maionese al basilico

½ cup egg substitute (or equivalent of 2 large egg yolks, see Note, above)
1 egg white
⅛ teaspoon white pepper
⅛ teaspoon ground cayenne pepper
¾ teaspoon salt
1 to 1½ cups pure olive oil
1 to 2 teaspoons light cream
4 tablespoons white-wine vinegar (or enough to make the mayonnaise rather pourable)
10 fresh basil leaves, chopped

This is a favorite for use with chilled appetizers and originally was developed to dress and garnish big buffet party dishes such as shrimp.

Place the egg substitute, the egg white, and the dry ingredients in a blender. Turn on the machine and add about ¼ cup of oil. Keep blending and slowly add another ¼ cup of oil.

When dressing begins to thicken, add the remaining oil in a steady stream. When the mayonnaise is really thick,

add the cream, blend briefly, add the vinegar, and blend again.

When the dressing is of a good pourable consistency, add the basil. Taste and adjust seasonings if necessary.

Yield: 3 cups, approximately

Parsley Mayonnaise

maionese al prezzemolo

Put the egg substitute in a blender. With the blender going, slowly pour in ⅔ cup of the olive oil. Run the blender at high speed until the mixture thickens. Add the lemon juice and the seasonings and blend again to mix well. The sauce is now a pourable sauce, good for fish and fowl alike. If you wish it to be thicker, turn on the motor, slowly pour the rest of the oil into the blender, and continue blending until the sauce is as thick as mayonnaise made with raw egg yolks.

Yield: about 1½ cups

½ cup egg substitute (or the equivalent of 2 large eggs, see Note, page 40)
⅔ to 1 cup olive oil
2 tablespoons lemon juice
½ teaspoon salt
⅛ teaspoon freshly ground white pepper, optional
¼ teaspoon dry mustard
5 sprigs of fresh flat-leaf parsley

Olive and Caper Sauce

salsa all'olive e capperi

2 lemons

2 tablespoons minced fresh flat-leaf
  parsley, plus several sprigs for
  garnish

1 tablespoon capers, rinsed, drained,
  and chopped

6 tablespoons olive oil

½ cup Sicilian olives (packed in
  brine), pitted

The definite flavor of this sauce balances well with the flavor and texture of deep-water, meaty fish such as cod and turbot, especially when poached.

Mix the juice of one lemon with the 2 tablespoons of parsley, capers, and olive oil, and process in a food processor or whisk well.

Chop the olives coarsely and stir them into the sauce.

Brush poached fish with the juice of the second lemon to get a deep lemon flavor well into the fish. Dress the fish with the sauce. Garnish with the parsley sprigs and serve.

Yield: 4 portions of sauce for 1 to 1¼ pounds of poached fish

Basic Tomato Sauce

salsa di pomodoro

This smooth, simple sauce is used in the preparation of many dishes in this book. If very ripe fresh tomatoes are at hand, use them: the sauce is instantly embellished.

4 tablespoons olive oil
4 cups peeled plum tomatoes, fresh or canned
1 carrot
1 celery rib
1 onion
4 or 5 sprigs of fresh flat-leaf parsley
2 teaspoons salt, or to taste
Freshly ground black pepper to taste

Put the olive oil in a big saucepan and cut the plum tomatoes into bite-size chunks over the pan so that no drop of juice is wasted. Coarsely chop the other vegetables and parsley and add to the olive oil. Bring to a boil, lower the heat, and cover and simmer for about 30 minutes. Uncover, taste for salt and pepper, adjust the seasonings if necessary, and simmer another 15 minutes or so, until the liquid has reduced and the tomatoes are practically dissolved. Put the whole mixture through a sieve or a food mill, and use it any way you wish.

Yield: 4 cups, or enough for 6 generous portions

NOTE: This sauce may be doubled or tripled, cooled, and then frozen in containers to fit your cooking demands.

Tomato and Basil Sauce

salsa di pomodoro e basilico

10 to 12 very ripe peeled tomatoes,
   or approximately 3 cups canned
4 tablespoons olive oil or unsalted
   butter
Salt to taste
A dozen fresh basil leaves, chopped
   coarsely

This sauce is a superior ingredient in a number of recipes, from sauces for pasta to pizza toppings.

Plump, very ripe plum tomatoes right from the garden give marvelous results. If you grow your own salad tomatoes, you will find superior results also when the tomatoes are picked at their peak. Canned plum tomatoes are satisfactory, but they are not quite the same (see page 56).

Core the tomatoes, and scoop the seedy portion into a sieve over a bowl. Break the pulp of the tomatoes into fork-size pieces and put them in the bowl. Press the seedy parts with your fingers or the back of a spoon to send all possible juice into the bowl. Discard the seeds.

Pour the olive oil into a sauté pan, add the tomato pieces and juice to the pan, and bring to a boil. Add the salt and basil. Stir, lower the heat, and simmer for about 15 minutes or until slightly reduced and the sauce coats a spoon.

Yield: 3 cups, approximately, or enough for 8 to 10 portions

Hot Tomato Sauce

salsa piccante al pomodoro

Place the olive oil, garlic, onion, carrot, and celery in a sauté pan, and cook about 10 minutes or until the vegetables are limp but not brown. Add the tomatoes and the wine and cook until the wine has evaporated and the tomatoes have softened.

Add the water, basil, and cayenne pepper. Bring back to a boil, lower the heat, and simmer for 20 minutes. Taste and adjust salt if necessary.

Yield: about 2 cups, or enough for 6 to 8 portions

2 to 3 tablespoons olive oil

1 to 2 garlic cloves, minced

1 small onion, minced

1 small carrot, peeled and chopped fine

½ celery rib, chopped fine, or ½ teaspoon celery salt

2 cups canned peeled plum tomatoes, crushed or mashed a bit

¼ cup dry white wine

1¾ cups water

2 teaspoons chopped fresh basil leaves, or 1 teaspoon dried

¼ teaspoon cayenne pepper

½ teaspoon salt (if using fresh celery)

Pesto

pesto alla Genovese

2 cups loosely packed fresh basil
    leaves
2 medium garlic cloves
⅔ cup (approximately 3 ounces)
    pine nuts
1 teaspoon salt
¾ to 1 cup olive oil
1 tablespoon freshly grated
    Parmesan cheese
1 tablespoon freshly grated pecorino
    cheese

Pesto alla Genovese *is the name of a classic basil-nut-garlic combination pounded to a paste consistency in a mortar with a pestle. With the addition of good olive oil, a sauce is developed to work marvelously with pasta and with poached fish. Today we forgo the mortar/pestle exercise and use a blender or food processor.*

Chop the basil and garlic coarsely. Crush the pine nuts with a rolling pin or meat pounder, and add them to the garlic and basil. Mix a bit and put in a blender or food processor. Add the salt and about half the olive oil and blend at low speed or process on/off until the herbs are minced.

Add the cheeses and blend or process at medium speed until everything is well amalgamated. Stop blending two or three times and scrape the mince from the sides of the blender.

Scrape the mixture into a small bowl. Beat in as much of the remaining oil as you wish to make the sauce as thin or thick as you desire.

Yield: 6 to 8 portions

Red Pesto

pesto rosso di Pantelleria

On the volcanic island of Pantelleria, southwest of Sicily, where agriculture spars with fishing to produce a rather special cuisine, red pesto takes top place. Islanders say the Genoese stole the idea for their garlic and basil (green) pesto. The basis of red pesto is made with the ripest, plumpest of plum tomatoes. Islanders sometimes use cheese, sometimes not, depending on the final use. We usually settle on the sauce without cheese when serving it with fish. One may use red pesto also on crostini for an appetizer or with pasta as a first course.

Some islanders use a half-dozen chopped green salty olives when making the sauce for a highly flavored grilled fish. Others add crushed pine nuts to give the sauce a bit more body. Both additions are perfectly valid as long as none of the flavors outdistances the others.

2 pounds fresh, very ripe plum tomatoes

2 cups loosely packed fresh basil leaves

3 garlic cloves

½ teaspoon salt

2 to 3 dashes of Tabasco, or to your taste

2 tablespoons olive oil

2 tablespoons capers, preferably packed in salt, well rinsed

1 tablespoon freshly grated pecorino cheese, optional

1 tablespoon freshly grated Parmesan cheese, optional

Blanch the tomatoes in boiling water a minute or two or until the skins pop wide open at the touch of a fork. Drain, cool slightly, and peel the tomatoes. Scoop out the seeds and juice into a sieve over a small bowl to reserve the juice. Cut the pulp into bits and add to the reserved juice. Chop the basil leaves and garlic coarsely and place in a blender. Add salt, Tabasco, and olive oil. Turn on the blender at a slow speed; start adding the tomato bits, juice, and capers; gradually accelerate the speed. Keep blending until a

sauce consistency is achieved. Return the speed to low and add the cheese(s) if using them. Place in a jar and let rest an hour or so—it gets better with time.

Yield: approximately 2 cups, enough for about 6 portions of fish

Walnut Sauce

salsa alle noci

1 garlic clove, minced
½ cup egg substitute (or the
  equivalent of 2 whole large eggs,
  see Note, page 40)
¾ cup olive oil
2 tablespoons dry white wine
1 tablespoon lemon juice
½ cup chopped walnuts
2 tablespoons chopped fresh flat-leaf
  parsley

Put the garlic in the bowl of the food processor. Add the egg substitute and process on/off until well mixed. With the motor on, slowly pour the olive oil into the egg mixture. Keep the motor on and add the wine and lemon juice. Stop the motor and stir in the walnuts and the parsley.

Yield: 1 cup, approximately, enough for 4 to 6 portions over broiled or poached fish

White Sauce

besciamella

Not hard to master, white sauce (béchamel) is an easy thickener that is basic to most cuisines of the Western world. The use of a small whisk will help remove any lumps. Salt and pepper is the usual flavoring, but we hope you will try the nutmeg, an ingredient almost always used in Italian white sauces, which enhances the taste no end.

If you make white sauce ahead of use time, cover with plastic wrap pressed down on the surface to prevent a "skin" from forming.

2 tablespoons unsalted butter
⅓ cup unbleached all-purpose flour
2 cups milk
¼ teaspoon freshly grated nutmeg
¼ teaspoon salt
⅛ teaspoon freshly ground white pepper

Melt the butter in a heavy 1-quart saucepan over low heat. Add the flour all at once, whisking with a small whisk as you add. Continue to cook and whisk for 1 minute and then pour in the milk in a steady stream as you whisk. Cook over medium heat, keeping the whisk going, for at least 4 minutes or until the sauce is thick and smooth and no longer tastes of uncooked flour.

Remove from heat, add the seasonings, and adjust if necessary.

Yield: 2 cups, or enough for 4 to 6 portions

Fish White Sauce

vellutata di pesce

4 tablespoons unsalted butter

¾ cup unbleached all-purpose flour

2 cups milk

Dash of salt and freshly ground
    black pepper

1 cup Basic Fish Stock I (page 166),
    heated

Juice of 1 lemon

5 sprigs of fresh flat-leaf parsley

The first time we made this version of white sauce using fish stock as well as milk, our enthusiasm was recorded with exclamation marks instead of comments for the seafood lasagne in which it starred.

Melt the butter in a skillet, stirring in the flour as you do so. Continue to stir and slowly add the milk. Stir and cook for about 3 minutes, adding the salt and pepper. Continue to stir and cook as you add the fish stock. Cook for about another minute or until the flour is completely cooked. Add the lemon juice, stir, and remove from heat.

Chop finely the parsley leaves and add them to the sauce. Serve immediately, hot, on fish or shellfish or cooled to layer lasagne.

Yield: 3 cups, or 6 to 8 portions of fish or lasagne

Mornay Sauce

salsa Mornay

Another familiar basic often used in saucing fish as well as in the composition of seafood tarts (page 78) and other larger gratins.

1 cup White Sauce (page 49)
1 egg yolk
1 cup light cream
2 tablespoons unsalted butter
3 tablespoons grated Gruyère cheese

Make the white sauce and keep over low heat.

Beat the egg yolk with the cream and pour the mixture into the heated sauce. Mix well and bring the sauce to a boil and let boil about 2 minutes. Remove from heat. Add the butter and when it has melted stir in the cheese.

Yield: 2 cups, or 4 to 6 portions

Herbs and Flavoring Plants

It takes a trip through the regions of Italy to discover there is more to fish flavoring than dear old lemon juice. Fish with its delicate flavor reacts so nicely to the gentle push and pull of an outside accent, and the aroma becomes enticing as the cooking proceeds. Furthermore, it isn't hard to get used to adding an herb.

Today, a great many markets increasingly offer fresh basil, sage, cilantro, dill, cress, and mint. Some say it is because the so-called nouvelle cuisine required the best of the fresh. Others feel that it is due to the ever-increasing love affair Americans have with new foods. It is also a recurrence of

a practice that goes back to the days when herbs were cultivated in kitchen gardens in Plymouth, Massachusetts.

Here is a beginning list of herbs that are especially good with fish. Many are generally found in green markets or produce sections of supermarkets, or you can grow your own. When we cannot find a fresh herb, we use dried herbs, but never more than half the amount of the fresh herb called for in the recipe. We suggest that you do likewise to begin and then adjust the amount to your taste.

Basil, an annual herb, basically comes in two types: it can grow high and bushy with big leaves or remain small and compact with tiny leaves like those of oregano. The plant, a member of the mint family, which came from Africa and Asia, made its way to Western Europe centuries ago.

Basil leaves are shiny and tender, can have a piquant or mild aroma, a rather peppery, clove-licorice taste, and go with tomatoes as salt goes with pepper. Basil is used in mayonnaise, with fish, in many types of salads, and as a garnish, adding a special flourish in taste as well as design. Scallops go well with basil as does swordfish. Basil paired with garlic is the heart of pesto, the richly flavored sauce that can dress virtually any poached fish and many of the grilled ones.

Basil may be preserved by any one of these three methods:

1) Wash and dry the leaves by spreading them out on clean dish towels; when completely dry, place them loosely in a jar with a cover (they will last about five days).
2) Coat the basil leaves with olive oil and place them in a jar with additional oil.
3) Mince one packed cup of basil leaves, blend the minced basil into ¼ pound butter, and freeze.

Basil preserved by the last two methods will keep for about three months.

Bay or *laurel leaf* is from an evergreen shrub or small tree and has been used for centuries as an aromatic part of soups, stews, sauces, and marinades for

fish and meat. It originated in Asia Minor and is now found cultivated or wild there, around the Mediterranean, in Northern Italy, and in California. In ancient times laurel was used to crown heroes and scholars. In the Middle Ages, laurel worked up to being a cure-all and was said to resist witchcraft.

The leaves are shiny and sturdy, not meant to be eaten but rather to be simmered as your food cooks and then removed. Some feel that the European leaves are superior to the Californian. Dried leaves last up to a year.

Capers are the buds of one of the prettiest flowers of a bush that has flourished in the Mediterranean area for more than two thousand years. Growers pick buds before they bloom and process them carefully by preserving them in vinegar and jarring them for sale around the world. On the island of Pantelleria, off the southwestern tip of Sicily, caper bushes spring out of the volcanic rock and grow wild or they are cultivated, bush by bush, alternating with grape vines. Island packers, however, disdain the use of vinegar and claim that their capers, which are bigger than most, are best preserved in salt.

Celery is another one of our favorite herbaceous plants that marries well with shellfish. A member of the carrot family, celery is found in northern Mediterranean countries wild, while it is cultivated almost everywhere. It is used in soups, stews, and salads.

Chives are an old faithful friend, hardy and good looking. They have sweet blossoms and tall, slender, oniony tasting stems to dress and enhance sauces for fish, mayonnaise, or add at the last moment to soups and vegetables. To use fresh all year long, chives can be grown in a pot on a sunny windowsill; freeze-dried chives are available in stores.

Coriander, another aromatic herb, is a member of the parsley family, the dried seeds of which work marvelously with meats, especially pork. The leaves, called cilantro, have a rather citrus flavor or mint touch when chopped and are

successfully paired with seafood and vegetables. Southwestern and Tex-Mex food call for cilantro a lot, as does Middle Eastern food.

Cress, a member of the mustard family, is cultivated as a leaf vegetable and is frequently used to garnish cold plates such as fish salads and mousses.

Dill, a native of Asia, is a favorite herb used fresh with fish; dried dill is found in pickles and vinegar. Sometimes referred to as the anise of the Scriptures, dill is a hardy annual that goes well with chowders as well as fish sauces.

Fennel, a member of the carrot family, goes back to ancient Greece where its original, Grecian name is *marathon*, from the region where it grew so profusely. If the archives serve, large fennel was first planted in central and southern Italy in the sixteenth century. Today, fennel with its anise flavor is a favorite vegetable when served raw with olive oil as a salad, or cooked in mussel soup and other fish dishes.

Garlic has been called the king of herbs for Latin countries, and it is used widely all over the world from China to Egypt, where the ancient Greeks and Romans first met it and brought it back home. It's hot and strong and a little goes a long way. So direct is garlic's approach to food, it frequently is not used whole or minced but just wiped around a bowl or over a slice of crusty bread before oil is added for toasted open-face sandwiches. In sauces, Italians generally use the whole clove, sautéed until golden and then discarded. But in the Italian sauce called *pesto*, minced garlic is paired with basil and held with olive oil for use with pasta, fish, and in Genoese minestrone. Contrary to many peoples' belief, Italian food is not loaded with garlic.

Lemon is probably first and foremost in flavoring seafood. Originally from the Far East, lemon trees are cultivated widely in Sicily, Calabria, the Sorrento peninsula, and around the northern lakes, especially Lake Garda. High in vitamin C, both peel and juice are used to bring out the fish flavors either during the cooking or as an added accent at serving time. Recently lemon oil has been featured in specialty stores and may be used as a substitute for lemon zest.

Sweet marjoram is a perennial herb, a member of the mint family, with small, soft leaves and a mild flavor that contributes gently to cheese and egg dishes as well as fish casseroles.

Oregano or wild marjoram, also a member of the mint family, is found in Europe and Asia and grows wild in southern Italy, where it is used to accent marinades and sauces, seafood, and Neapolitan pizzas. Oregano grown in southern Italy is far more aromatic than that found elsewhere and has an intense, rather spicy flavor that is heightened in drying.

Parsley, the most ubiquitous of the herbs, is a member of the carrot family. Bright green, found in markets everywhere, grown in gardens annually, it frequently takes its place as a garnish. Its slightly peppery flavor is also a nice addition to soups, stews, mayonnaise, and other sauces for both meat and fish. The flat-leaf, or Italian, parsley is thought by many to be more flavorful than curly-leaf parsley, and hence a number of the recipes in this collection call for flat-leaf parsley. We also use parsley stems by themselves as a base to keep a fish from sticking to its baking dish.

Hot pepper is used in a great many Italian dishes to brighten the flavor and accent a dish. In Italy and in America, one can buy dried hot red pepper pods or ground red pepper, which is made from the same plant. The hot red pepper is identified as chili pepper or cayenne. One dictionary says "chili, the pod of any species of *capsicum* especially *capsicum frutescens*, the common pepper of the garden, occurring in many varieties that range from mild to hot, having pungent seeds also ranging from mild to hot."

The little box we buy at the supermarket says "One of the hottest spices, Ground Red Pepper is made from hot *capsicum* peppers." The encyclopedia says the *capsicum frutescens* species is believed to have been brought to Europe by Columbus. Powdered pepper, like the pepper pods themselves, should be added at the start of cooking to mellow the pungent flavor. Since tastes vary so much, we recommend about ¼ teaspoon of powdered red pepper or one small cayenne

pepper pod, seeded, for 4 servings. Add more if you wish after your sauce has simmered for a while and you have tasted it.

Rosemary grows wild along the Tyrranean coast of Italy as well as in a number of other places where the nights are humid and the soil a bit on the rocky and arid side. Another member of the mint family, it is used frequently with roast lamb, and is considered a strong flavoring. It is often used as a marinade for barbecued meat and fish such as monkfish and eels on skewers.

Saffron, that glorious addition to *risotto* and *zuppa di pesce* was brought from Asia Minor to the Mediterranean by the Arabs and spread around southern Europe by the Crusaders. Today Spain, France, Italy, and Austria all grow it and vie for top listing as a market source. It is also grown in Afghanistan, China, and Pennsylvania, where the Amish use it in their dishes. Its scent and flavor are slightly bitter, which blends nicely with the dishes it enhances. While saffron's color turns everything it touches a golden hue, its price is also golden because the stamen, the flavoring part of the flower it comes from, is minuscule: 176 pounds of saffron flowers are reduced to 1 kilo or 2.2 pounds of stamens, which, when dried, produce only 2½ ounces of divine flavor for which there is no substitute.

Sage, another mint family member, is the flavoring that comes to our minds at the mention of trout. Along the shores of Lake Garda, in northern Italy, trout is served baked, bathed in butter, and touched with fresh sage. Sage is also used in fish marinades.

Tomatoes, not an herb but a fruit and, oh my, what a flavoring. Columbus never knew what miracles the land he discovered would bring to the tables of the world. Italy uses the tomato for pasta, pizza, rice, sauces, soups, and as a much loved vegetable. While the tomato is available year-round in the United States, the taste does, indeed, differ from season to season, growing place to growing place. Real tomato lovers, whenever possible, grow their own, even on balconies. In the

kitchen, the favored tomato for sauces is the plum tomato, which has a more generous pulp than a salad tomato. When choosing a canned brand, it is up to you; we look for the cans of tomatoes that have been put up without tomato paste or purée. We use tomato paste sparingly, and even though sun-dried tomatoes have become rather trendy lately in America, they, too, are used very sparingly.

Vinegar is indeed a flavoring element. In Italy, red-wine vinegar is used a great deal by and large, although when we make a basic fish stock we tend to reach for the white cider vinegar. Balsamic vinegar, which takes about twenty-five good long years (sometimes even more) to produce when made in the authentic fashion, is a marvel to use sparingly with salads.

Garnishes

Having followed the old rule about garnishes (a sprig of parsley and a slice of lemon) for years, we finally got around to making a few garnishes that are easy to learn, easy to do, and look very professional alongside almost any dish. If you have an extra minute, here are a few of our favorites, which do not require fancy tools or funny ingredients.

Cabbage Flower Peel back and remove the outer, heavier leaves of a small red cabbage. With a sharp knife, cut off the top third of the cabbage in a saw-toothed pattern. Using the same sharp knife, circle the central core and cut it out. Spread the cabbage leaves apart, thus making a petal-like effect. You now have a cabbage flower that may be used as a dish for a dip, mayonnaise, olives, etc.

Cucumber Chain With the seedless, extra-long European cucumber, you can cut curls long enough to encircle plates of seafood salads. Cut a length of unpeeled cucumber and score the skin with a vegetable peeler. Insert a wooden skewer through the center of the cucumber.

Cut through the cucumber to the skewer at a slight angle, slowly turning as you cut in a continuous spiral. Remove the skewer and stretch the cucumber gently to open up a chain of connected curls.

Onion Flowers The easiest of all garnishes: choose a well-rounded, medium-size onion and peel off its outer skin. Leave the root end intact but cut off any dangling roots.

Starting at the top of the onion, make a cut down toward the root end, stopping about half an inch from the end. This cut should be deep into the center of the onion. Make a second cut in the same fashion and then continue until you have gone all the way around the onion. It is just like slicing slivers without detaching them.

Once cut, place the onion in a bowl of warm water and let it soak for five minutes. This starts the opening of the onion. Replace the warm water with ice water and the onion flower will open even wider. When it is removed from the water to dry a bit on paper toweling, the onion smell has gone and the vegetable looks rather like a chrysanthemum.

Parsley and Lemon This garnish is, of course, the most familiar of all, especially for fish. We use the flat-leaf parsley nearly all the time for cooking but the curly parsley to garnish any plate. If the diner has to squeeze his own lemon, wedges cut about ½ inch thick are fine. If the lemon is sheer decoration, we like to cut it in ⅛-inch-wide slices and then cut once into the center and twist the slice to make it stand out more.

Tomato Rose This may be our favorite decoration for an aspic, a seafood salad, or a simple platter of fish fillets. Use a sharp, small paring knife to peel the skin of a medium-size tomato. Start at the blossom end of the tomato and cut a flat round just a bit bigger than a quarter before continuing to peel the tomato. This flat round acts as a base for the rose.

Keep the peeled skin as thin as possible and make a strip about 4 inches long. Peel a second strip about 3 inches long.

Coil the first strip loosely around the base. Coil the second strip more tightly and place it into the center of the loosely coiled strip.

Gently spread open the coiled strips to shape a rose in bloom, which may be placed directly on a serving platter. If you wish, tuck a large leaf of flat-leaf parsley under the rose. Tomato roses may be kept on a small plate, covered with plastic wrap, for up to four days if you use firm, fresh tomatoes.

Wine

There is an Italian saying that we have evoked from time to time: "A meal without wine is like a day without sun." Whether you use wine to make the sauce or to flavor the recipe, or you just have a nice glass to accompany a favorite food, wine is important. While we cannot go into vast paragraphs for filling your cellar, we would like to say just a few words.

Many, many of the recipes in this book carry the advice "add dry white wine." It is good advice because wine brings out all the best in the sauce, makes it more defined, and certainly adds a contrasting flavor to the fish, which in turn completes the dish. The problem is how to define what to use. A dry white wine should be crisp, not overly fruity in taste, and not overly potent in aroma. And it should be a good wine, not wildly expensive but certainly not a cheap, throwaway wine. You can kill any dish by using poor quality wine; definitely avoid all wines labeled "cooking wine."

Thus, our modest rule is use good wine if you can. If you don't wish to use wine or can't find a wine to fit your needs, then go without. A touch of lemon juice is a valid alternative. A dry white vermouth can add an even more complementary flavor, since vermouth is flavored with a touch of aromatic herbs. And finally, when you lift your glass for a first sip, we recommend another Italian saying: "Salute," which means "to your health."

Antipasti

Olives and Anchovies

Anchovy and Mozzarella Toasts

Hot Sauce with Vegetables

Artichokes with Anchovy Dressing

Prawn Cocktail

Crabmeat Cocktail

Traditional Venetian Crabmeat Cocktail

Margherita Seafood Cocktail

Seafood Cocktail

Shrimp Cocktail

Crabmeat Tartlets

Seafood in Puff Pastry

Shrimp Tartlets

Shrimp Tart

Shrimp Puffs

Seafood Toasts

Oyster Fritters

Mussels in Mustard Sauce

Mussels on the Half Shell

Mussels with Aromatic Herbs

Mussels with Sardine Butter in Aspic

Razor Clam Antipasto

Savory Squid

Peppers Stuffed with Tuna

Tomatoes Stuffed with Tuna

If everyone descends on us for a holiday, there is bound to be a meal that takes a bit of tug and pull to get together. During the hullabaloo of arrivals and greetings someone invariably turns out an appetizer, even if only a lovely piece of cheese with crusty bread. In those cases, *antipasti* serve to hold everyone off while we cook the main meal. For planned, serious, special occasions, be they dinners or buffets, appetizers should tease the palate and tantalize the appetite. Contrary to custom in many popular restaurants, this course should be relatively small, consist of few choices, and should rarely be substituted for the whole meal. (Let the Latin roots of the word then come to the fore: *ante-prandium*, "before the meal.") This is the practice in Italy.

Olives and Anchovies

antipasto d'olive e alici

½ *medium onion, minced*
1 *garlic clove, halved*
4 *anchovy fillets, chopped coarsely*
⅛ *teaspoon dried oregano (a pinch)*
¾ *cup olive oil*
1½ *pounds black olives, packed in
    brine*
Fresh basil or parsley for garnish

This is probably the easiest of all flavored antipasti as it goes together in no time and can be eaten without plates—just remember to have paper napkins handy.

Place the onion, garlic, anchovies, and oregano in a sauté pan. Add the olive oil and cook over medium heat for about 5 minutes or until the onion bits and garlic are soft, the anchovies more or less melted.

Pit the olives and place them in a suitable bowl. Strain the pan juices over the olives. Garnish as you wish and serve.

Yield: 6 to 8 portions

Anchovy and Mozzarella Toasts

crostini alle alici e mozzarella

This simple preparation packs a lot of taste and a lot of tradition. In Rome it was (and it still is) a great competitor with pizza as a pre- or after-movie snack. If cut into dainty pieces it is also excellent for cocktail toasts, and as an antipasto proper it is a tuneup for the taste buds while waiting for the first course to come off the stove.

8 slices Italian bread, baguette style
6 thin slices mozzarella
3 tablespoons olive oil
2 tablespoons unsalted butter, melted
6 anchovy fillets

Preheat the oven to 450 degrees Fahrenheit.

Trim the bread slices to an even size, about 3 inches in diameter, cutting off the crusts at the same time. Place 4 slices vertically in each of two small ovenproof casseroles. Place the mozzarella slices between the bread slices. Dribble olive oil over all.

Put in the oven and toast for 5 to 8 minutes.

Melt the butter in a small saucepan. Mash the anchovies into the butter. Pour the hot anchovy butter over the toasts when they come out of the oven.

Yield: 2 portions, or more when the crostini *are cut in smaller pieces*

Hot Sauce with Vegetables

bagna cauda

VEGETABLES:

4 cardoons, optional

Juice of 1 lemon

1 red bell pepper

1 green bell pepper

*5 white celery ribs from the center
    of the bunch*

½ head small cauliflower

5 small carrots

*5 or 6 cabbage leaves, preferably
    from the center*

SAUCE:

6 garlic cloves

½ cup milk

5 tablespoons unsalted butter

1 dozen anchovy fillets

1 cup olive oil

Salt to taste

A list of antipasti in a fish cookery book must include this one, which marries the touch of a dozen anchovies to olive oil and fresh, tender, small vegetables. It is a dipping dish that generations of wine lovers have used to stay the appetite while enjoying a glass of wine. Cardoons, a perennial Mediterranean plant that is similar to celery but with sturdier and larger stalks and bulbs, are an important part of the vegetable list for bagna cauda *in Italy. If you can find them in your market, or grow them in your garden, they are well worth your attention.* Bagna cauda *is served with the sauce kept hot in a chafing dish; the dipping can be done with fingers or with those long forks used for fondue.*

There are, as usual, variations on the theme: try bagna cauda *with other vegetables that have the right texture as well as taste for the sauce: broccoli flowers, zucchini pieces, even a Belgian endive leaf or two. Also, we found that some people like the sauce even better when a dash of cream is worked into it to thicken it ever so slightly.*

Wash the cardoons, peel off the stringiest ribs, cut the stems into 3-inch lengths, and soak in water with the juice of the lemon for an hour.

To make the sauce, peel the garlic cloves and let them stand in the milk for an hour to cut their sharpness.

Melt the butter over very low heat in an earthenware casserole. Mince the garlic, or press it, and sauté in the butter for 5 minutes. Mash the anchovies into a paste and stir into the butter. Slowly stir in the olive oil. Continue cooking over very low heat, stirring occasionally, for 35 to 40 minutes. Taste for salt and add if necessary.

While the sauce cooks, prepare the rest of the vegetables. Core and cut the peppers in thin strips. Wash the celery ribs and cut them in half lengthwise. Break the cauliflower into florets. Peel the carrots and cut them in half, lengthwise. Cut the cabbage leaves into manageable pieces.

When the sauce is ready, transfer it from the stove to a warming device on the table. It must be kept warm while everybody gets a chance to dip. We find that placing the warming device in the center of a serving platter, with the vegetables encircling it, is quite satisfactory.

Yield: 6 portions

Artichokes with Anchovy Dressing

carciofi in salsa d'acciuga

3 anchovy fillets
3 cocktail onions, drained and
    halved
1 teaspoon Dijon-style mustard
3 tablespoons olive oil
2 tablespoons red-wine vinegar
Freshly ground white pepper to taste
5 ounces frozen artichoke hearts,
    cooked and drained

One avocado, halved, may be substituted for the artichokes for a variation on this theme.

In a mortar or small food processor, mash the anchovies and onions to a paste.

Stir in the mustard, oil, and vinegar, and work with the pestle or process until the sauce is smooth and homogenized. Add a sprinkling of white pepper to taste, and mix again.

Place cooked, cooled artichoke hearts on a plate. Pour the sauce over the artichokes and serve.

Yield: 2 portions

Prawn Cocktail

antipasto di scampi

If you are lucky enough to find prawns (cousins to the lobster and known as langoustine *in French), this is a quite wonderful way to serve them—in a rather fancy sauce that is also perfect for large shrimp. Prawns are also called Norway lobster and they are found all the way from Iceland to Morocco and throughout the western and central Mediterranean as well as in the Adriatic Sea.*

1 pound prawns or large shrimp, unpeeled
1 hard-boiled egg yolk
1 teaspoon Dijon-style mustard
3 tablespoons olive oil
Juice of ½ lemon
6 tablespoons tomato ketchup
¼ teaspoon white wine Worcestershire sauce
2 tablespoons dry sherry
2 tablespoons heavy cream
Salt to taste
Freshly ground white pepper to taste
6 leaves Bibb lettuce

Prepare the prawns or shrimp by cooking them in boiling, salted water (10 minutes for the prawns, 3 minutes or until coral red for the large shrimp). While they cool, place the egg yolk in a blender. Add the mustard. Turn on the blender to low speed and add the oil slowly and then add the lemon juice. Stop the blender, add the Worcestershire sauce, sherry, cream, salt, and pepper, and blend very briefly. Chill well.

Shell the prawns by removing the tail from the body; cut the shell on the underside of the tail and lift out the meat. Or shell and then devein the shrimp by removing the black vein along the curve of the shrimp.

At serving time, put a perfect lettuce leaf on each of six plates and divide the prawns or shrimp evenly onto the lettuce. Spoon some cocktail sauce over each plate.

Yield: 6 portions

Crabmeat Cocktail

antipasto di granseola

1 pound cooked crabmeat
12 leaves Bibb lettuce
4 hard-boiled egg yolks
¼ teaspoon salt
⅛ teaspoon white pepper, or to taste
Dash of Worcestershire sauce
1 tablespoon chopped fresh basil
⅔ cup heavy cream
Juice of ½ lemon
Dash of white-wine vinegar,
    optional

The spiny, or spider, crab found in the northern Adriatic has an intense sea flavor, which explains the fondness the Venetians have for this crustacean, which they use to make their famous crabmeat cocktail. Our Pacific or Atlantic crabs (snow, stone, king, Dungeness) are larger in size and have a more delicate taste. Canned crabmeat is quite acceptable.

Drain the crabmeat thoroughly and go through it carefully to remove any bits of shell. Separate and core the Bibb lettuce, wash and drain it; set the leaves aside to dry.

Put the egg yolks in a blender. Add the salt, pepper, Worcestershire sauce, and basil. Work the yolks until creamy. Slowly add the cream.

Taste for salt and adjust. Slowly add the lemon juice.

Line 6 large cocktail glasses or small bowls with the lettuce. Divide the crabmeat among the bowls. Pour the sauce over the crab. For heightened flavor, sprinkle a drop or two of vinegar on each dish.

Yield: 6 portions

Traditional Venetian Crabmeat Cocktail

granseola alla veneziana

Shred the crabmeat into a small bowl. Mix in the parsley. Add the lemon juice and olive oil and mix well. Add salt if necessary and pepper. Chill thoroughly and serve on chilled plates or in chilled crab shells.

Yield: 6 portions

1 pound cooked crabmeat
2 tablespoons minced fresh flat-leaf parsley
Juice of 1 lemon
3 tablespoons virgin olive oil
Salt to taste
Freshly ground white pepper to taste

Margherita Seafood Cocktail

antipasto di mare Margherita

½ *pound small squid, cleaned (page 16)*

1 quart Basic Fish Stock I (page 166)

½ *pound baby cherrystone clams*

½ *pound mussels, scrubbed, "beards" removed*

½ *pound shrimp*

1 tablespoon capers, rinsed and drained

1 tablespoon chopped fresh flat-leaf parsley

Juice of 1 lemon, or to taste

4 tablespoons olive oil

Salt and freshly ground white pepper to taste

Four kinds of seafood, fish broth, capers, and lemon are the main ingredients for this antipasto from the sea. The squid is one of the few creatures that can be cooked either very rapidly or for over 15 minutes. In this case, the 20-minute cooking in the fish broth enhances the squid flavor; adding the clams, mussels, and shrimp toward the end of the cooking span leaves them tender but not overcooked.

Seafood cocktail may be kept covered in the refrigerator for up to 10 hours, after which and just before serving, add the capers and the parsley.

Cut the squid sacs in rings, the tentacles in half lengthwise. Bring the fish stock to a boil, add the squid, and let boil gently for 15 minutes. Add the clams and mussels and cook about 3 minutes or until the shells open. Add the shrimp and cook another 2 minutes or until the shrimp are a bright coral color.

Scoop out the shellfish and when cool enough to handle, remove and discard the shells, letting the juices fall back into the pan. Place clams, mussels, and shrimp in a bowl. Scoop out the squid and add to the bowl.

Chop the capers and add them along with the parsley to the seafood. Dress with the lemon juice and olive oil.

Refrigerate for about an hour before serving, at which time, toss, taste, and add salt and pepper to please.

Yield: 4 portions

Seafood Cocktail

antipasto di mare

Shell and clean the shrimp, and butterfly each by making a sharp, deep incision along its back. Add the vinegar to 2 quarts of boiling, lightly salted water. Add the shrimp and cook for 2 to 3 minutes or until coral pink. Scoop out the shrimp and let cool. Clean and cut the squid (page 16) and blanch it in the shrimp water for 1 minute. Drain and cool it right away in a pot of cold water. Place the shrimp, squid, and celery slices in a large bowl. Add the oil, lemon juice, parsley, and the salt and pepper. Mix and let marinate for an hour.

At serving time, place a lettuce leaf on each of 6 hors d'oeuvres plates. Add a portion of the shrimp-squid-celery mixture to each plate, dress with the marinade. Garnish with lemon slices and serve.

Yield: 6 portions

½ pound medium shrimp
2 tablespoons white-wine vinegar
1½ pounds squid
½ pound celery, sliced thin
½ cup olive oil
¼ cup lemon juice
¼ cup fresh flat-leaf parsley leaves, washed and chopped
½ teaspoon salt
½ teaspoon freshly ground white pepper
6 Bibb lettuce leaves
Lemon slices for garnish

Shrimp Cocktail

cocktail di gamberi

1 small head Bibb lettuce

30 medium shrimp, approximately
    1¼ pounds

1 recipe Parsley Mayonnaise (page
    41)

1 tablespoon Worcestershire sauce

2 tablespoons tomato juice

2 tablespoons lemon juice

¼ teaspoon powdered white pepper

4 tomatoes

Core the lettuce, separate the leaves, wash, drain, and pat dry with paper towels.

Cook the unshelled shrimp for 2 to 3 minutes in boiling salted water. Cool them under running cold water; strip off the shells but leave the tails on. Devein if necessary.

Mix the parsley mayonnaise with the Worcestershire sauce, tomato juice, lemon juice, and pepper.

Cut each tomato into 8 wedges.

Use the lettuce to line the bottom of each cocktail glass or bowl. Hang 5 shrimp over the edge of each glass, tails on the outside, alternating them with tomato wedges.

At serving time, dribble the mayonnaise over the backs of the shrimp and the tomatoes, letting some of it collect on the lettuce.

Yield: 6 portions

Crabmeat Tartlets

barchette di granchio

Once you've made a batch of Short Crust Pastry, it is time to practice tartlets with seafood. Also called barquettes, these small pastries are a particular draw for any formal or informal occasion. The "little boats" can carry different loads, such as shrimp (see Shrimp Tartlets, page 78) or scallops, or anything else that strikes your fancy.

1 recipe Short Crust Pastry (page 305), enough for 12 small tartlet forms
8 ounces crabmeat (canned)
1 tablespoon Marsala
1 teaspoon lemon juice
1 dash of Tabasco
8 to 10 fresh mushrooms, approximately 3 ounces
1½ tablespoons unsalted butter
Salt and freshly ground black pepper to taste
1 teaspoon unbleached all-purpose flour
¼ cup milk
1 egg yolk
Unflavored breadcrumbs

Preheat the oven to 400 degrees Fahrenheit.

Roll out the pastry dough and cut it in even rectangles just a little larger than your tartlet forms. Line the forms with the rectangles, pressing the dough gently all around. Or put all the tartlet forms, face up, as close together as possible, place the rolled dough over them, pushing it down gently into each form. Pass a rolling pin over them, letting the pressure of the pin force the tartlet rims to cut the dough to the correct size. One way or the other, once the forms are lined with dough, cover with aluminum foil and weight them down with pastry weights, beans, or rice.

Bake for about 15 minutes or until toast colored.

Remove weights and foil and let cool.

Marinate the crabmeat in the Marsala, lemon juice, and Tabasco for 10 minutes. Clean and thinly slice the mushrooms.

Melt 1 tablespoon of the butter in a small saucepan and sauté the mushrooms in it. Add the salt and pepper, and continue cooking until the mushrooms release their natural juices (about 4 minutes). Scoop the mushrooms out of the pan and add to the crabmeat.

Melt the remaining butter in the pan juices over low heat. Whisk in the flour and cook 1 minute. Add the milk and cook, stirring, until beginning to thicken. Whisk in the egg yolk. Continue to cook for three more minutes, or a total of 4 minutes.

Add the egg sauce to the crabmeat and mushrooms, and mix again. Fill the tartlet shells with the mixture. Sprinkle with breadcrumbs and place under a preheated broiler for 5 minutes.

Yield: 6 portions

Seafood in Puff Pastry

pasta sfogliata alla pescatora

Preheat the oven to 400 degrees Fahrenheit.

Bring the fish stock or water and salt, carrot, onion, celery, and bay leaf to a boil. Add the shrimp shells if you have them. Lower the heat, and simmer for 20 to 30 minutes.

Bake your pastry shells for 7 to 8 minutes.

If using sea scallops, slice them in half. When the broth is ready, cook the seafood, each type by itself, by dropping it into the broth, bringing the broth back to the boil, and letting each cook 1 minute longer. Place the cooked seafood in a bowl.

Remove the pastry shells from the oven, scoop out the pastry center, and ready the shells on a platter. Keep them warm in cooling oven.

Make the white sauce, using 2 cups of fish stock instead of the milk called for in the recipe. Taste the sauce for final flavor, adjust if necessary. Add the cooked seafood, stirring over low heat until the seafood is reasonably hot. Divide the seafood into the pastry shells and serve.

Yield: 12 portions

2 to 3 cups Basic Fish Stock I (page 166) or 3 cups water

1 teaspoon salt

1 carrot

1 onion

1 celery rib

1 bay leaf

1 pound combined seafood (shrimps, scallops, squid), cleaned and shells reserved

12 puff pastry cups (fresh Rough Puff Pastry, page 304) or commercial frozen puff pastry

1 recipe White Sauce (page 49)

Shrimp Tartlets

tartine di gamberi

1 recipe Short Crust Pastry (page 305)

1 pound fresh medium shrimp

3 cups Basic Fish Stock II (page 168), or 3 cups boiling salted water

1 cup Mornay Sauce (page 51)

¼ cup grated Parmesan cheese

Sprigs of fresh parsley for garnish, optional

Preheat the oven to 400 degrees Fahrenheit.

Roll out the pastry dough and cut it in rectangles just a little larger than your tartlet forms. Line the forms with the rectangles, pressing the dough gently all around. Or, put all the tartlet forms as close together as possible, place the rolled dough over them, and push it down gently into each form. Pass a rolling pin over them, letting the pressure of the pin force the tartlet rims to cut the dough the correct size. One way or the other, once the forms are lined with dough, cover this with aluminum foil and weight it down with pastry weights, beans, or rice.

Bake for about 15 minutes or until toast colored. Remove weights and foil and let cool.

Cook the shrimp in boiling fish stock or water for about 1 minute. Remove from broth, peel, and devein. Divide the shrimp evenly among the tartlets. Cover with the Mornay sauce and sprinkle with the cheese.

Put back in the oven just long enough to melt the cheese topping a bit and heat the tartlets through. Garnish with a few leaves of parsley.

Yield: 6 large or 12 small filled tartlets

Shrimp Tart

crostata di gamberi

Originally this recipe was for scampi or prawn tails, and it could double as a hot hors d'oeuvre or a fancy luncheon dish. But it isn't always easy to find langoustines (also called Dublin Bay prawns), and the conversion to shrimp works well.

1 recipe Short Crust Pastry (page 305)
2 cups sliced mushrooms
3 tablespoons unsalted butter
1½ pounds uncooked large shrimp or prawns, peeled
1¼ cups White Sauce (page 49)
3 tablespoons Basic Tomato Sauce (page 43), or canned commercial tomato sauce
Pinch of celery salt
Freshly ground white pepper

Preheat the oven to 400 degrees Fahrenheit.

Line an 8-inch tart pan with the pastry; cover with aluminum foil and pastry weights. Bake for 15 minutes. Remove from the oven, lift out the foil and weights, and return to bake another 5 to 7 minutes or until browned.

Sauté the mushroom slices in the butter for about 5 minutes or until they have given up their juices. Add the shrimp (or scampi) and cook another 2 to 3 minutes or until bright coral red and cooked but still tender.

Stir together the white sauce and tomato sauce, adding the celery salt and pepper to taste. Add the sauce to the shrimp and heat through.

Pour the shrimp and sauce into the baked crust and place in the oven for about 5 minutes or until glazed.

Yield: 6 portions

Shrimp Puffs

bigné di gamberi

1 recipe Cream Puff Pastry (page
  308)
2 cans (8½ ounces total) tiny, whole
  shrimp
½ teaspoon cayenne pepper
1 tablespoon chopped fresh flat-leaf
  parsley
Dash of freshly grated nutmeg
Vegetable oil for frying

While most cream puffs are sweet and baked in the oven to be served for dessert, these puffs, flavored with shrimp and nutmeg, are deep-fried and served hot as appetizers. The addition of a touch of cayenne pepper puts the puffs in the celebration category.

Make the pastry. Drain and mince the shrimp. Mix the shrimp bits, cayenne, parsley, and nutmeg into the dough.

Bring the vegetable oil to 300 degrees Fahrenheit. Scoop a tablespoon of dough and, with the help of another spoon, let it drop into the oil. Repeat a few times, without crowding the oil. When the first puffs are golden and well puffed up, remove with a slotted spoon and drain on paper towels. Keep the *bigné* warm while frying the rest of the dough.

Yield: 2 dozen, approximately

Seafood Toasts

crostini con frutti di mare

Preheat the oven to 425 degrees Fahrenheit.

Put the olive oil in a sauté pan large enough to hold the seafood. Heat over medium heat.

Drain the seafood carefully and sauté in the oil for a minute.

Add the Mornay sauce and sprinkle with a touch of white pepper to your taste. Mix lightly.

Cut the crusts off the bread slices and then cut the slices in rectangles about 2 inches by 1 inch or to your own design. Fry them to golden brown in the oil-butter mixture.

After the bread slices are fried, remove them to a cookie sheet. Spread with the seafood. Briefly fry the breadcrumbs in the remaining butter and oil and sprinkle over the seafood.

Place the crostini in the oven for about 5 minutes or until browned. Serve immediately.

Yield: 2 dozen, approximately, or 6 to 8 portions

2 tablespoons olive oil, approximately

¼ cup small shrimp, shelled and chopped (or ½ cup tiny canned shrimp*)

¼ cup fresh mussels, shelled and chopped (or ½ cup canned smoked mussels*)

¼ cup fresh clams, shelled and chopped (or ½ cup canned baby clams*)

1 cup Mornay Sauce (page 51), approximately

Freshly ground white pepper to taste

6 slices day-old white Italian-style bread

2 tablespoons olive oil mixed with 2 tablespoons unsalted butter

4 tablespoons unflavored breadcrumbs

* Approximately three ounces

Oyster Fritters

bigné di ostriche

1 recipe Egg Batter (page 29)
3 dozen oysters, shucked
Vegetable oil for frying
3 lemons, quartered

While almost everyone knows how delicious a fresh oyster on the half shell can be, not all of us are familiar with oyster fritters. For those who really never got the hang of opening an oyster, this is the ideal way to use fresh, shucked oysters and delight the people you dine with.

Make the batter and place in the refrigerator for at least 30 minutes or up to 3 hours.

Place the oysters and their liquid in a large sauté pan over medium heat. Bring to a boil and remove the pan immediately from the heat. Let the oysters cool, and when cool remove them from their liquid, drain well, and pat dry with paper toweling.

Bring the vegetable oil to frying heat (375 degrees Fahrenheit), dip a few oysters at a time in the batter and then in the frying oil. When golden brown, remove the oysters to a hot plate and continue to dip in batter and fry those that remain. Place the quartered lemons around and about the plate of fritters and serve.

Yield: 6 portions

Mussels in Mustard Sauce

cozze in salsa piccante

You can't begin to name the many, many ways to use the versatile mussel. Sleek and black when cleaned, soft and gently rich on the inside, the mussel, whether farm-grown or picked off the coast of Maine, is served in many fashions. This is a piquant old favorite.

2 pounds fresh mussels, cleaned, "beards" removed
2 tablespoons unsalted butter
2 tablespoons unbleached all-purpose flour
1 tablespoon red-wine vinegar
2 tablespoons Dijon-style mustard
2 generous dashes of Tabasco
Salt, optional
1 tablespoon minced fresh flat-leaf parsley

Put the cleaned mussels in a pot with ¼ cup of water, cover, and steam for 3 to 5 minutes or until the shells have opened.

When the mussels are cool enough to handle, separate the shells, discarding the mussel-free halves and separating the mussel from the half to which it clings. Place the mussel on that half shell on a warm plate and place in a warm oven.

Filter the liquid through a cheesecloth-lined sieve and reserve.

Melt the butter in a saucepan, add the flour, and stir rapidly with a whisk. Cook over low heat for 3 minutes, then slowly add ¾ cup of mussel broth, stirring as you add. Bring to a low boil, stir in the vinegar and mustard, and cook 2 minutes more or until creamy and of a sauce consistency. Finally, add the Tabasco, taste for salt, and adjust if you wish, and stir in the parsley. Spoon a bit of hot sauce over each mussel and serve.

Yield: 6 portions

Mussels on the Half Shell

cozze crude al basilico

1 pound fresh mussels, scrubbed,
   "beards" removed

4 to 6 tablespoons olive oil

1 dozen basil leaves, washed, patted
   dry, coarsely chopped

1 garlic clove

Freshly ground white pepper

This antipasto is for a sit-down meal, but it is such a treat that it is well worth the small amount of time needed to set the table and begin.

Check the mussels to make sure they are all well closed, discarding any that remain open.

Pour enough of the olive oil in a big sauté pan to cover the bottom, add half the basil leaves, the garlic, and the mussels.

Place over moderately high heat, cover the pan, and cook for a minute or two until the mussels open. Discard any mussels that do not open.

Scoop out the mussels, remove them from their shells, and place them back on half shells on a serving plate. Strain the pan juices through a very fine sieve, add pepper to taste, and pour a bit on each mussel. Add a drop or two of the remaining olive oil to each and then sprinkle with the remaining coarsely chopped basil leaves.

Yield: 4 to 6 portions

Mussels with Aromatic Herbs

cozze agli aromi

Place the mussels in a bowl of ice water to let any possible sand leach out. Put the olive oil in a small saucepan and sauté in it the crushed garlic and the scallions. When they are limp, stir in the basil, rosemary, fennel, and mint. When everything is well mixed, add the wine. Raise the heat and when the wine is almost evaporated, add the warm water and let boil slowly for a few minutes.

Pour this broth into a pot large enough to hold the mussels. Bring it to a boil, drain the mussels, and add them to the pot.

Cover and cook 3 to 5 minutes, or until the mussels have opened. With a slotted spoon, scoop out the mussels, discarding any that did not open, and letting all possible liquid drain back into the broth. When cool enough to handle, separate the mussels from their shells. Completely open the shells, discarding the top half. Place the remaining shell halves, with a mussel in each one, on a cookie sheet.

Filter the broth through a fine sieve into a saucepan. Whisk into it the flour, and bring to a slow boil, stirring constantly. Add the butter, cayenne, and cheese. Taste and adjust for salt and pepper, and cook, stirring, until it all thickens to the consistency of a thin béchamel. Let cool a little and then, with a teaspoon, pour some sauce on each mussel in its half shell. Sprinkle with a pinch of breadcrumbs and put under a broiler for 2 or 3 minutes. Serve immediately.

1 pound fresh mussels, scrubbed, "beards" removed

1½ tablespoons olive oil

2 garlic cloves, crushed

3 scallions, minced (1 tablespoon)

3 or 4 leaves basil, minced (1 tablespoon)

1 sprig rosemary, minced (1 tablespoon)

1½ teaspoons fennel seeds, crushed

3 to 4 fresh mint leaves, minced (1 tablespoon)

1 cup dry white wine

½ cup warm water

1 tablespoon unbleached all-purpose flour

1 tablespoon unsalted butter

⅛ to ¼ teaspoon cayenne pepper, or to taste

2 tablespoons freshly grated pecorino *cheese*

Salt and freshly ground black pepper to taste

2 tablespoons unflavored breadcrumbs (or as necessary)

Yield: 4 portions

Mussels with Sardine Butter in Aspic

cozze con sardine in gelatina

4 pounds mussels, scrubbed,
    "beards" removed

1 cup dry white wine

½ envelope plain gelatin

¼ cup cold water

6 ounces sardines, canned in olive
    oil, drained

6 tablespoons unsalted butter,
    softened

Sprigs of fresh curly or flat-leaf
    parsley for garnish

Steam the mussels in the wine in a covered pot about 3 to 5 minutes or until the shells open. Remove the mussels from the liquid, discarding any that have not opened. When cool enough to handle, take the mussels from their shells, letting the liquid drop back into the pot.

Reduce the liquid in the pot to ¾ cup. Melt the gelatin in the cold water, and completely dissolve it in the still hot mussel pan liquid. Strain that liquid through cheesecloth into a small bowl and place the bowl over ice in a larger bowl to cool until it is syrupy.

Mash the sardines into the butter; choose the best-looking half shells for the number of mussels you have and put a touch of the sardine butter in each shell. Place the mussels back in the half shells and put them on a plate. Pour the now-syrupy gelatin over the filled shells and let cool completely. Decorate with parsley.

Yield: 6 portions

Razor Clam Antipasto

antipasto di cannolicchi

Razor clams, long tubular mollusks, are regular and prized fare in Adriatic fish markets. There they are about 5 inches long, while Atlantic razor clams are closer to 7 to 9 inches long and about one inch in diameter. Like all mollusks, they will toughen up if overcooked. So, steam them and remove them from the heat almost as soon as they open.

Brush clean the clams and put them to soak in running cold water for 10 minutes. Put a half cup of water in a large frying pan, add the clams, cover, and bring to a boil. As soon as the shells are open, turn off the heat, remove the clams from the shells, letting the juice fall back into the pan. Set the clams aside, and filter and reserve the juice.

Put 4 tablespoons of the olive oil in a sauté pan and sauté the garlic cloves until browned and then discard them.

Pit the olives and chop them coarsely, and add to the flavored oil together with the parsley and hot pepper. Stir well and add the wine. Let cook over low heat. Put the remaining tablespoon of olive oil in a small frying pan, stir in the breadcrumbs, and stir and cook over moderate heat until toast colored. Add 3 tablespoons of the cooked breadcrumbs to the olive-parsley sauce, stirring well. Pour ¾ cup of clam juice into the sauce. Meanwhile, cube the

12 razor clams

5 tablespoons olive oil

2 garlic cloves

10 green Sicilian-style olives

4 tablespoons minced fresh flat-leaf parsley

½ teaspoon cayenne pepper, or 2 to 3 dashes of Tabasco

½ cup dry white wine

4 tablespoons unflavored breadcrumbs

¾ cup clam juice

2 tablespoons lemon juice

6 crisp lettuce or Belgian endive leaves

clams, discarding the tips if you wish, and add the clams to the sauce. Turn off the heat, stir, and add the lemon juice. Adjust the liquids according to your taste: more clam juice for more sauce or more of the remaining breadcrumbs for a thicker texture. Serve on crisp lettuce leaves or Belgian endive leaves.

Yield: 6 portions

Savory Squid

calamari all'appetitosa

1½ pounds squid, fresh or frozen
6 tablespoons olive oil
1 dried cayenne pepper pod, seeded, or 2 generous dashes of Tabasco
2 garlic cloves, split in half
3 tablespoons unsalted butter
2 tablespoons minced fresh flat-leaf parsley
2½ tablespoons unflavored breadcrumbs
Juice of 1 lemon
Salt to taste

If using frozen squid, thaw overnight in the refrigerator or under running cold water. Clean the squid (page 16). Cut the bodies in ½-inch rings, the larger tentacles in half lengthwise.

Blanch the squid in boiling, salted water for 1 minute, drain, and rinse in cold water.

Put the oil in a sauté pan with the pepper pod and garlic and sauté over brisk heat until the garlic is browned and the pepper pod dark, or add Tabasco if using.

Remove the flavorings and add butter, parsley, and breadcrumbs, and stir.

Add the squid and the lemon juice and taste for salt. Adjust flavorings if necessary. Serve hot.

Yield: 4 portions

Peppers Stuffed with Tuna

peperoni ripieni al tonno

Preheat the oven to 400 degrees Fahrenheit.

Soak the bread briefly under running water. Squeeze it well, discard the crusts, and shred the remaining bread into a bowl.

Drain the tuna and reserve the oil; chop the fish together coarsely with the olives. Add to the shredded bread. Moisten the mixture with the tuna oil and enough of the olive oil to make it cling together. Add the salt and pepper and mix well.

Wash the peppers, cut them in half lengthwise, and remove seeds and cores. Fill the halves with the tuna mixture and put them in an oiled baking dish.

Bake in preheated oven for 15 to 20 minutes, or until the peppers are tender to a fork. Serve hot or cold.

Yield: 6 portions

3 to 4 slices day-old Italian bread, baguette style

1 6½-ounce can light tuna (packed in olive oil)

24 Sicilian black olives (packed in brine), pitted

4 tablespoons olive oil

¼ teaspoon salt

¼ teaspoon freshly ground black pepper

6 bell peppers (red, green, or yellow)

Tomatoes Stuffed with Tuna

pomodori al tonno

6 medium, firm salad tomatoes
Salt
2 hard-boiled eggs
1 3½-ounce can light tuna (packed
   in olive oil)
1 tablespoon capers
1 tablespoon chopped fresh flat-leaf
   parsley
Freshly ground white pepper
1 cup commercial or Parsley
   Mayonnaise (page 41)

Cut off the tops, or upper fourth, of each tomato and reserve. Scoop out the seeds and pulp and drain through a sieve, reserving the juice. Salt the tomato shells lightly and turn them upside down to drain.

Chop the fleshy part of the reserved tops. Finely chop the hard-boiled eggs and put them in a mixing bowl with the tuna and some of its olive oil, capers, and parsley. Mix well. Add the chopped tomato tops and enough juice to make a paste; add pepper to taste.

Add half the mayonnaise to the tuna-egg paste, mix well, and stuff the tomato shells. Chill 30 minutes before serving. Top with the remaining mayonnaise.

Yield: 6 portions

Salads

Italians use the salad after the entrée as a palate refresher, generally with a dressing no more complicated than a simple vinaigrette. Fish salads, however, tend to be more involved and a bit richer than the usual mixed salad greens, with or without other vegetables. The fish salad in Italy goes back to the cold table, part of the original antipasto of the Romans, and to the grand dinners of the Renaissance. Rounds of lobster meat on a bed of saffron-poached sole fillets, decorated with tiny shrimps and flowers of calamari tentacles surrounded by poached quail eggs, all under crystal-clear wine aspic would just do for a simple picnic. Today's offerings are not quite so elaborate, but we do use fish salads for buffets or to accompany a summer "al fresco" meal. Of course, we are not ashamed to admit turning a fish salad into an entire summer meal. Fish salads fit well, also, in the antipasto department. It's in your hands.

Fish Salad

insalata di pesce

1½ to 2 pounds fish fillets (white,
    black, or striped sea bass, fresh
    cod, or haddock)
2 bay leaves
3 hard-boiled eggs
1 dozen green Sicilian-style olives
    (packed in brine)
2 ounces (about a handful) frozen
    green beans
2 tablespoons frozen peas
1 heart Boston or Bibb lettuce
1 cup commercial mayonnaise or
    Parsley Mayonnaise (page 41)
Juice of 1 lemon
1 tablespoon capers, rinsed and
    drained

Put the fish fillets in cold water with the bay leaves and bring the pot to a boil. Lower the heat and simmer until the fillets are cooked (the flesh is opaque and begins to flake easily—the exact time depends on the thickness of the fillet but probably no more than 10 minutes maximum).

Lift the fish out of the water carefully and set aside to cool and drain.

Cut the hard-boiled eggs in quarters or sixths. Pit the olives. Cook the frozen vegetables in boiling salted water until just tender or steam them sprinkled with a bit of salt.

Wash the lettuce and pat dry the leaves.

Place the largest of the leaves around the sides of a salad bowl. Cut the remaining lettuce in strips and place in the bottom of the salad bowl.

Cut the fish fillets, now cooled, into strips about 1 inch wide and place them over the lettuce.

Mix the mayonnaise with the lemon juice and dribble half of it over the fish fillets. Add the peas, the beans, and the capers. Add the last of the mayonnaise. Place the olives and the egg slices decoratively over all and put the bowl in the refrigerator until serving time.

Yield: 4 to 6 portions

Four Fish Salad

insalata ai quattro pesci

This salad uses both canned and fresh seafood to the benefit of all.

Scrub the mussels clean and place them in a frying pan with the garlic and olive oil. Cover, raise the heat to medium, and cook for about 4 minutes or until they have opened. Lift the mussels from their pan and remove them from their shells and place in a bowl.

Drain the tuna, reserving the oil, and place with the mussels. Drain the salmon of its water, check and remove any tiny bones. Add the salmon to the other two fish.

If using fresh shrimp, peel them and sauté in the mussels' pan for about 3 minutes or until cooked and nicely coral colored. Scoop from the pan with a slotted spoon and add to the other fish.

Mix the mayonnaise with the reserved olive oil, the mustard, brandy, paprika, and a touch of salt and pepper.

Wash the escarole leaves, pat dry, and line a salad bowl with them. When it is time to serve, carefully place the four fish on the salad leaves, spoon the mayonnaise evenly over all, and serve.

Yield: 4 portions

2 pounds fresh mussels
1 garlic clove, crushed
1½ tablespoons olive oil
3½ ounces canned light tuna
   (packed in olive oil)
¼ pound canned salmon
½ pound fresh small shrimp, or 2
   4¼-ounce cans tiny whole shrimp
1 cup commercial mayonnaise or
   Parsley Mayonnaise (page 41)
1 teaspoon Dijon-style mustard
2 tablespoons brandy
Dash of paprika
Salt and freshly ground white
   pepper to taste
1 heart curly escarole

Genoese Fish Salad

cappon magro

2 garlic cloves, halved

1½ cups cooked, diced, sliced, or julienne-cut beets (canned are fine)

1½ cups fresh cooked string beans

1½ cups fresh cooked cauliflower florets

½ cup olive oil

¼ cup red-wine vinegar

3 cups poached fish (such as halibut, salmon, sea bass, or lobster; use a combination)

1½ dozen medium shrimp, cooked, shelled, deveined

3 heads Bibb lettuce, washed, trimmed, patted dry

6 celery ribs, cut in thin julienne slices

1 cup pitted ripe olives

12 anchovy fillets

4 hard-boiled eggs, quartered

3 ripe tomatoes

1 recipe Pesto (page 46)

This particular production could be named the fish salad of all fish salads. Everything you ever listed as a salad ingredient (see note below for variations) seems to be included, as well as one (oyster plant or salsify) that has virtually disappeared from the American, British, and Italian markets. It is a wonderful platter for a party and we recommend it highly, with or without the virtually unavailable oyster plant.

These vegetables have been chosen for their color as well as taste and texture. You can, if you wish, reduce the amount of one or two of the choices and substitute boiled, small red potatoes, carrots, or artichoke hearts.

Rub a large, relatively deep platter with the garlic cloves. Place the cooked, cooled vegetables in separate bowls. Mix the oil and vinegar together and dress and toss the vegetables with the dressing and arrange them in the center of the platter.

Flake the fish gently. Arrange the fish and the shrimp, alternating the two if you wish to make a colorful ring, around the vegetables that are centered on the platter.

Finally, make a ring of the prettiest lettuce leaves around the fish. Add as nicely as you can the celery, olives, the anchovy fillets, and eggs.

Cut the tomatoes in six or eight sections, discarding the watery centers if using winter tomatoes so that you

have nothing but firm, bright, curved pieces to spread here and there around the outer edge.

Make the pesto and serve it separately.

Yield: 8 to 10 portions

Mushroom Salad

insalata di funghi e acciughe

This is another example of using the anchovy to enhance the mayonnaise and come to the rescue of what would otherwise be an everyday salad. Anchovies are terrific partners in many dishes as well as when used as seasoners and have been for centuries in many European cuisines. They heighten and add flavor, accent, and a bit of salt, without any "fishy" taste.

1 pound fresh mushrooms
1 garlic clove
6 flat anchovy fillets, drained and minced
¼ cup minced fresh flat-leaf parsley
2 hard-boiled eggs, yolks mashed with a fork and whites reserved for garnish
½ cup olive oil
3 tablespoons lemon juice, approximately
Salt to taste
Lettuce leaves for garnish

Clean and cut the mushrooms in thin wedges and set aside.

Using a garlic press, squeeze the juice of the garlic clove into your salad bowl, or just rub the clove hard against the side of the bowl. Add the anchovies, parsley, and egg yolks, and mix well.

Gradually whisk in the olive oil until the sauce is the consistency of mayonnaise. Slowly whisk in the lemon juice until the sauce is creamy. Taste for salt and adjust.

Add the mushrooms to the anchovy mayonnaise, toss, and serve on lettuce leaves. The whites of the hard-boiled eggs may be chopped fine and sprinkled around the mushrooms as decoration.

Yield: 6 portions

Rice Salad

insalata di riso

2 cups Arborio (or Vialone)
    Italian rice

4 anchovy fillets, minced

½ cup black and green pitted olives,
    halved

2 tablespoons capers, drained

1 red bell pepper, in thin julienne
    strips

1 green or yellow bell pepper, in thin
    julienne strips

2 cups fresh or frozen peas and
    carrots

2 6½-ounce cans light tuna (packed
    in olive oil)

½ cup extra-virgin olive oil

Juice of 2 lemons

Salt and freshly ground black
    pepper

2 hard-boiled eggs for garnish,
    optional

Fresh parsley or radicchio or Bibb
    lettuce leaves for garnish,
    optional

A rice salad may sound rather bland, but this particular dish, ideal for summer buffets, comes from Turin, where the rice is dressed with extra-virgin olive oil and brightened with summer vegetables while anchovies, capers, olives, and lemon juice provide lively accents.

When imported Arborio or Vialone rice is not available, we turn to American types. This salad is perfectly delicious using short- or medium-grain rice.

Cook the rice in 5 cups of boiling, salted water until tender. Drain the rice, run cold water over it, and drain again thoroughly. Place the rice in a large mixing bowl.

Add the anchovies, the olives, and the capers to the rice. Add the strips of sweet peppers and toss gently.

Cook the peas and carrots to the tender-crisp stage, drain, rinse with cold water, and add to the rice.

Break up the tuna with a fork and add it to the rice along with its oil. Dress the entire bowl with olive oil and lemon juice. Taste for salt and pepper and add if necessary. Chill at least 30 minutes before serving.

At serving time, toss the salad again lightly and place it on an appropriate platter. Decorate with sliced eggs and salad greens, if you wish.

Yield: 12 portions

Shrimp and Belgian Endive

gamberetti alla belga

This is a good example of the influence of American cuisine in Italian cookery: the use of ketchup in connection with shellfish. In a form of disguised flattery, Italy has on the market a tomato condiment called "Rubra," a close and much used imitation of ketchup. But in the last decade or so, ketchup has come into its own and its name—and use—is more evident and widespread.

¾ pound small shrimp
2 tablespoons white-wine vinegar
1 bay leaf
½ lemon
3 or 4 peppercorns
2 large heads Belgian endive
½ cup commercial mayonnaise
1 tablespoon lemon juice
2 tablespoons heavy cream
*3 generous tablespoons tomato
    ketchup*
Dash of paprika

Cook the shrimp in boiling salted water to which you have added the vinegar, bay leaf, lemon, and peppercorns, for about 3 minutes or until they turn coral colored. Drain and let cool.

Remove the largest and most perfect of the endive leaves and set aside for use in the final preparation. Cut the core from the remaining centers of the endive and slice half of these leaves in thin rounds and half in thin strips.

Place the mayonnaise in a bowl, add the lemon juice, and mix well. Add the cream, the ketchup, and the paprika and mix again until smooth. Add the cooled, cooked shrimp and the rounds of endive and mix again.

On each of four plates, make a ring of the large endive leaves. Place the thin strips of endive in the center of the ring. Divide the dressed shrimp evenly on the centers of the plates and serve.

Yield: 4 portions

Shrimp and Pasta Salad

insalata di pasta coi gamberi

1¼ pounds macaroni (medium
    shells, penne, rotini, ziti)

1 dozen black olives, pitted

1 red bell pepper, cored and diced

1 green bell pepper, cored and diced

1 small cucumber, peeled, seeded,
    and diced

½ medium onion, peeled and
    minced

3 celery ribs, sliced thin

1 cup Anchovy-Garlic Salad
    Dressing (page 36) or Parsley
    Mayonnaise (page 41)

1 pound medium shrimp

2 tablespoons cider vinegar

1 bay leaf

½ lemon

3 or 4 peppercorns

6 tomato roses (page 58) or small
    tomatoes

1 dozen sprigs of fresh curly parsley

2 hearts salad greens

Cook the pasta *al dente* in boiling, salted water. Drain well, rinse under cold water, and place in a large bowl. Add the olives, the prepared vegetables, and the dressing or mayonnaise and mix well.

Cook the shrimp 3 to 5 minutes in boiling, salted water to which you have added the vinegar, bay leaf, lemon, and peppercorns. Drain thoroughly, rinse in cold water, and pat dry with paper towels.

Make 6 tomato roses for garnish or cut tomatoes into thin slivers. Wash and trim the parsley sprigs, discarding any damaged leaves. Wash and pat dry the salad greens.

When it is time to serve, the salad may be mounded on a platter, surrounded by greens, and decorated with the shrimp, tomato roses or tomatoes, and the parsley leaves. For individual plates, make a ring of greens, fill with salad, and decorate with the shrimp, tomato roses, and parsley.

Yield: 6 generous portions

Shrimp and Scallops in Aspic

insalata di scampi e capesante

Working with aspic, brightly colored shrimp, white scallops, julienne strips of sweet red pepper and a bit of green fresh parsley can be lots of fun. Once a cook has successfully set a first dish in aspic, the game is just beginning: it is interesting to work out designs that are as pleasant to the palate as to the eye. Be sure to have ice cubes on hand.

The only thing to remember is that if you load the ring or mold with too many vegetables, they will give off their own liquids over prolonged chilling and spoil the gelatin a bit. Vegetable pieces do best if rolled in jelling aspic before being placed in the mold.

4 cups clarified Basic Fish Stock I (page 166) or clear chicken stock
4 envelopes unflavored gelatin
½ pound medium shrimp, poached, peeled, and deveined
½ pound scallops, poached and cut in thin rounds
1 dozen small black pitted olives
1 small red bell pepper, cut in thin julienne strips
Sprigs of flat-leaf parsley
Fresh chives
2 hearts curly endive for garnish

Make the aspic using the instructions on page 292. Place the bowl in a larger bowl of ice or in the refrigerator, until the aspic begins to jell and reaches a syrupy consistency. At the same time, set a ring pan over ice and thoroughly chill it. Separately chill the seafood, olives, and red pepper.

When the aspic begins to jell, pour about a half cup into your ring pan and swirl it around to solidify on the sides and bottom. Chill the pan briefly and repeat the coating process.

Begin the design which, when the aspic is turned out on a platter, will be the top of your finished dish: dip the parsley sprigs in the jelling aspic and place them in little three-sprig bunches evenly around the bottom of the pan.

Pour a bit of aspic over the parsley and when that is set, distribute the shrimp and rounds of scallops alternately, making a second layer of the dish. Pour in more aspic to cover, adjusting your design as need be. Allow to set. By this time, the depth in the pan will allow you to make the julienne strips of pepper stand up around the edge. Now, add more aspic, another layer of shrimp and scallops, and some more aspic.

Roll the olives in the aspic and then place them around the pan, and criss-cross the chives on the top. Add the last of the aspic.

Place the mold in the refrigerator with a piece of wrap to cover and chill thoroughly for about 2 hours.

Before serving, dip the mold very briefly in hot water, place a plate over the top, and turn it out. Stick little pieces of hearts of curly endive around the entire border.

Yield: 12 portions

Summer Salad with Tuna

insalata fantasia

This is an old standby that serves as a salad, an entire meal in the summer, or an appetizer. It all depends on how much you put on the plate.

Circle a platter or individual salad plates with the greens. Garnish symmetrically with the tomatoes and the pepper strips. Place shell beans in the center. Flake the tuna over the beans and add the onion rings and olives. Place the egg quarters around the edge of the salad. Drizzle the olive oil and vinegar over all, and season with salt and pepper. Serve with hot slices of Italian-style bread.

Yield: 2 to 4 servings, depending on appetite

* NOTE: For a mild taste, soak onion slivers in ice water for about 15 minutes before assembling the salad.

1 handful clean, cut-up salad greens
4 tomato wedges or 4 cherry tomatoes, halved
4 thin strips red bell pepper
4 thin strips green bell pepper
1 15½-ounce can shell beans, rinsed
1 3½-ounce can light tuna (packed in olive oil)
6 slivers or rounds red onions or Vidalia onions in season *
4 large pitted olives
1 hard-boiled egg, quartered
2 tablespoons olive oil
1 tablespoon red-wine vinegar
Salt and freshly ground black pepper to taste
Italian-style bread

Tuna and Bean Salad

insalata di fagioli e tonno

2 1-pound cans shell beans, or 3
    pounds fresh shell beans
1 6½-ounce can light tuna (packed
    in olive oil)
3 tablespoons olive oil
2 tablespoons red-wine vinegar
Salt and freshly ground black
    pepper to taste
1 medium red onion, optional
Italian-style bread

A simpler, more basic version of the preceding salad, and a very traditional Tuscan one. A year-round preparation, it is particularly appreciated in the summer when it can take advantage of fresh shell beans and turn easily into a satisfying one-dish lunch.

If using canned shelled beans: drain their liquid, rinse under water, and let drain again.

If using fresh beans: shell and put to boil in abundant water, lightly salted. As soon as they reach the boiling point, turn heat off and let the beans cool in their water. Bring back to a boil and turn heat off right away. Test, and if not ready, let cool in the hot water. Do not overcook; test again in 5 minutes, and when done, drain and rinse in cool water.

Put the beans and tuna with its oil in a salad bowl, add the olive oil, wine vinegar, and salt and pepper, and toss gently.

Slice the onion thinly (soaking the slivers in cold water for 10 to 15 minutes will make them crisper and sweeter) and let each person add to their serving. Accompany with slices of hot Italian-style bread.

Yield: 4 to 6 portions

Tuna and Chickpea Salad

insalata di ceci e tonno

Put the tuna and its oil in a salad bowl and break it up with a fork. Drain the chickpeas, discarding the liquid, and add them to the tuna.

Slice the onion into slivers and the celery into very thin slices, discarding the leaves, and add to the salad bowl. Add the olive oil, toss well, and add the salt, pepper, and vinegar. Toss again and serve with hot slices of Italian-style bread.

Yield: 6 portions

1 6½-ounce can light tuna (packed in olive oil)
2 15½-ounce cans chickpeas
1 Bermuda onion
3 celery ribs
2 tablespoons olive oil
Salt to taste
Freshly ground black pepper
2 tablespoons red-wine vinegar
Italian-style bread

VI

Fishing Partners:
Pasta, Couscous, Rice, Polenta

PASTA
Homemade Pasta
Green Pasta
Egg-White Pasta

CLAM SAUCES, NEAPOLITAN STYLE
Baby Clams and White Sauce with Vermicelli
Baby Clams and Tomato Sauce with Vermicelli
Cherrystone Clams with Vermicelli
Baby Clams and Tuna Sauce with Tonnarelli
Baby Clams, Scallops, and Shrimp in Tomato and Basil Sauce with Linguine
Crabmeat Sauce with Thin Spaghetti
Crabmeat and Tomato and Basil Sauce with Linguine
Lobster Sauce with Fettuccine
Lobster, Salmon Roe, and Cream Sauce with Linguine
Lobster, Caviar, and Sour Cream Sauce with Fettuccine

Mussels and Shrimp in Tomato and Basil Sauce with Linguine

Mussels and Squid in Tomato and Basil Sauce with Linguine

Smoked Salmon and Salmon Roe with Linguine

Scallops and Shrimp with Penne

Scallops and Asparagus in Cream Sauce with Pasta Bows

Scallops and Spinach in Tomato and Sour Cream Sauce with Linguine

Shrimp Flamed with Brandy in Tomato and Basil Sauce with Fettuccine

Squid in Tomato Sauce with Spaghetti

Fresh Tuna in Tomato Sauce with Macaroni

FILLED PASTA DISHES

Fish Packets

Fish Tortelli

Sea Bass and Turbot in Ravioli

Sole, Shrimp, and Caviar in Ravioli

Seafood Lasagne

Sole and Mushroom Lasagne

COUSCOUS

Sicilian Couscous I

Sicilian Couscous II

RICE

Shrimp Risotto, Venetian Style

Shellfish with Rice

Lobster Risotto

POLENTA

Salt Cod with Chard and Polenta

Swordfish in Spicy Sauce with Polenta

Fresh Tuna in Tomato Sauce with Polenta

O f all the glories that Italian cuisine has put on our table, perhaps the most heartwarming, friendly, and satisfying are those that mix fish with pasta, rice, or polenta. Following are but a few samples of the thousands of possible combinations. Because of their size and sturdy nature, which allows them to stand up well to their partners, shellfish and mollusks tend to appear more frequently than other fish in this chapter. Some require the company of egg pasta, homemade or store-bought (made with all-purpose flour and eggs), while others are more comfortable with commercial dry pasta (made with semolina flour and water). The choice is not just by whim: the shapes and consistency of certain types of pasta better complement the sauces they accompany. Sometimes there is the added element of tradition, as in the classic *vermicelli alle vongole*: probably the clam sauce would work just as well with spaghetti but definitely not as well with egg fettuccine.

There is a tendency to consider homemade pasta superior—more elegant and refined—to commercial pasta. The determination is not valid, since each has qualities that are more appropriate for a particular dish and that come to the fore for different occasions.

While the quality of homemade pasta is literally in your hands, there are myriad brands of commercial pasta on the market. Our recommendation is to check the ingredients list on the package: if it specifies that the pasta is made with "durum wheat semolina" or simply "semolina," you are off to a good start. The simplest advice is to try the several brands available to you and then stick with the one that works best for you.

The easiest way to spoil a homemade or commercial pasta is by not cooking it properly or, horrors! overcooking it and turning it into mush. Essential is a pot large enough to hold a quart of water for every 3 ounces of pasta, approximately. Bring the water to a rolling boil, add 1 teaspoon of salt for each quart of water, and, when it comes back to a boil, plunge the pasta into it; as soon as it is limp stir it gently around with a wooden spoon and cover the pot so that the water comes back to a boil as quickly as possible. Stir it once in a while; for commercial pasta follow the timing recommended on the box. But it is advisable, somewhat before the time is up, to fish out a strand or piece of pasta and taste it: if it is cooked through but with a hint of a core to it, it is done—*al dente*—as it should be. That means cooked, but still with some fight left for your teeth.

Fresh homemade pasta cooks much faster—from two to five minutes, depending on thickness and how long it has dried, but the best way to know when it is done is, again, by tasting it.

Once cooked, drain the pasta thoroughly, dress it with the warm sauce, and serve as soon as possible. It should come to the table piping hot; serving it on warm plates is a good practice. Rinsing pasta in cold water is absolutely forbidden, permitted only under special dispensation (e.g.: for preparing lasagne.)

Cold pasta is allowed in a very few instances, as in pasta salads—which, by the way, are American inspired.

Pasta

Homemade Pasta—Egg Pasta

pasta fatta in casa—pasta all'uovo

Once "homemade" really meant "handmade." It implied the use of a sizable pastry board, of a three-foot-long rolling pin, plus a reasonable amount of elbow grease and cleanup time. It involved the making of a crater of flour on the board,

breaking eggs into it, turning the whole thing into a ball of dough, kneading it, rolling it into a thin sheet, and finally cutting it. With the advent of the food processor and the pasta machine, all the fuss is gone and making pasta is a cinch.

The ingredients for making traditional pasta are only eggs and unbleached all-purpose flour (some suggest the use of semolina flour; while this is fine for commercial pasta, it takes away from the the lightness and texture that makes homemade pasta different). Generally, a 1-egg batch is considered equal to 1 serving of pasta, 2 eggs for 2. . . . But then, as the number of portions grows (and depending on final use and appetites) we follow a process of de-escalation: 3 eggs for 4 to 5 servings, 4 eggs for 5 to 6 servings, 5 eggs for 7 to 8, and so on. The basic proportion is, approximately:

¾ cup unbleached all-purpose flour

1 large egg

1 pinch (⅛ teaspoon) of salt

The approximation is due to the fact that eggs and flour can vary, as can conditions of temperature and humidity, and so they will combine in slightly different proportions.

Put flour and salt in the bowl of a food processor with the steel blade. (An average processor can easily make a 4-egg/3-cups-of-flour batch; for more, it is advisable to make two or more batches.)

Turn on/off for a second to fluff the flour. Lightly beat the egg(s) in a separate bowl, start the processor, and slowly pour in the eggs. Process on/off for a minute or so: the mixture should turn into pellets, more or less the size of pepper grains, that will stick together when pinched. If the mixture is more like coarse meal, process again, adding a tablespoon of water at a time, until it reaches the pellet stage. If a ball of dough forms, then add a little bit of flour at a time until the ball breaks into pellets. Once you get to this stage, pour the pellets into a bowl and squeeze them all together and knead the resulting dough into a soft, nonsticky ball. If using more than 1 egg, divide the dough into fist-size pieces, flatten them, and cover them so that they do not dry out.

Set up the pasta machine and start sending the first piece through its rollers set at their widest gap. Without changing that setting, fold the dough in half and pass

it through the rollers, folding it each time, five or six times or until the dough is well kneaded and smooth. The dough should not be sticky: if it is, dust it lightly with flour. Now you can narrow the rollers' gap one step with each pass until you reach the desired thinness. The dough now has reached the exalted state of pasta.

Continue with remaining dough, spreading out each finished strip on a clean dish towel. The final thing to do is to cut the pasta strips into cuts or ribbons of the desired width. Pasta machines on the market come with two, sometimes three cutters; generally they are calibrated for very thin "angel hair," ⅛-inch-wide "linguine," and ¼-inch "fettuccine." Different pasta machines have somewhat different calibrations and additional cutters. The instructions that come with the hardware are pretty reliable. But most reliable of all will be your experience: after a few sessions you will be an accomplished pasta maker.

For the smaller, filled pasta, such as ravioli and tortelloni, there are two ways to go:

1) If making the filled pasta by hand, cut the pasta sheets into 2-inch by 2-inch squares or rounds 2 inches in diameter, using a round pastry cutter or a knife. The rule is to work as quickly as you can. Fill and fold and seal shut while the pasta is still moist enough to stick together when pressed. If it is not, dampen a finger and run it around the edges where the pasta is to be sealed. Pasta strips may be covered with a damp, very well wrung out clean dish towel while they await your deft fingers.

2) If using a ravioli form (which resembles a covered ice-cube tray and is about 12 inches in length), cut two strips of pasta, one the length of the form and the second about 15 inches long. Place the longer of the two strips loosely over the half of the form with 12 depressions. Carefully push the pasta down into each depression to ready it for the filling. Fill the depressions and cover them with the second and shorter strip of pasta. Cover the pasta with the top of the form and press lightly, thus cutting out 12 individual ravioli.

After you have your pasta cut the way you wish, the cuts may again be placed on the dish towel to dry slightly or completely before being cooked. Very fresh pasta cooks in the aforementioned two minutes; fresh egg pasta that has been dried takes about five minutes.

There are a few traditional variations of homemade pasta, but the need not to

leave well enough alone has produced some outlandish productions: garlic pasta, basil pasta, parsley pasta, pepper pasta . . . *ad infinitum*. To us these pastas, by proposing definite (read: overpowering) flavors, defeat the basic purpose of pasta: a clear-cut texture with a relatively neutral taste, ready and willing to absorb all that a sauce has to give and make it its own.

Among the traditional types is *pasta verde*: green pasta or "spinach pasta." Its flavor doesn't fight what it is coupled with, and its color can stand on its own (as in *fettuccine verdi*). It is also particularly pleasant to the taste and the eye when mixed with golden egg pasta (as in *fettuccine paglia e fieno*: straw and hay) or when it is used in alternating layers in lasagne.

The basic ingredients are unbleached all-purpose flour, eggs, and "spinach eggs" (roughly the size of 5 ounces of spinach, cooked and squeezed dry).

Green Pasta

pasta verde

If using fresh spinach: wash and remove the stems. Cook the leaves briefly in as little water as possible with ½ teaspoon salt. Drain thoroughly, pressing the spinach against the sides of the sieve. (If you have cheesecloth handy, wrap the cooked spinach in it and squeeze dry.) Mince the spinach well.

If using frozen spinach leaves, cook until tender in boiling salted water, drain and squeeze dry as above and mince. In your hand, the squeezed spinach should be roughly the size of an egg.

Place the flour, spinach, and ¼ teaspoon salt in the bowl of a food processor equipped with the cutting blade, and process on/off until spinach is further minced and well mixed with the flour. Beat the eggs lightly and, with

5 ounces fresh or frozen spinach leaves (½ 10-ounce package, frozen)
¾ teaspoon salt
2¼ cups unbleached all-purpose flour
2 large eggs

the motor on, slowly pour them into the processor bowl. Process on/off until the mixture forms small pellets about the size of pepper grains. Most probably you will have to add a little more flour, because the spinach, no matter how well squeezed dry, will keep supplying moisture to the mix. Once you have reached the pellet stage, proceed as for egg pasta (page 111). Do not be discouraged when you get to the rolling/kneading if for the first few passes through the rollers the dough looks rather ragged. Soon it will smooth out and at the final pass it will look and feel like green silk.

Yield: 4 portions

If the cholesterol in the egg pasta and the butter in some of the sauces are not in your diet, substitutes for either one are available. Several brands of egg substitute can be found on the market, and only by trying can you decide which one is for you. The egg substitutes do work remarkably well for pasta: substitute the eggs with the brand's suggested amount of liquid and not even an expert will know the difference. However, if you wish to make pasta with just egg whites, here is the way:

Egg-White Pasta

pasta chiara

2¼ *cups unbleached all-purpose*
   flour
3 *egg whites*
2 *tablespoons dry white wine*

Place the flour in the food processor with the steel blade. Briefly beat the egg whites with the wine. With the processor on, pour in the egg whites and wine and proceed as with the previous recipe.

Yield: 4 portions

As for the butter in the sauces, we substitute olive oil whenever we can. But for butter, too, there are alternatives, and some work better than others, especially when subjected to cooking heat. Again, it is up to you to decide when and which brand to use.

One thing is for sure: the ever-marvelous American market can get ingredients to please the palate, to turn out dishes as close to the authentic Italian fare as possible. You, too, can be like the Italian consumer who insists that his dish be tasty even if it doesn't use all the butter or fats of yesterday's tradition.

Clam Sauces, Neapolitan Style

The following three clam sauce recipes for use with vermicelli are variations on a theme which could very well be Napoli's anthem. There is an old saying that describes the incomparable beauty of the city's gulf: "See Naples and, then, you may die." But, we like to add, not before having had some *vermicelli alle vongole*. It is impossible to duplicate the whole *mise en scène*, or the local original ingredients: their clams, their pasta, their San Marzano tomatoes, or their dry white wine from the Vesuvius slopes. But you can get close to the experience if you follow your taste buds, get the freshest and smallest cherrystone clams. If you must use canned baby clams, do not overcook them—they should just warm up in the sauce. We use canned baby clams in the recipes calling for baby clams. We do not recommend chowder clams. Serve pasta and sauce as they come off the stove: toss and stir, eat . . . and let your imagination soar. Do not ground it by sprinkling cheese over *vermicelli alle vongole* or (almost) any other pasta with fish, for that matter: that *is* punished by death, not only in Naples but in all Italy.

In place of the cheese, when serving fish sauce with pasta, many cooks use toasted breadcrumbs: place a teaspoon or so of olive oil in a small sauté pan, add a tablespoon of breadcrumbs, and toast and stir until the breadcrumbs are nicely browned. This gives not only a nice touch to the dish but adds a bit of contrasting crunch and flavor that rounds the dish off nicely.

Baby Clams and White Sauce with Vermicelli

vermicelli alle vongole in bianco

SAUCE:

2 dried cayenne pepper pods, seeded,
    or ¼ teaspoon ground cayenne
⅓ cup olive oil
2 whole garlic cloves
1 10-ounce can baby clams,
    drained, liquid reserved
¼ cup dry white wine
½ cup coarsely chopped fresh flat-
    leaf parsley, approximately
Salt and freshly ground black
    pepper to taste
¼ cup unflavored breadcrumbs
    toasted in a small amount of
    olive oil

PASTA:

14 ounces vermicelli (or thin
    spaghetti)
4 quarts boiling water
4 teaspoons salt

Put the pepper pods, if using them, in the oil in the pan and sauté over medium heat, adding the peeled garlic as you sauté. When both flavorings are browned, remove them and add the clams, half the reserved clam juice, and raise the heat. When boiling nicely, add the white wine and cook until it has evaporated. Lower the heat, sprinkle in the ground red pepper, if using it, and half of the parsley, and simmer gently for about 5 minutes. Taste for salt and pepper and add to please. Meanwhile, toast the breadcrumbs in the olive oil until golden brown and cook the pasta in abundant boiling, salted water until *al dente*, cooked but still with a bit of bite to it. Drain thoroughly and add it to the clam sauce.

If the clam sauce needs more liquid (depends on how high the simmering went), add a bit more of the reserved clam juice.

Serve sprinkled with the toasted breadcrumbs and the reserved chopped parsley.

Yield: 4 portions

Baby Clams and Tomato Sauce with Vermicelli

vermicelli alle vongole al sugo

Put the oil, garlic, and pepper pod in a large sauté pan and sauté until the garlic is golden and the pepper dark brown. Remove both flavorings and add the tomatoes. Bring to a boil; add the wine and 5 tablespoons of the clam liquid. Add the white pepper. Taste for salt, and add if the clam juice wasn't particularly salty. Mash the tomatoes with a fork, bring back to a boil, and then lower the heat. Cook 15 minutes to reduce the sauce, stirring once in a while. Add the clams and parsley, stir, and keep warm on very low heat.

Meanwhile, cook the pasta in boiling, salted water. Drain thoroughly when cooked *al dente* and toss with the sauce in its pan over high heat for a moment or two. Serve hot, sprinkled with the toasted breadcrumbs.

Yield: 4 portions

SAUCE:
4 tablespoons olive oil
2 garlic cloves
1 dried cayenne pepper pod, seeded
2 cups canned peeled plum
    tomatoes, or 1 pound fresh ripe
    plum tomatoes, blanched and
    peeled
¼ cup dry white wine
1 10-ounce can baby clams,
    drained, liquid reserved
Freshly ground white pepper to taste
Salt to taste
2 to 3 tablespoons chopped fresh flat-
    leaf parsley
4 tablespoons unflavored
    breadcrumbs toasted in a small
    amount of olive oil

PASTA:
14 ounces vermicelli (or thin
    spaghetti)
4 quarts water
4 teaspoons salt

Cherrystone Clams with Vermicelli

vermicelli alle vongole

SAUCE:

3 to 4 pounds fresh, smallest possible cherrystone clams

⅓ cup olive oil

2 whole garlic cloves

2 dried cayenne pepper pods, seeded, or ¼ teaspoon ground cayenne

½ cup dry white wine

2 tablespoons chopped fresh flat-leaf parsley

3 to 4 tablespoons unflavored breadcrumbs toasted in a small amount of olive oil

PASTA:

14 ounces vermicelli (or thin spaghetti)

4 quarts water

4 teaspoons salt

Put the clams in a large (10- to 11-inch) sauté pan with enough olive oil to cover the pan bottom. Cover the pan and place over high heat for 2 to 3 minutes or until the shells open.

Scoop the clams from the pan and remove all but a few from their shells. Reserve the clams in the shells for garnishing.

Strain the clam juice and oil through a very fine sieve lined with cheesecloth and reserve. Place remaining olive oil in the sauté pan and add the garlic cloves and the pepper pods. Sauté until the garlic is golden and the pepper deep brown. Remove the flavorings and add the wine and bring up the heat.

Cook until the wine has evaporated (about 2 minutes). Add ground cayenne if using it, half the reserved clam liquid, the parsley, and the shelled clams, and cook a minute more.

Meanwhile, cook the vermicelli in boiling, salted water until *al dente* and then drain. Toss the pasta with the sauce in the hot sauté pan and divide among 4 plates, garnish with the clams still in their shells and a sprinkling of toasted breadcrumbs.

Yield: 4 portions

Baby Clams and Tuna Sauce with Tonnarelli

tonnarelli, tonno, e vongole

If using homemade tonnarelli, make according to recipe before proceeding with next step.

Drain the clams, reserving the clam juice. Sauté the garlic and the pepper pod, if using it, in the olive oil and remove the two flavorings when well browned. Add the Tabasco, if using it, and clams, stir, and add the tuna with its oil, breaking up the tuna a bit with a fork.

Add half the clam juice, black pepper, and 1½ table-spoons of the parsley. Simmer about 10 minutes or until the sauce has reduced and thickened. If at this stage the sauce becomes too dry, add more clam juice. (Clam juice tends to be rather salty, so pay great attention. A dash or two of white wine is also a good lengthener.) Check for salt and add to your taste.

Meanwhile, cook the tonnarelli in boiling, salted wa-ter about 3 minutes, or *al dente*. If using spaghetti, cook in boiling, salted water for about 12 minutes.

Serve the sauce on the tonnarelli, sprinkled with the last of the parsley and the toasted breadcrumbs.

Yield: 6 portions

NOTE: Tonnarelli are square-cut strands of pasta that are similar in size to thin linguine. Roll the pasta as thick as the spaghetti cut on the pasta machine is wide and cut it accordingly by hand if your machine doesn't have a tonnarelli cut.

PASTA:

1 4-egg batch Homemade Pasta, tonnarelli cut (page 110), or 1¼ pounds spaghetti

6 quarts water

6 teaspoons salt

SAUCE:

1 10-ounce can baby clams

1 garlic clove

1 dried cayenne pepper pod, seeded, or 3 or 4 drops Tabasco

2 tablespoons olive oil

1 6½-ounce can light tuna, packed in olive oil

Freshly ground black pepper to taste

2 tablespoons chopped fresh flat-leaf parsley

1 teaspoon salt, optional

3 tablespoons unflavored breadcrumbs toasted in a small amount of olive oil

Baby Clams, Scallops, and Shrimp in Tomato and Basil Sauce with Linguine

linguine pescatore

SAUCE:

3 tablespoons unsalted butter

3 cups very ripe peeled plum tomatoes, crushed, or 3 cups Tomato and Basil Sauce (page 44)

½ teaspoon dried oregano

¼ cup olive oil

2 garlic cloves, minced

¼ teaspoon ground cayenne pepper, or dash of Tabasco, optional

4 tablespoons coarsely chopped flat-leaf parsley

3 ounces medium shrimp (about 8), peeled

3 ounces scallops (if using the big sea scallops, cut in half)

¼ cup dry white wine

Salt to taste

5 ounces baby clams, canned

2 tablespoons unflavored breadcrumbs toasted in a small amount of olive oil

All the various Mediterranean fishing ports, Italian as well as French, scoop together variations of this "fisherman's" sauce, touched with ripe tomatoes, a bit of butter, a hint (more if you wish) of garlic, and fresh shellfish. The scallops may be bay or deep sea.

This sauce may be prepared ahead of time as well as multiplied for greater numbers and reheated just as the pasta is cooked.

Melt the butter, add the tomatoes and oregano, and cook over medium heat about 20 minutes or until of a sauce consistency (coats a spoon). Or heat the tomato and basil sauce.

In a large saucepan, heat the olive oil and sauté the garlic until translucent. Add the cayenne or Tabasco, half the parsley, the shrimp, the scallops, and cook 3 minutes. Add the wine and cook 3 more minutes or until the wine has evaporated.

Add the tomato sauce to the shellfish pan, stir, taste, and add salt as necessary. Add the clams (reserving the liquid). If by this time the combined sauce has become a bit too dense, use some of the reserved clam juice to lengthen it.

Cook the linguine in abundant boiling, salted water until *al dente*. Drain well and toss and mix with the sauce. Serve with the last of the parsley and the toasted breadcrumbs.

Yield: 4 portions

PASTA:

1 3-egg batch Homemade Pasta, linguine cut (page 110), or 14 ounces commercial linguine

4 quarts water

4 teaspoons salt

Crabmeat Sauce with Thin Spaghetti

spaghettini al granchio

This is another elegant, tasty dish that, with a minimum of dexterity, can be ready by the time the spaghettini is cooked. Just to get a jump on things, the toasted breadcrumbs may be prepared ahead of time.

Bring the water to a boil, add salt, and cook the pasta.

Meanwhile, put the olive oil in a skillet and sauté the garlic in it. When golden, remove the garlic, and add the anchovies to the oil. Over low heat, mash and stir the anchovies until they are almost dissolved in the oil. Add the crabmeat and the parsley, stir, and remove from heat.

When the pasta is cooked *al dente*, drain it well, dress with the crabmeat sauce, sprinkle with the breadcrumbs, toss, and serve.

Yield: 4 portions

PASTA:

4 quarts boiling water

4 teaspoons salt

14 ounces thin spaghetti

SAUCE:

4 tablespoons olive oil

1 garlic clove, halved

3 anchovy fillets

6 ounces fancy lump crabmeat, canned

2 tablespoons chopped fresh flat-leaf parsley

3 tablespoons unflavored breadcrumbs toasted in a small amount of olive oil

Crabmeat and Tomato and Basil Sauce with Linguine

linguine rosa al granchio

PASTA:

7 ounces linguine

3 quarts water

3 teaspoons salt

SAUCE:

*½ cup Tomato and Basil Sauce
    (page 44)*

*2 tablespoons chopped fresh flat-leaf
    parsley*

3 tablespoons light cream

Dash of Tabasco, optional

1 ounce vodka

*3 ounces fancy lump crabmeat,
    canned*

Put the linguine in abundant boiling salted water and when it comes back to a boil cook it *al dente* (about 12 minutes).

Heat the tomato sauce in a sauté pan large enough to hold the pasta when cooked. Add half the parsley and the light cream and simmer for about 3 minutes.

Add the Tabasco, if using it, and the vodka and cook another minute or two until the vodka has almost evaporated.

Add the cooked, drained pasta to the sauce and toss. Add the crabmeat, mix gently, and serve sprinkled with the rest of the chopped parsley.

Yield: 2 portions

Lobster Sauce with Fettuccine

fettuccine all'astice

Cook the whole lobster in boiling, salted water for 12 minutes after the water comes back to a boil. Remove from the water, cool slightly, and shell. Cut the lobster meat into bite-size pieces, the tail into rounds. Heat the olive oil in a sauté pan, add the garlic, sauté until golden, and discard. Add the Tabasco, anchovies, celery, and parsley. Sauté until the flavorings are limp but not browned. Stir in the lobster meat and remove from heat.

Meanwhile, make and cook the fettuccine in abundant boiling, salted water. Drain well and place on warmed plates that should already be blessed with ½ tablespoon butter each. Toss well, add the sauce, and serve.

Yield: 2 portions

SAUCE:
*1 1¼-pound lobster, uncooked, or
    about 6 ounces cooked lobster
    meat*
2 tablespoons olive oil
1 garlic clove, peeled
*Dash of Tabasco or sprinkling of
    cayenne pepper to taste*
2 anchovy fillets, mashed
½ celery rib, minced
*5 sprigs of fresh flat-leaf parsley,
    minced*
1 tablespoon unsalted butter

PASTA:
*1 2-egg batch Homemade Pasta,
    fettuccine cut (page 110)*
3 quarts water
3 teaspoons salt

Lobster, Salmon Roe, and Cream Sauce with Linguine

linguine alla panna, astice e caviale

PASTA:

1 2-egg recipe Homemade Pasta,
*   linguine cut (page 110), or 7*
*   ounces commercial linguine*
4 quarts water
4 teaspoons salt

SAUCE:

2 tablespoons unsalted butter
4 ounces cooked lobster meat
¼ cup heavy cream
1 ounce salmon roe caviar (about 3
*   rounded teaspoons)*
1 hard-boiled egg yolk, grated
1 hard-boiled egg white, grated
1 tablespoon fresh or freeze-dried
*   chives, approximately*
Juice of ½ lemon (1½ tablespoons)

Adding caviar to lobster and both to pasta could seem a sybaritic touch designed just for a fall-of-the-Roman-empire banquet. We find that the addition of a little caviar gives just the right accent to turn a simple dish into a simply elegant one.

Black and red lumpfish roe, golden whitefish roe, and domestic black, small-grain sturgeon caviar are available in many supermarkets. For pasta sauces we prefer the softer, larger, bright red salmon roe caviar. It is big and fat and adds a nice, positive, nonsalty taste when you chomp into it. We reserve imported, expensive caviars to be served by themselves for special occasions.

If using freshly made pasta, prepare it first and place on clean dish towels while you make the sauce.

If using commercial pasta, put the water on to boil, add the salt, and when the water boils, cook the pasta.

To make the sauce, melt the butter in a small saucepan. Cut up the lobster meat, half in rounds and half diced, and add to the butter. Stir in the cream and cook on very low heat while the pasta cooks.

If using freshly made pasta, cook it in boiling, salted water after the sauce is made, and then drain the pasta

thoroughly and divide between two warmed individual pasta plates. Put half the sauce on each portion and mix well. Put the caviar on top of the pasta, sprinkle with the egg yolk, surround the pasta with the egg white, and sprinkle on the chives. Add the lemon juice and let each diner toss his or her own pasta.

Yield: 2 portions

Lobster, Caviar, and Sour Cream Sauce with Fettuccine

fettuccine all'aragosta e caviale

PASTA:

1 2-egg batch Homemade Pasta,
  fettuccine cut (page 110), or 7
  ounces commercial fettuccine
4 quarts water
4 teaspoons salt

SAUCE:

2 tablespoons unsalted butter
4 ounces cooked lobster meat
2 heaping tablespoons sour cream
1½ ounces caviar of your choice
1 heaping tablespoon coarsely
  chopped fresh flat-leaf parsley

If using freshly made pasta, prepare it first and put on kitchen towels to dry slightly. Put the pasta water on to boil.

Melt the butter in a small saucepan. Dice the lobster meat and add to the butter, keeping it on the lowest heat.

Meanwhile, salt the boiling water and cook the pasta. (If using commercial fettuccine you will find the cooking time longer and may wish to remove the butter sauce from the heat until the pasta is cooked.)

Drain the pasta well, toss it with the butter and lobster, and serve it on two warmed plates. Put a heaping tablespoon of sour cream on top of the pasta. Add the caviar and sprinkle with a bit of parsley.

Yield: 2 portions

Mussels and Shrimp in Tomato and Basil Sauce with Linguine

Linguine al pomodoro con cozze e gamberi

If using homemade pasta, prepare it first and put on a kitchen towel to dry. Put the water for the pasta on to boil.

Put 2 tablespoons of the olive oil and the water in a large sauté pan with a good cover. Add 1 of the garlic cloves and the mussels. Place over high heat, covered, and cook for a minute or two until the mussels have opened. Remove the pan from the heat and let cool a moment. Discard any mussels that have failed to open. Take the opened mussels from their shells, letting the juice fall back into the sauté pan. Add the Tabasco. Reserve mussels and strain the juices through cheesecloth over them.

Mince the remaining garlic and put it in a second pan with the rest of the olive oil and sauté until the garlic is slightly golden. Add the shrimp to the pan and the mushrooms and sauté 2 minutes or until the shrimp is a good coral color.

Add the brandy and let cook until it has evaporated. Add the mussels and strained juices as well as the tomato sauce and the baby clams. Add the cream. Cook and stir 30 seconds or until heated through. Remove from heat.

Cook the linguine in boiling, salted water until it is *al dente*. (Commercial linguine takes about 8 to 10 minutes to cook while homemade pasta should take between 3 and

PASTA:

1 4-egg batch Homemade Pasta, linguine cut (page 110), or 1¼ pounds commercial linguine

6 quarts water

6 teaspoons salt

SAUCE:

½ cup olive oil

1 tablespoon water

3 garlic cloves, peeled

1 dozen (approximately ½ pound) fresh mussels, cleaned

Dash of Tabasco

1 dozen (approximately 8 ounces) medium shrimp, peeled

6 large (approximately 4 ounces) mushrooms, sliced

⅓ cup brandy

2 cups Tomato and Basil Sauce (page 44)

6 tablespoons (approximately 3 ounces) canned whole baby clams, drained

4 tablespoons heavy cream

2 tablespoons chopped fresh flat-leaf parsley

5, depending on how dry it was allowed to become.) Drain thoroughly and place in 6 hot pasta plates. Add the sauce proportionately. Garnish with a sprinkling of chopped parsley and serve.

Yield: 6 portions

Mussels and Squid in Tomato and Basil Sauce with Linguine

linguine al pomodoro con cozze e calamari

PASTA:

1 4-egg batch Homemade Pasta, linguine cut (page 110), or 1¼ pounds commercial linguine

6 quarts water

6 teaspoons salt

SAUCE:

1 pound mussels

⅓ cup olive oil

1 cup dry white wine

1 small onion, slivered

1 garlic clove, peeled

1 pound small squid, cleaned and cut (page 16)

3 cups Tomato and Basil Sauce (page 44)

Salt and freshly ground white pepper to taste

If using homemade pasta, prepare it first and put on a kitchen towel to dry. Put the pasta water on to boil.

Remove the "beards" from the mussels and scrub them well. Place 4 tablespoons of the olive oil in a large sauté pan along with the mussels. Cover the pan, bring it to a high heat, add a touch of the white wine, cover again, and cook about 2 minutes or until the mussels have opened. Remove the mussels from their shells over the pan. Reserve the mussels and strain the pan's juices through cheesecloth over them.

Place the remaining olive oil in the sauté pan. Add the onion and the garlic and sauté over high heat until the onion is limp. Add the squid. Cook 1 minute over high heat until the squid starts to turn lavender and pink. Add the last of the wine and cook until evaporated.

Meanwhile, when the water boils, put in the pasta, bring back to a boil, and cook about 10 minutes or until *al dente*.

Remove the garlic from the sauté pan and add the tomato and basil sauce and the reserved mussels and their liquid. Cook 2 minutes or until heated through. Taste for seasonings and add salt and pepper to taste.

Drain the pasta, add it to the sauce, toss well over high heat, and serve.

Yield: 6 portions

Smoked Salmon and Salmon Roe with Linguine

linguine al caviale e salmone

Cook the pasta in boiling, salted water.

Meanwhile, put the two creams in a warm stainless-steel bowl. When the pasta is cooked, drain it well and toss it in the cream.

Add the smoked salmon and about half the caviar, and toss again. Place in two warmed individual pasta plates or bowls.

Sprinkle each serving with a bit of chopped parsley and divide the remaining caviar between the two plates. Serve at once.

Yield: 2 portions

PASTA:

7 ounces commercial linguine
4 quarts boiling water
4 teaspoons salt

SAUCE:

⅔ cup sour cream, at room temperature
¼ cup light cream, at room temperature
2 ounces smoked salmon, cut in inch-long julienne strips
2 ounces salmon roe
1 tablespoon chopped fresh flat-leaf parsley

Scallops and Shrimp
with Penne

penne, cape sante e gamberi

PASTA:

7 ounces penne (or other short pasta cut)

3 quarts water

3 teaspoons salt

SAUCE:

6 ounces fresh bay scallops

4 ounces medium shrimp (approximately 6)

3 tablespoons olive oil

1 garlic clove, peeled

¼ to ½ teaspoon salt, or to taste

Freshly ground black pepper

2 teaspoons capers, drained

2 tablespoons chopped fresh flat-leaf parsley

Tabasco, optional

Juice of ½ lemon

1 teaspoon "quick mixing" flour*

Light, easy, and quick to make is the best description of this dish. It can be put together and be served in about 20 minutes.

Put the pasta to cook in boiling, salted water.

Rinse the scallops well, and peel and devein the shrimp. Place the oil and garlic in a saucepan and sauté until garlic is browned. Discard the garlic and add the scallops and shrimp and sauté for about 3 minutes.

Add the salt, pepper, capers, and parsley, and stir, and cook another 2 minutes.

Season with the Tabasco to your taste and add the lemon juice. Stir in the flour and cook until a slightly thick sauce of the pan's juices has developed.

Drain the pasta when it is cooked *al dente* (about 8 to 10 minutes) and add it to the shrimp-scallop pan. Mix well and serve.

Yield: 2 portions

* NOTE: "Quick mixing" flour takes the fear out of sauce making for those who do not wish to blend flour and butter to thicken a sauce. It doesn't tend to lump up and cooks in about 3 minutes.

Scallops and Asparagus in Cream Sauce with Pasta Bows

farfalle, asparagi, e capesante

This dish is quite capable of being a main course or an opening course for a meal with a light entrée. Easy to multiply if friends drop in unexpectedly.

Put the dried mushrooms in a small bowl, cover with warm water, and let soak for 10 minutes.

Heat the olive oil in a saucepan and add the shallot. Cook and stir until limp. Lift the mushrooms from their water, letting any sand remain in the bottom of the bowl. Slice the mushrooms thinly. Add them to the shallot and cook about 2 minutes. Add the scallops and cook for another 3 minutes. Season with salt and pepper. Add the vermouth and when it has partially evaporated, add the cooked asparagus. Stir, add the cream, and lower the heat.

Put the pasta to cook in boiling, salted water 8 to 10 minutes or until it is *al dente*. Drain and add to the sauce. Stir, and serve sprinkled with the chopped parsley.

Yield: 2 portions

SAUCE:

1½ ounces dried porcini mushrooms
3 tablespoons olive oil
1 shallot, peeled and minced
7 ounces scallops
Salt and freshly ground white
    pepper to taste
2 tablespoons dry white vermouth
7 ounces fresh asparagus, cut in
    1-inch lengths and cooked lying
    flat in 3 inches of boiling salted
    water for 3 to 4 minutes
1 cup heavy cream
1½ tablespoons chopped fresh flat-
    leaf parsley

PASTA:

7 ounces pasta (bows or thin
    mostaccioli)
3 quarts boiling water
3 teaspoons salt

Scallops and Spinach in Tomato and Sour Cream Sauce with Linguine

linguine all'Anna

SAUCE:

⅓ cup olive oil

2 to 3 garlic cloves, peeled

⅛ teaspoon ground red pepper, or dash of Tabasco to taste

3 cups canned peeled plum tomatoes, puréed

1 pound scallops

6 ounces fresh spinach leaves, washed

2 tablespoons sour cream or low-fat yogurt

PASTA:

14 ounces linguine

4 quarts water

4 teaspoons salt

Heat all but 2 tablespoons of the olive oil in a large sauté pan. Add the garlic and sauté until golden and then remove. Add the red pepper or Tabasco and the puréed tomatoes, and simmer about 15 minutes.

Cook the pasta in abundant boiling, salted water.

While the pasta cooks, heat the last of the olive oil in a separate sauté pan and sauté the scallops about 3 minutes. Add the spinach and sauté 1 minute. Add the tomato sauce and sour cream or yogurt and mix well. Remove from heat.

When the pasta has cooked about 8 to 10 minutes and is *al dente*, drain it thoroughly, toss it with the sauce, and serve.

Yield: 4 portions

Shrimp Flamed with Brandy in Tomato and Basil Sauce with Fettuccine

fettuccine coi gamberi al brandy

Put the tomato sauce in a sauté pan, add pepper and Tabasco. Bring the pan to a boil, lower the heat, and add the parsley. Stir and remove from heat.

If you are using freshly made pasta, prepare it at this point.

Bring the water to a boil, add salt, and cook the pasta *al dente*. While the pasta cooks, melt the butter in a second sauté pan, add the shrimp, stir, and cook for 2 minutes. Add the brandy and flame it. Stir in the tomato sauce and mix everything over moderate heat.

Drain the pasta thoroughly and place either in 4 individual pasta plates or one large serving bowl. Dress with the warm sauce and serve.

Yield: 4 portions

SAUCE:

2 cups Tomato and Basil Sauce (page 44)
Freshly ground white pepper to taste
Dash of Tabasco
¼ cup chopped fresh flat-leaf parsley
2 tablespoons unsalted butter
6 ounces shrimp, peeled
¼ cup brandy, warmed

PASTA:

1 3-egg batch Homemade Pasta, fettuccine cut (page 110), or 14 ounces commercial fettuccine
4 quarts water
4 teaspoons salt

Squid in Tomato Sauce with Spaghetti

spaghetti con calamari

SAUCE:

⅓ cup olive oil or enough to cover
    pan bottom
1 garlic clove, minced
½ small onion, minced
10 sprigs of fresh flat-leaf parsley,
    minced
1 pound squid, cleaned (page 16),
    cut in rounds, tentacles cut in
    half
1 pound canned peeled plum
    tomatoes, coarsely chopped
1 teaspoon salt
¼ teaspoon freshly ground white
    pepper

PASTA:

1 pound spaghetti
6 quarts water
2 tablespoons salt

Place the olive oil in a large saucepan. Add the garlic, onion, and half the parsley leaves. Cook over medium heat until limp. Add the cut-up squid, tomatoes, salt, and pepper, and cook about 20 minutes, or until the squid is tender. (If the sauce has reduced too much, add a few tablespoons of water.) Cook the pasta in boiling, salted water until tender, *al dente*, cooked but with a bit of bite to it, about 13 minutes. Drain and place in a warmed deep platter. Cover with the squid sauce and sprinkle with the remaining chopped parsley.

Yield: 4 portions

Fresh Tuna in Tomato Sauce with Macaroni

bucatini al pomodoro e tonno

Poach the tuna in water to cover with the vinegar, peppercorns, bay leaf, celery, and carrot.

While the tuna poaches, place the olive oil in a sauté pan, and sauté the garlic, anchovies, and onion over medium heat. When the garlic is soft and golden, discard it and add the tomatoes, crushing them a bit as they go into the pan. Simmer for about 15 minutes or until the sauce coats a spoon and is slightly reduced.

Add half the tuna, drained, and the oregano and pepper and simmer another 5 minutes or until the tuna flakes very easily.

Cook the pasta, drain it well, and toss it with the sauce. Serve in warmed pasta plates or bowls, adding the remaining tuna bits to the portions and garnish with the breadcrumbs.

Yield: 4 portions

NOTE: While the names of different shapes of dried commercial pasta tend to vary from manufacturer to manufacturer, we have tried to stick to the Italian name or names, depending on the original birthplace, so to speak. *Bucatini* (a Northern Italian name) or *perciatelli* (a Southern Italian name) are the same cut—slightly thicker than regular spaghetti and slightly thinner than regular macaroni, but they do have a hole in them, which means the sauce gets nicely trapped and therefore more appreciated.

SAUCE:

1¼ to 1½ *pounds fresh tuna, cut in*
    1-inch cubes
1½ *tablespoons red-wine vinegar or*
    white-wine vinegar
4 *peppercorns*
1 *bay leaf*
1 *celery rib*
1 *carrot*
¼ *cup olive oil*
1 *garlic clove*
3 *anchovies, minced*
½ *onion, minced*
2 *cups peeled plum tomatoes*
½ *teaspoon dried oregano*
Freshly ground black pepper to taste
¼ *cup unflavored breadcrumbs*
    toasted in a small amount of
    olive oil

PASTA:

14 *ounces macaroni* (perciatelli *or*
    bucatini)
4 *quarts water*
4 *teaspoons salt*

Filled Pasta Dishes

Fish Packets

chicche di pesce

FILLING:

*1 pound salmon, halibut, pollock, or
    fresh tuna*

*1 tablespoon minced fresh flat-leaf
    parsley*

½ teaspoon dried thyme

1 teaspoon grated lemon rind

*⅛ teaspoon freshly ground white
    pepper*

1 egg yolk

Salt to taste

PASTA:

*1 2-egg batch Homemade Pasta
    (page 110) or 1 1-egg batch
    Green Pasta (page 113)*

*3 to 4 cups Basic Fish Stock II for
    cooking packets (page 168)*

SAUCE:

*2 cups Tomato and Basil Sauce
    (page 44)*

*2 teaspoons chopped fresh or freeze-
    dried chives, approximately*

*These little "packets" of pasta, filled with gently sea-
soned fish, are a twisted version of ravioli because
chicche (kick-ay)—a children's name for candies—
have their wrappers sealed at each end with a twist.
Chicche can be made with green or plain pasta, and
the filling can be made with almost any solid, flavorful fish.*

To make the filling, put the fish in the bowl of a food
processor, steel blade in place. Add the parsley, thyme,
lemon rind, and pepper, and process, adding the egg just
as soon as the fish is minced. When a thick paste has been
reached, taste for salt and adjust if necessary. Let rest,
chilled, for at least 30 minutes.

    Make the pasta, roll it out as thin as possible, and cut
in 2½-inch by 3½-inch rectangles. With a pastry bag,
fitted with a ¼-inch tip, pipe a bit of the filling down the
center of each rectangle, leaving about ½ inch on either
end. Fold one edge of the pasta covering the filling, and
close by bringing up the other side. Twist the two ends

shut. Bring the fish stock to a boil in a wide-bottomed pan and place the packets in a single layer to cook for about 5 to 8 minutes.

Strain the tomato sauce and heat it thoroughly.

To serve, place a swirl of tomato sauce on each diner's plate, top with fish packets, dot with more sauce, sprinkle with chives, and serve.

Yield: 6 portions

Fish Tortelli

tortelli di pesce

FILLING:

7 ounces firm-fleshed fish such as
    hake, scorpion fish, or monkfish
1 small onion, minced
3 to 4 tablespoons olive oil or
    enough to coat bottom of pan
½ cup dry white wine
Pinch of salt
Pinch of freshly ground white
    pepper
2 egg yolks
1 ounce grated Parmesan cheese

PASTA:

3 cups unbleached all-purpose flour
2 eggs
3 tablespoons dry white wine

SAUCE:

Melted butter to please or 1 to 1½
    cups Basic Tomato Sauce (page
    43)

*If you have a fine fish broth on hand, cook the tortelli
in it and serve with a good sprinkling of freshly
ground white pepper.*

Cut the fish fillets in small pieces. Put the minced onion in
the oil and sauté until limp. Add the fish, and cook for
about 3 minutes. Add the wine, salt, and pepper, and cook
over medium heat until the wine has evaporated.

When the fish is cooked, place it in the bowl of a food
processor along with the onion and process until a soft
paste has formed. Add the egg yolks and the Parmesan
cheese and process on/off until well mixed.

Mix the pasta dough according to directions for Egg-
White Pasta, page 114. Prepare the ravioli forms according
to the directions on page 112.

Place the filling in even dabs on half the pasta. Cover
with the remaining half and cut rounds with a pastry
cutter, enclosing the filling and pressing the dough together.

Cook the tortelli in boiling, salted water until *al dente*.
Remove from the water, place on a warmed serving platter, and dress with either melted butter or with the tomato
sauce.

Yield: 4 to 6 portions

Sea Bass and Turbot in Ravioli

ravioli di pesce alla Ligure

To make the pasta, place the flour in a food processor, add the eggs and wine, and process on/off until little pellets of dough are formed. If too dry, add a touch of lukewarm water and process again. Continue as on page 111 until a dough has been formed. Roll to the thickness of a dime, and cover with a piece of plastic wrap until the filling is ready.

Place the fish fillets in a clean food processor bowl and process until a good paste has formed. Add the spinach, the chard, cheeses, marjoram, egg yolk, salt, and pepper, and process on/off until well mixed.

Drop half teaspoons of the filling, evenly spaced (about an inch between fillings) on half the dough (instructions on page 112). Cover with the remaining half of dough and cut out the ravioli using a pastry cutter. Or use a ravioli form (see page 112) and fill the form and seal as directed.

Open the mussels by putting them in a large sauté pan with the water; cover the pan and raise the heat for about 3 minutes or until all the mussels have opened. Discard any that do not open. Remove the mussels from their shells and chop them coarsely.

Clean out the sauté pan, add the oil, garlic, and parsley, and sauté briefly. Add the tomatoes and simmer for about 10 minutes or until reduced and the sauce rather

PASTA:

3 cups unbleached all-purpose flour
2 large eggs
3 tablespoons dry white wine
Warm water
Salt

FILLING:

5 ounces sea bass fillet
5 ounces turbot fillet
5 ounces spinach leaves, washed
4 ounces Swiss chard leaves, washed
4 teaspoons grated Parmesan cheese
3 ounces ricotta
2 teaspoons fresh marjoram
1 egg yolk
Salt to please
Pinch of freshly ground white
   pepper

SAUCE:

2 pounds fresh mussels, scrubbed,
   beards removed
¼ cup water
2 to 3 tablespoons olive oil

1 garlic clove, peeled and crushed
1 tablespoon minced fresh flat-leaf
  parsley
10 ounces peeled plum tomatoes
Salt

coats a spoon. Taste for salt and adjust if necessary. Remove the garlic and add the chopped mussels. Remove from heat.

Cook the ravioli in boiling, salted water 5 minutes or until *al dente*. Drain and place in a deep serving platter. Cover with the sauce.

Yield: 4 to 6 portions

Sole, Shrimp, and Caviar in Ravioli

ravioli di specie

Make the pasta, adding the teaspoon of olive oil as you mix the dough. Roll out in two even thin strips, and cover them with a sheet of plastic wrap to keep moist.

To make the filling, cut off the crusts of the bread slices and place the bread to soak in the cream.

Mince the shallot and sauté it with the leek in the olive oil until soft. Add the sole. Peel the shrimp and add them to the sauté pan. Add salt and pepper to your taste, turn up the heat, add the wine, and cook over high heat until the liquids have been evaporated.

Put the contents of the sauté pan into a food mill or food processor and mince finely. Add the bread (without squeezing away the cream) and mix well to form a good paste.

Place the filling by the teaspoonful on one strip of the pasta, leaving about 1 to 1½ inches between each spoonful. Cover with the remaining strip of pasta. Or use a ravioli-making machine (page 112).

Cook the ravioli in boiling salted water until the pasta is *al dente,* about 5 minutes. Drain well.

Meanwhile, make the sauce. Mince the 2 shallots and add them to the white wine in a sauté pan and heat until reduced by a quarter. Add the cream if using it and the herbs. Stir, add the cooked ravioli, and sauté ever so briefly over high heat. Finally, add the caviar and serve.

Yield: 4 to 6 portions (about 50 ravioli)

PASTA:

1 2-egg batch Homemade Pasta (page 110)

1 teaspoon olive oil

FILLING:

3 slices day-old bread

1¾ cups light cream

1 shallot, peeled

White part of 1 leek, minced

2 tablespoons olive oil

7 to 8 ounces fillet of sole

7 to 8 ounces unpeeled shrimp

Salt and freshly ground white pepper

⅓ cup dry white wine

SAUCE:

2 shallots

1 cup dry white wine

1 to 2 tablespoons light cream, optional

2 teaspoons chopped flat-leaf parsley

½ teaspoon dried thyme

½ teaspoon dried marjoram

1 heaping tablespoon salmon caviar

Seafood Lasagne

lasagne di magro

PASTA:

1 3-egg batch Homemade Pasta (page 110), Green Pasta (page 113), or 8-ounce package "no boil" lasagne sheets

SAUCE AND FISH:

1 recipe White Sauce (page 49), doubled

2 tablespoons chopped fresh flat-leaf parsley

1 recipe Basic Fish Stock I (page 166)

1 pound fresh salmon

1 pound sole fillets

1 pound fresh small shrimp, shelled and deveined

4 to 6 large shrimp for garnish, optional

8 tablespoons unsalted butter

3 anchovy fillets

12 ounces fresh mushrooms, sliced

1 ounce dried Italian porcini mushrooms, soaked in warm water for 10 to 15 minutes

⅛ teaspoon freshly ground white pepper

½ cup unflavored breadcrumbs

¼ cup grated Parmesan cheese

Once upon a time, when the Roman Catholic Church was very strict about meatless meals during Lent and the vigil days of Saints' Days, lasagne with seafood came into its own. Light, full of fish and flavor, it can make a meal. We use it for a host of holidays, guests, and a family who love fish.

If you wish to make it with your own pasta dough, see page 113 and make the Green Pasta, which adds a special touch to the dish and keeps it on the delicate side. Commercially packaged lasagne strips can be used, but they are slightly heavier. The precooked "no boil" lasagne sheets are really good for layering a lasagne quickly and give nice results.

If using Homemade Pasta or Green Pasta, cut it into wide strips as long as your pan is wide, about 3 to a layer. Cook the strips, a few at a time, for 2 to 3 minutes in boiling, salted water. Remove and spread on clean kitchen towels.

Make the white sauce, adding the chopped parsley after about 2 minutes of cooking. When smooth and thick, set aside to cool with plastic wrap pressed down on the surface.

Heat four cups of fish stock in a suitable saucepan and poach the salmon until it is on the edge of flaking. Remove the salmon to a platter and poach the sole for a minute or so.

Remove the sole to a platter and poach the shrimp about 1 minute.

Cut the salmon in small bite-size pieces and butterfly the large shrimp if using them for garnish.

Melt 3 tablespoons of butter in a saucepan. Add the anchovies, stir, and add the fresh mushrooms. Cook about 4 minutes. Don't drain the porcini mushrooms, just lift them out of their water with a fork, leaving whatever dirt there may be in the cup. Cut in pieces the size of the fresh mushrooms and add them to the pan.

When the anchovies have more or less disintegrated and the fresh mushrooms have given up their juices, add the pepper, stir, and remove from heat.

Preheat the oven to 350 degrees Fahrenheit.

Butter your baking pan, dust with some of the breadcrumbs. Place pasta strips (fresh or "no boil") overlapping a bit to cover the pan bottom. Spread sole fillets to cover the pasta, reserving one, and dot with about half the small shrimp.

Using a pastry bag, make four ribbons of white sauce running over the fish from end to end of the pan, or drop tablespoons of white sauce about 2 inches apart. Cover with pasta strips.

The second layer of the lasagne consists of half of the mushroom mixture and four more ribbons of white sauce. Cover with more pasta strips.

For the third layer, cover the pasta with about ¾ of the salmon bits. Add the white sauce as before and cover with pasta strips.

Use the last of the sole, salmon bits, and remaining small shrimp for the final layer. Add the white sauce and

the final layer of pasta strips. Sprinkle this layer with the last of the mushrooms, dot with the last of the white sauce, position the large shrimps, and sprinkle with the remaining breadcrumbs.

Melt the remaining butter and drizzle it back and forth over the breadcrumbs. Sprinkle with the Parmesan cheese.

Bake for 30 minutes and then let rest 15 minutes before cutting.

Yield: 10 portions

Sole and Mushroom Lasagne

lasagne con sogliole e funghi

One of the favorite topics of Italian food buffs is Renaissance cooking, that magnificent cookery said to have been brought to France from Italy by way of the head chef for Catherine de Médicis who married the Duke of Orléans (later Henry II) in 1533. Whatever the history, the cuisine is prized, and there are some who feel that the following is typical of those times.

This is one of the dishes in which you may substitute perch fillets for the small sole fillets. You may also use frozen sole or perch fillets for this recipe. Thaw them in the refrigerator, pat dry, and cook immediately.

Although the commercial "no boil" lasagne sheets are quite satisfactory here, we do not recommend the use of regular commercial lasagne pasta for this dish as it is generally too thick and heavy for the delicate texture of this lasagne.

Make the pasta according to the recipe. Cut in pieces as long as your baking dish is wide. Cook the pasta cuts a few at a time in boiling, salted water until *al dente*. Remove with tongs, dip into cold water to cool a moment, and spread on a clean dish towel. (If using "no boil" pasta, skip this step.)

Dredge the fillets in flour, patting them gently to remove excess, and sauté them briefly in 3 to 4 table-spoons of butter until toast brown on both sides, a matter

PASTA:

1 3-egg batch Homemade Pasta (page 110) or 8-ounce package "no boil" lasagne sheets

SAUCE AND FISH:

1 pound small sole fillets, approximately

Unbleached all-purpose flour to coat the fillets

5 to 6 tablespoons unsalted butter (or half butter/half olive oil) plus additional butter for greasing the baking dish and dotting top of lasagne

1 to 2 tablespoons dry white wine

Salt and freshly ground white pepper to taste

1 batch Mornay Sauce (page 51)

Scant teaspoon freshly grated nutmeg

8 ounces fresh mushrooms or 1 ounce dried porcini mushrooms

of 2 to 3 minutes. Add the wine as the second sides brown and season with salt and white pepper.

Prepare the Mornay sauce, adding the nutmeg to flavor. Clean the fresh mushrooms, slice, and sauté them in about 2 tablespoons of butter.

If using dried mushrooms, soak them 10 to 15 minutes in warm water. Lift the mushrooms out of the water, letting any sand settle in the bottom of the glass or bowl. Cut up coarsely and proceed as you would with fresh mushrooms.

Preheat the oven to 350 degrees Fahrenheit.

Butter the baking dish. Place a layer of lasagne cuts, slightly overlapping, on the bottom of the dish. Spread a layer of the cooked fillets. Follow with a layer of pasta, a layer of Mornay sauce, another of pasta, then sole, mushrooms, Mornay, and pasta. Make as many layerings as you can, depending on the size of the dish, and finish by dotting the top layer of lasagne with butter.

Bake for about 25 minutes or until well cooked and heated through. Let rest about 10 minutes before serving.

Yield: 6 portions

Couscous

Sicilian Couscous I

cuscusu

Just about six centuries ago, the Arabs occupied Sicily for a while. Their influence is still felt today in architecture, culture, and gastronomy. Sicilians have taken some Arab tastes and styles of cooking and made them their own: couscous, tiny grains of semolina, became cuscusu and assumed a new aspect. Instead of the North African pairing with lamb, couscous was spiced up and served with a ragout of fish flavored with herbs, almonds, and aromas—such as cinnamon, cloves, and nutmeg—rarely associated with Italian fish dishes.

Cuscusu *proper is homemade with semolina flour and is quite an elaborate process, which can be adequately circumvented by using "instant" couscous. There is no loss of taste or texture and a great saving of fuss and time.*

The final success of couscous rests with the fish and the fish broth: the more different types of fish, the better. It is best to coordinate with your fish dealer and let him know of your desires. The fish broth requires fish heads and bones (called racks), which your vendor can order if his supply comes without them. Solid-fleshed, flavorful fish—that will stand the cooking without falling apart—is what we are after here.

FISH:

1½ pounds fish, approximately, cut in pieces (e.g., swordfish, monkfish, halibut, grouper, black sea bass, gray mullet)

½ pound fresh shrimp, shelled and cleaned, shells reserved for broth

½ pound squid, cleaned and cut (page 16)

Meat of a 1-pound lobster, cooked and cut in chunks, optional

BROTH:

4 tablespoons olive oil

4 garlic cloves, peeled and mashed

1 large onion, chopped

2 anchovy fillets, chopped

3 bay leaves

2 to 3 sprigs of fresh flat-leaf parsley

4 to 5 fresh basil leaves

1 teaspoon peppercorns

½ teaspoon salt

6½ cups warm water

2 pounds "racks," or "chowder
    fish," approximately
Reserved shrimp shells
½ cup dry white wine
1 cup Basic Tomato Sauce (page
    43)
2 tablespoons tomato paste
¼ teaspoon ground cayenne pepper
2 teaspoons salt

COUSCOUS:
1 cup water
1 packet (.005 ounce) Italian
    powdered saffron
⅛ teaspoon powdered cinnamon
⅛ teaspoon powdered cloves
⅛ teaspoon powdered nutmeg
1 10-ounce package instant couscous

The fish broth may be prepared ahead of time. Since it freezes well, it is worthwhile making a larger batch to use for other dishes or for a very probable return performance.

If your fish can be purchased intact, and if you are not too fussy, do as they do in the islands: after you have cut off the head and tails for the broth, chop the cleaned fish and cook the pieces with the bones in. You will have to be able to deal with boning the fish at the table, but it is a process that boosts the taste enormously. You will need a finger bowl or two plus some extra napkins—it is a production but worth every minute of it. Here is a cuscusu *for a party of six.*

Refrigerate prepared seafood in separate containers until needed.

In a large soup pot, put oil, garlic, onion, anchovies, bay leaves, parsley, basil, peppercorns, and salt, and sauté, stirring, over brisk heat for 2 minutes. Add ½ cup warm water, and when almost evaporated put in the fish racks (or chowder fish) and the shrimp shells. Stir around for a minute or so, then add the wine and cook until it has almost evaporated.

Add the tomato sauce, tomato paste, and cayenne pepper. Stir, and when well amalgamated, add the remaining warm water and the salt. Bring to a boil, cover the pot, and let simmer for 30 minutes, then skim the broth with a slotted spoon and simmer for another 15 to 20 minutes. Let cool a little, then filter the broth through a fine sieve into a bowl or adequate container. Taste and adjust for salt and spiciness. The broth should have a certain zip to it: if needed, stir in more red pepper.

Put 1½ cups of fish broth, 1 cup of water, and the saffron, cinnamon, cloves, and nutmeg in a 2-quart soup pot and bring to a boil. Pour into it the couscous, stir well, cover the pot and turn off the heat. Let stand 5 minutes.

In a large saucepan, put the rest of the broth and bring to a boil. Put into it the prepared fish, beginning with the more firm-fleshed kind. When the broth comes back to a boil, put in the next and so on.

With the last, add the shrimp and after a minute the squid. Boil gently a minute more (do not overcook), add the optional lobster meat, and turn off the heat. Scoop out the fish with a slotted spoon and keep warm.

Fluff up the couscous in its pot, stir in a ladleful of broth and apportion on warm soup plates, making a hollow in the center of each helping. Into this place the fish and serve. Put the remaining hot broth into a soup terrine and let the guests add it to their plates as they please.

Yield: 6 portions

Sicilian Couscous II

BROTH AND RAGOUT:

*4 pounds varied fresh fish (e.g., ½
    pound shrimp, ½ pound mussels,
    some monkfish, haddock, cod,
    halibut, whiting, or butterfish; if
    following feast day tradition,
    also include the meat of a 1¼-
    pound lobster)*

1 onion

*1 dried cayenne pepper pod, or ¼
    teaspoon ground cayenne pepper*

½ cup olive oil

¾ cup almonds, peeled

4 garlic cloves

*2 tablespoons chopped fresh flat-leaf
    parsley*

*2 cups canned plum tomatoes,
    chopped*

*1 teaspoon freshly ground white
    pepper, or to taste*

3 quarts warm water

2 teaspoons salt, approximately

*Traditionally, Sicilians dress a couscous bowl for a
feast day with lobster as follows: place the couscous in
the center of a deep platter; slice the lobster tail in
rounds and place on top of the couscous with the claws
at either end; cut the peppers in julienne strips and set
them around the edge of the platter. Sprinkle the entire
glory with a handful of sweet peas, cooked in boiling
salted water until just tender.*

This variation of cuscusu *is flavored with almonds for a party of eight.*

Clean the fish as necessary, saving the heads, tails, bones,
and shrimp shells. (See headnote, page 147.) Slice the
onion in slivers, sauté with the pepper pod (if using) in the
olive oil in a large pot until the onion is translucent and
the pepper dark brown. Discard the pepper.

In a food processor equipped with the metal blade,
process the almonds, garlic, and parsley together until
well minced. Add to the onions and stir and cook 3
minutes. Add the tomatoes, white pepper, and ground
cayenne pepper (if using it) and cook until the ingredients
are well blended.

Add the warm water and salt, and bring the pot to a
boil. Add the fish heads, tails, bones, and shells. Cook 20
minutes. While cooking, add the mussels and retrieve
them with a slotted spoon the minute they open, and set
them aside for later use.

When the broth is cooked, strain it into a new pot and

keep warm over low heat. Discard the fish heads and bones and shrimp shells.

Put 1½ cups fish broth, 1 cup of water, and the saffron, olive oil, salt, and cinnamon in a 2-quart soup pot and bring to a boil. Add the couscous, stir, cover, and turn off the heat. Keep in a warm place until the fish is done. Fluff up the couscous before serving it.

Put the fish in the remaining broth according to texture, the meatier fish first. Bring the broth back to a boil, and cook about 10 minutes. Add the more delicate fish, and keep the broth boiling gently for 5 minutes. Add the shrimp and cook 3 minutes. Stir in the mussels.

To serve, put the fish in its broth in a hot soup tureen. Serve each plate with a ladle or two of couscous and a variety of fish, garnished with the lobster, pepper slices, and peas.

Yield: 8 portions

COUSCOUS:

1 cup water

1 packet (.005 ounce) Italian powdered saffron

¼ cup olive oil

½ teaspoon salt, approximately

½ teaspoon cinnamon

1 pound "instant" couscous

GARNISH:

Slices of lobster tails and claws

Red, green, and yellow bell peppers in julienne slices

5 ounces cooked frozen green peas

Rice

Another partner that works well with fish and fish sauces is rice. In Italy rice (*riso*) appears as a first course and is handled as diversely and lovingly as a dish of pasta. It is seldom used as an accompaniment. Once almost exclusively a northern dish, especially as *risotto*, today it is at home all over the country. Italy grows most of its rice and divides it into rice suitable for soups and rice more suitable for *risotto*, with somewhat rounder grains which tend to fatten up with the cooking, absorbing the liquids and sauces with which they are cooked while still retaining a certain firmness. The most common types imported in this country (under different brand labels) are Arborio and Vialone. They are available in Italian markets and specialty stores and we make reasonable efforts to get them. But when we cannot readily find Italian rice, we substitute American medium-grain rice (such as River Rice) which reacts as Italian rice does and contributes to the sauce and is as close to us as the nearest supermarket. American instant rice, however, is definitely a no-no for *risotto*.

You can cook rice by pouring it into a boiling liquid and, a few minutes before its final cooking time, adding the flavoring sauce. For a traditional *risotto* the method is slightly more involved and finally more rewarding. It starts by sautéing minced onion in butter until limp and golden, then adding the rice and cooking it until it begins to crackle. Then a warm cooking liquid—generally a chicken, beef, or fish broth—is added, stirring, a ladle or two at a time. When this is absorbed, more is added and so on until, close to final cooking, the rice's partner is added. The whole process can take up to 30 minutes.

Years ago, perhaps even before our grandmothers' time, risotto was traditionally made this way, and no one was ever allowed to break the rules. However, with the passage of time and cooking stoves, pots, hands, and schedules, the rules are bent a little bit. By and large, when the oil is flavored, the other flavors are in, and liquid is added from time to time and not necessarily by the single ladle or ½ cup at a time for over 20 minutes, it is still called *risotto*. Steamed or plain rice cooked with salted water in one dose (the American method) is never called *risotto*.

There are different schools of thought about the final consistency of a *risotto*. Some say that it should be so thick that when served it remains in a mound on the plate. Others say it should be *all' onda*, or loose enough to make "waves" on the plate when it is served. You can decide on your preference, and arrive at it by adding more or less liquid.

The important fact is that, no matter how you cook it, rice should not be overcooked: each grain should be cooked through but still retain its shape and individuality—*al dente*, as it were— and all kept together by a certain creaminess produced by the combination of broth, sauce, and the rice-released starch.

Shrimp Risotto, Venetian Style

risotto alla veneziana

This is a favorite that is made in the classic Italian risotto fashion using only as much liquid as the rice can absorb at each addition. The flavor is enhanced by the shrimp broth and its shells.

1 pound medium shrimp, shells on
½ cup olive oil
1 medium onion, quartered
12 fresh basil leaves, plus additional
    small leaves for garnish
2 garlic cloves, peeled
5 sprigs of fresh flat-leaf parsley
5 cups water
6 tablespoons unsalted butter
1½ cup Arborio rice or medium-
    grain American rice
½ teaspoon salt

Shell and devein the shrimp and sauté the shells in half the olive oil for at least 10 minutes to render the flavor.

While the shells cook in the oil, put the onion, half the basil, garlic, and half the parsley sprigs with the shrimp in boiling, salted water. Cook for 2 to 3 minutes, or until the shrimp are coral colored. Scoop out the shrimp, and set them aside. Bring the shrimp water back to a boil and then simmer for 15 minutes. Strain through a cheesecloth-lined sieve and reserve.

Remove the shrimp shells from the olive oil and add it to the butter with the rest of the oil in a large saucepan. Chop the remaining basil leaves, except those for garnish, and add them with the rice to the oil/butter mixture. Cook until the rice crackles and is coated with the butter and oil. Add ½ cup of the shrimp broth. Cook over medium heat, adding more broth as addition is absorbed, ½ cup at a time, and stirring at each addition. Add the shrimp when the rice is nearly cooked, after about 15 minutes, and check for salt and add as needed. Add the last of the shrimp broth, and chop remaining parsley leaves and stir them into the rice. Cook until the rice is very plumped up and tender. Scoop the risotto into a heated serving bowl, place pairs of small basil leaves over the mound of rice and shrimp, and serve.

Yield: 6 portions

Shellfish with Rice

riso ai frutti di mare

Clean the squid (page 16), cut the sacs in rings, the tentacles in half. Peel the shrimp.

Heat the olive oil in a large sauté pan, add the garlic, cook it until golden, and then discard it. Add the squid, shrimp, and cayenne pepper. Cook and stir 1 to 2 minutes or until the squid tentacles turn slightly purple and the shrimp coral. Add the wine and cook until evaporated.

In a separate pan, place the mussels with just a touch of water and cook, covered, over high heat until the mussels open, a matter of minutes. Remove the mussels from their shells (discarding any that remain closed) and add to the squid pan. Strain the mussel liquid through a fine sieve and add it to the squid pan. Add the baby clams and 2 or 3 tablespoons of their liquid. Turn off the heat, cover the pan, and keep warm.

Heat the oil in a heavy saucepan. Add the onion and cook until very limp and almost translucent. Add the rice and stir and cook until the rice crackles. Add the hot fish broth (or lightly salted hot water). Bring to a boil, lower the heat, and simmer, covered, about 13 minutes or until cooked, stirring a couple of times. Stir in the squid, shellfish, and all their cooking liquids. Taste for salt; adjust if necessary. Add the parsley and the butter and cook, stirring gently, for another minute. Serve on warm plates.

Yield: 6 portions

½ pound small to medium squid
½ pound medium shrimp
3 tablespoons olive oil
2 garlic cloves
¼ teaspoon ground cayenne pepper, or to taste
½ cup dry white wine
½ pound mussels
4 ounces canned baby clams, liquid reserved
4 tablespoons olive oil
1 small onion, minced
1½ cups imported Italian rice or medium-grain rice
3 cups hot, clear fish broth or water
Salt to taste (if using water, about 1 teaspoon)
3 tablespoons chopped fresh flat-leaf parsley
2 tablespoons unsalted butter

Lobster Risotto

risotto all'astice

1¼- to 1½-pound lobster*
2 tablespoons unsalted butter
3 tablespoons olive oil
1 celery rib, minced
1 small onion, minced
1 garlic clove, minced
2 cups Arborio rice or American
    medium-grain rice
1 teaspoon salt
5 tablespoons dry sherry
4½ cups hot chicken broth,
    approximately
1 packet (.005 ounce) powdered
    Italian saffron
2 to 3 tablespoons chopped fresh flat-
    leaf parsley

Poach the lobster, making sure the water is abundant, at least 6 quarts, and as salty as sea water. When the water boils, put in the lobster and bring the pot back to a simmer. Simmer 10 minutes per pound.

When the lobster is cool enough to handle easily, remove the meat from the shell. Slice the tail in neat rounds and reserve. Cut up the rest of the meat in ¼- to ½-inch pieces. Reserve the roe if you wish.

Melt the butter with the oil in a large saucepan. Add the celery, onion, and garlic and sauté until they are limp. Add the rice and salt. Continue to cook until the rice crackles. Add the sherry and cook until it has evaporated.

Add the hot broth. Sprinkle the saffron into the rice and stir well. Lower the heat and cook for about 15 minutes, stirring from time to time. Stir in more broth if the rice should dry out too much. Add lobster meat after about 12 minutes of cooking time.

When the rice is tender, stir again and serve on hot plates. Dress each plate with the reserved lobster rounds, the roe if you wish, and chopped parsley. Serve immediately.

Yield: 6 portions

*NOTE: A 1½-pound lobster yields about 1½ cups of lobster meat, which turns out to be about 6 to 7 ounces or a little more than half a can of the frozen, canned lobster from Prince Edward Island, available in many supermarkets. If making *risotto* for a party of more than six, we find the canned lobster a rather nice substitute for fresh lobster.

Polenta

As of recently, polenta has found its deserved spot in the culinary limelight, egged on by the rediscovery of *cucina rustica*, a cuisine that emphasizes old peasant dishes (reworked and trimmed to conform to modern trends, naturally). Polenta was once the basic staple of northern Italian regions—especially the Veneto—as much as rice was for Lombardy and Piedmont and pasta was for the southern regions.

A sturdy affair, polenta serves the same functions that rice, pasta, and bread had for the non-polenta-eating Italian tables: the support for the basic nutritional elements—meat, fish, or vegetable—of the region.

Polenta today tends to appears more as an accompaniment or trim to a fancy dish, in the form of dainty wedges grilled or fried. Or, the way we prefer it, as a thinner version of its old self and the carrier for a sauce: an ideal one-dish meal.

The makings for polenta can be found on the market as yellow cornmeal (coarse ground) or as *harina de mais* in Spanish-American markets or, imported from Italy, as "instant polenta." We have become particularly fond of the last, since not only is it very good, but it cuts the cooking time down to 5 minutes from the 30 to 40 minutes that the regular one requires.

Traditionally the cooked, steaming polenta was poured and allowed to spread over a large board and then the sauce was dolloped over it. The diners sat around the board and ate from it as from a common plate, marking out with their forks a portion—their private turf—in front of themselves. Once that portion was finished, another one was staked out. The most territory went to the hungriest . . . or fastest. To change the routine of a dinner, especially when children and grandchildren are with us, we follow the old tradition: it makes for a lively, different way of sharing (literally and metaphorically) a warm meal.

Try it.

Salt Cod with Chard and Polenta

polenta, erbette, e baccalà

FISH:

1 pound dried salt cod, soaked
   (page 17)

SAUCE:

4 tablespoons olive oil
3 garlic cloves, crushed
1 medium onion, slivered
1 carrot, minced
1 celery rib, minced
¼ teaspoon ground cayenne pepper
Salt to taste
½ cup dry white wine
2 cups canned peeled plum
   tomatoes, coarsely chopped
1 pound Swiss chard, washed

POLENTA:

1 package Italian "instant"
   polenta or 1⅓ cups American
   cornmeal
7 cups cold water
2½ teaspoons salt
3 tablespoons unsalted butter

This dish makes its home in central Italy, in the region of the Marches. Its particularity rests in the ingenious addition of Swiss chard (or spinach) to the fish. The resulting stew is served on top of steaming-hot polenta.

Drain and cut the cod into 1- to 2-inch square pieces and set aside.

Heat the oil in a large sauté pan, brown the garlic and then discard it. Add the onion, carrot, celery, and pepper to the flavored oil. Sprinkle with a bit of salt and cook until the vegetables are wilted. Raise the heat, add the wine, and cook until the wine has evaporated. Add the tomatoes, bring to a boil, then simmer for 15 to 20 minutes.

Add the cod to the sauce. Poach for 10 minutes.

Bring about a cup of water to a boil, briefly drain the chard, and add it to the boiling water. Cook until *al dente* (wilted but still slightly crisp). Drain the chard, squeeze it dry, chop coarsely, and add it to the simmering sauce. Cook another 5 minutes.

If using instant polenta (it cooks in about 5 minutes) follow the instructions on the box. If using regular cornmeal, stir it in half the cold water. Bring the remaining 3½ cups of water to a boil, pour into it the cornmeal/cold water mixture and bring back to a boil, stirring con-

stantly. Add the salt and the butter, lower the heat to a simmer, and cook, stirring frequently, about 30 minutes.

Scoop or pour the cooked polenta on entrée plates. Spoon the sauce over the polenta. Keep any remaining sauce warm in a terrine for repeat customers.

Yield: 6 portions

Swordfish in Spicy Sauce with Polenta

polentina e pescespada

This is a happy wedding between a northern and a southern Italian dish. The classic northern polenta here becomes a polentina, a thinner version thereof, dressed with the swordfish stew. For a sturdier dish, substitute the swordfish with fresh tuna; for a more delicate one use halibut.

1 small green bell pepper
½ cup green Spanish olives, with or without pimiento
4 tablespoons olive oil
¼ teaspoon salt
½ teaspoon freshly ground black pepper
¼ cup dry white wine or warm water
1 28-ounce can peeled plum tomatoes
¼ to ½ teaspoon ground cayenne pepper
1½ pounds swordfish, approximately
¾ cup instant polenta or cornmeal
2 tablespoons unsalted butter

Wash, remove seeds and stem, and cut the pepper in ¼-inch cubes. Drain the olives and chop them. Put the olive oil, pepper cubes, and olives in a large sauté pan. Add the salt and black pepper and stir-cook for 3 to 4 minutes. Add the wine (or ¼ cup warm water) and stir until evaporated. Put the peeled tomatoes with their liquid in a bowl and mash them roughly with a fork and add them to the

pan with the pepper and olives. Bring to a boil, add the cayenne pepper (to taste: the dish should be on the hot side) and simmer the sauce for 20 minutes, or until reduced by about a quarter. Cut the swordfish in roughly 3- by 3-inch pieces, about ½ inch thick, and add to the sauce. Poach them in the simmering sauce for 5 minutes, or until the swordfish is cooked through. If the fish, in cooking, has added moisture to the sauce, scoop the fish out and boil the sauce down for 3 to 4 minutes longer, stirring, until the watery part has evaporated and the whole is of sauce consistency. Turn heat off, put fish back in the pan, and keep warm.

Make a *polentina* with ¾ cup of Italian instant polenta cooked in 5½ cups of lightly salted boiling water to which the butter has been added. Cook, stirring, for 5 to 6 minutes. (If using cornmeal, use the same proportions. For cooking, see page 158.)

Pour the *polentina* on flat serving dishes so that it spreads out to cover the plate, apportion fish and sauce over them, and serve.

Yield: 4 portions

Fresh Tuna in Tomato Sauce with Polenta

ragù di tonno fresco

This ragù *is equally delicious served on small-cut macaroni (penne, rigatoni).*

Mince together, almost to a paste, the parsley, basil, celery, carrot, and onion. Sauté it in the olive oil over medium heat. Add the salt and pepper to taste, stir, and cook until all is golden and limp. To accelerate the process, add 2 or 3 tablespoons of warm water and let evaporate completely.

With a sharp knife, cut the fresh tuna in small cubes (¼ inch, approximately) and sauté it in the pan with the minced vegetables. When the tuna has lost its raw color, raise the heat, add the wine, and cover. Mash the tomatoes well and add them to the pan. Stir in the cloves and the lemon zest and let the *ragù* cook, covered, at a low simmer for 20 to 25 minutes. Stir once in a while and add, if necessary, a few tablespoons of warm water or tomato juice to achieve sauce consistency. Put in a tureen in a warm place.

Make a polenta (page 158) with the "instant polenta," or with the cornmeal and serve on plates with each individual spooning the *ragù* from the tureen.

Yield: 4 portions

1 cup loosely packed fresh flat-leaf parsley

5 to 6 fresh basil leaves

1 celery rib

1 medium carrot

1 medium onion

4 tablespoons olive oil

Salt and freshly ground black pepper to taste

1 pound fresh tuna

1 cup dry red wine

2 cups canned plum tomatoes and their juice

⅛ teaspoon powdered cloves

2 tablespoons grated zest of lemon

Tomato juice, optional

¾ cup instant polenta or cornmeal

2 tablespoons unsalted butter

5 cups water

VII

Soups

Bouillabaisse, cacciucco, cioppino, chowder, fish stew, *zuppa di pesce*—there are a lot of names for one of the most delicious, enticing, and perhaps the pleasantest way to cook fish: soup.

A whole host of people steer clear of fish soup for preconceived, sometimes rather silly notions: it takes too long, it calls for odd fish, it means a lot of stewing and stirring, it is very difficult. But in a reasonably up-to-date kitchen with a half-decent market, all the above fears can be thrown out and you can get down to making a glorious soup worthy of the best cooks in any town.

Most of the soups in this chapter fall into one of two categories, those that begin with the use of an already-made fish stock, and those that make their own base as they cook.

We shall start with a genuine fish stock that goes well with virtually any fish, can be made ahead of time, will keep in the refrigerator, freezes well, and maintains itself frozen for up to 3 months.

In the second type of soup that makes its own base, many of its ingredients hardly vary from one dish to another. Like the French *mirepoix* (a constant and gentle mince of herbs for flavoring), the ingredients are very versatile: olive oil, hint of garlic, touch of hot pepper, splash of dry white wine, sometimes celery, perhaps a bit of tomato, and your base begins. The fish is usually added according to how fast each species cooks, and the whole process doesn't take long, certainly not the time it takes to make a number of other equally great soups.

Finally, before you get out your pot or pan, remember that the very word *soup*

usually implies something more liquid than solid, something that serves as an opener for dinner. However, a great, great many of these savory dishes are more solid than liquid, more fish than broth, more fun than most of their names can tell you, and thus more main course. If, at first glance, they appear closely related it is because they are: geographically—at least by American standards—their origins are practically next door to each other. And yet, when they finally arrive at table, their various nuances in the making will add up to quite different tastes. They have been chosen for their flavor as well as for their adaptability to the American home, markets, and palates.

Basic Fish Stock I

brodo di pesce

Following is the basic recipe for fish stock. It makes about 4 quarts as a base for use in other soups or to hold, frozen, for future occasions. I use a large, stainless-steel stockpot for this.

½ cup olive oil*
4 garlic cloves, peeled
2 dried cayenne pepper pods, seeded,
    or ½ teaspoon ground red pepper
8 anchovy fillets, chopped
½ cup chopped fresh flat-leaf parsley
3 cups canned peeled plum tomatoes
2 cups dry white wine
5 pounds fish bones, tails, heads
    (racks)
2 celery ribs with leaves

Sauté in the olive oil in a large stockpot the garlic and pepper pods (if using this form) until golden and dark brown respectively. Discard the two flavorings. Add the anchovies and parsley to the flavored oil and sauté briefly. Add the tomatoes, the ground red pepper if using it, and the wine, and cook for a minute. Add the fish bones, heads, tails, and all the vegetables. Pour in the water to cover and bring slowly to a simmer. Let the pot simmer semicovered for about an hour.

Line a big strainer with double cheesecloth and strain the fish broth into a new pot. Add about half the salt,

taste, and add more if you like. If you wish to add a bit of pepper at this time, it is your choice.

The broth may be used immediately (as in Lobster Soup, page 184) or it may be frozen in containers for future use.

Yield: about 4 quarts

* NOTE: If you have on hand a reserve of Garlic, Olive Oil, and Hot Red Pepper Sauce (page 37), use it in place of the oil, garlic, and cayenne pepper listed. We have found specialty stores that sell garlic-flavored olive oil, which you may want to use for this dish and in others calling for flavored olive oil.

2 carrots, peeled
2 bay leaves
2 medium onions
Cold water to cover (about 3½ quarts)
4 teaspoons salt, approximately
Freshly ground black pepper, optional

Basic Fish Stock II

3 quarts water, approximately

2 cups white vinegar, or 1 quart
*   dry white wine, or ½ cup lemon*
*   juice*

1 large onion

2 carrots

2 celery ribs with leaves

2 bay leaves

5 sprigs of fresh flat-leaf parsley

2 basil leaves

1 sprig of thyme

5 peppercorns

3 teaspoons salt, or to your taste

4 to 5 pounds fish racks (bones,
*   heads, and tails) and shrimp*
*   shells, optional, depending on*
*   your use**

This is the stock we use when poaching fish. In cooks' parlance it is court bouillon; our copy of the cookery encyclopedia lists no less than fourteen court bouillons for fish, so this is only one. Our formula uses either vinegar and water, wine and water, or lemon juice. When cooked with fish bones or after poaching a fish in it and reduced, it is called fumet, *or essence, and it may be clarified and used in aspic.*

Place all the ingredients in a soup pot or fish poacher. Bring to a boil, lower the heat, and simmer for at least 30 minutes.

* NOTE: If poaching fish, do not use the fish bones or shells, and allow the broth to cool before lowering the fish into the liquid.

If aspic is your goal, use the fish bones as they will aid in the gelling process.

Or, you may wish to use the broth to make white sauce for Seafood Lasagne (page 142). In any case for the last two types of use, strain the broth through three layers of cheesecloth. If you wish to clarify the broth even more, bring it to a boil, add 3 egg whites, boil vigorously about 5 minutes, and then let cool. The egg whites collect almost any particles and can be scooped off the top of the broth.

Cioppino

ciuppin

Here is a fish soup that has many versions: in San Francisco it is called cioppino *and it is made by fishermen using local West Coast fish and red wine. In Liguria, where the soup came from, it is called* ciuppin *and uses white wine and the accent of ginger. Both versions call for tomatoes, but the Italian recipe forbids tomato paste. We prefer the soup as we had it in Liguria.*

Clean, bone, and wash the fish. Cut the squid sacs in ¼-inch-wide strips, large tentacles in half.

Put the fish heads, tails, and bones in water to cover. Add salt, bring to a boil, reduce heat, and let simmer for about 20 minutes.

To make the soup, place the olive oil in a deep top-of-the-stove casserole.

Mince the onion, carrot, celery, garlic, parsley, and anchovies finely; chop the now-softened mushrooms coarsely and put them all to cook over medium heat. When these flavorings are soft but not browned, add the squid, stir, and cook 3 minutes. Add the longest-cooking pieces of cut-up fish and cook for 2 or 3 minutes. Add the more tender fish and sauté over high heat. Add salt and pepper and white wine and cook until the wine has almost evaporated.

Add the tomatoes and stir in the ginger. Pouring through a fine strainer, add enough of the fish broth to

FISH:

3½ *pounds varied small fish from the following list: sea bass, striped bass, grey sole, striped or black mullet, lobster, crab, hogfish, scup, sea robin, tautog*

½ *pound cleaned squid (page 16)*
Salt to taste

SOUP:

4 tablespoons olive oil
1 small onion
1 small carrot
1 small celery rib
3 garlic cloves
3 or 4 sprigs of fresh flat-leaf parsley
4 anchovy fillets
¾ *to 1 ounce dried porcini mushrooms, soaked in warm water*
Salt and freshly ground black pepper to taste
1 cup dry white wine
10 ounces canned peeled plum tomatoes, drained and mashed

¼ teaspoon powdered ginger, or 2
   thin slices fresh
4 slices Italian-style bread, deep-
   fried in olive oil or toasted
1 tablespoon chopped fresh flat-leaf
   parsley

just cover the fish. Bring to a boil, lower the heat, and cook another 3 minutes.

Remove the sturdier pieces of fish and set aside in a warm place. Scoop all the smaller fish, now falling apart, into a strainer and push the pieces through into the pot.

Add the solid chunks of fish. Stir and taste. Adjust seasonings if necessary and serve in warmed soup plates with fried or toasted bread in the bottom. Sprinkle with parsley.

Yield: 4 to 6 portions

Fish Soup from Ortona

zuppa di pesce d'Ortona

*In this soup, the use of roasted sweet bell pepper, oreg-
ano, and saffron produces a rather sophisticated difference. We use fish that are what you would choose in
the little Adriatic fishing village of Ortona. Let your
market be the guide, but stay away from fatty types of
fish such as mackerel, or the sturdier ones such as tuna
and swordfish. Ideally this soup should be made in a
large sauté pan so that all the fish cook in one layer; the
dish will be closer to a stew than the other fish soups in
this chapter.*

Chop off any heads and tails of the fish, shell the shrimp,
and reserve, refrigerated, until needed.

Put the olive oil in a large sauté pan (or soup pot) and
sauté the pepper pod in it until dark brown. Discard the
pepper and let the oil cool a moment before adding the
plum tomatoes. Then raise the heat until the tomatoes
start to boil. Lower the heat and simmer 10 minutes, or
until the tomatoes have blended nicely with the oil and
the liquid has been reduced a bit.

Add the roasted pepper strips, the oregano, salt, and
pepper, and bring the pot to a boil. Add the wine and saffron, and continue cooking until it has evaporated. Cover
the pot, lower the heat, and cook for about 10 minutes.

In the meantime, put the reserved fish heads, tails,
and shrimp shells into another pot with water to cover
(about a quart) with 1 teaspoon salt. Bring to a boil,

FISH:

½ *pound fresh cod fillet (or hake,
    pout, whiting, haddock)*

1 *small red snapper (or 2 or 3 fillets
    ocean perch)*

½ *pound halibut steak*

½ *pound medium shrimp*

1 *pound mussels, cleaned*

½ *pound squid, cleaned and cut in
    rings (page 16)*

1 *teaspoon salt*

SOUP:

4 *tablespoons olive oil*

1 *dried cayenne pepper pod, seeded*

2 *cups peeled plum tomatoes, cut in
    chunks*

1 *red or green bell pepper, roasted,
    peeled, and cut in strips (page
    35)*

¼ *teaspoon dried oregano*

½ *teaspoon salt, or to taste*

Freshly ground black pepper

½ *cup dry white wine*

1 *packet (.005 ounce) Italian
    powdered saffron*

*2 tablespoons chopped fresh flat-leaf
  parsley*
*4 slices Italian-style bread, toasted
  or deep-fried*

lower the heat, and simmer for 15 minutes; then strain the broth from the fish heads into the sauté pan with the tomato mixture. Let the soup reduce at a slow boil for 5 minutes.

Cut the cod in half and add it to the sauté pan (or first soup pot). When it boils, add the red snapper. When it boils again, add the halibut, return the pot to a boil, lower the heat, and simmer about 5 minutes. The timing here is important: the minute the red snapper and halibut are almost done, add the shrimp.

As soon as the shrimp are cooked (about 2 minutes), add the mussels and squid and cover the pot. Cook about 3 minutes longer, or until the mussels have opened up. Discard any unopened mussels. Sprinkle the soup with the chopped parsley. Serve with the toasted or fried bread.

Yield: 4 to 6 portions

Fisherman's Soup

zuppa di pesce alla marinara

The method for making this soup belongs under the heading "another way to skin a cat." Instead of adding broth or making it as the soup cooks, this dish uses ready-made simple tomato sauce—accented by wine—to fill the bowl.

If you want a slightly less thick soup, thin it with a few tablespoons of hot water.

Put the flavored oil in a sauté pan over high heat. Add the clams and mussels, and when all the shells have opened (about 3 minutes—discard any that have not by this point), add the wine. Let the wine evaporate and add the tomato sauce, scallops, shrimp, and squid, and cook another 2 minutes.

Add the Tabasco, taste for salt, and add if necessary. Serve in soup bowls on a slice of fried or toasted Italian bread and garnish with parsley.

Yield: 4 portions

4 tablespoons Garlic, Olive Oil, and Hot Red Pepper Sauce (page 37)
½ pound littleneck clams
1 pound mussels, approximately
1½ cups dry white wine
1½ cups Basic Tomato Sauce (page 43)
¼ pound scallops
¼ pound shrimp, shelled
2 or 3 squid, cleaned
Dash of Tabasco
Salt to taste
Toasted or deep-fried Italian-style bread slices, optional
1 tablespoon chopped fresh curly or flat-leaf parsley

Fish Soup from Genoa

zuppa di pesce alla genovese

FISH:

2½ to 3 pounds assorted fish from
the following list: turbot, skate,
red snapper, sea bass, monkfish
1 pound squid, approximately
1 pound mussels

SOUP:

4 tablespoons olive oil, or enough to
cover soup pot bottom
½ medium onion, minced
1 celery rib with leaves
5 sprigs of fresh flat-leaf parsley
1 bay leaf
1 cup dry white wine
3 anchovy fillets, minced
1 quart Basic Fish Stock II (page
168)

FINAL TOUCH:

¼ cup olive oil
1 garlic clove
1 cayenne pepper pod, seeded
¼ cup chopped fresh flat-leaf parsley
4 to 6 slices Italian or French
bread, deep-fried or toasted

Cut the fish into reasonable pieces (about the size of your soup spoon) and separate according to speed of cooking.

Clean the squid (page 16) and cut the tentacles in half, the bodies in rings. Clean the mussels and remove the beards.

Put oil in a soup pot, add the onion, the celery, the parsley sprigs, and the bay leaf. Cook over moderate heat until onion is limp. Add the squid and sauté 1 minute. Add the wine and cook until it has evaporated. Add the minced anchovies and the longer-cooking fish. Cover with fish stock, bring to a boil, and cook 3 minutes. Add the rest of the fish and cook 5 minutes. Add the mussels and cook until they open, about 1 to 2 minutes. Discard any mussels that have not opened, and remove the pot from the heat.

During the last 5 minutes of cooking, in a small saucepan put 2 to 3 tablespoons of olive oil (see Note, page 167), or just enough to cover the bottom of the pan. Add the garlic and pepper pod and cook over medium heat until the garlic is golden, the pepper dark brown. Remove both flavorings and add the chopped parsley. Strain the broth through a cheesecloth-lined strainer into another pot over a very low heat. Stir in the garlic-pepper sauce.

Distribute the fish fairly in four deep soup bowls with the fried or toasted bread in the bottom. Ladle the soup over the fish. Decorate with the open mussels and serve.

Yield: 4 to 6 portions

Roman Fish Soup

zuppa di pesce alla romana

Rome is situated about thirty miles to the north of the resort town of Anzio, known for its fish soup, and about fifty miles to the south of Civitavecchia, a busy port also known for its fish soup. Being the capital city, Rome claims this recipe as her own. It could come from any or all three of them. It can be made from scratch or utilizing a basic fish stock.

Clean the squid (page 16) and mussels and peel the shrimp. Clean and scale the fish or have it done at the market. Leave the head and tails on for best results.

Heat the olive oil, garlic, and pepper (see Note, page 167) in a soup pot over medium heat. When the garlic is golden and the pepper a deep brown, remove and discard them and add the squid. Cook for 2 minutes or until the squid has changed color to pink and lavender. Add the wine and cook until it has almost evaporated. Add the tomatoes, tomato paste, and salt to the pot. Bring to a boil and cook 10 to 15 minutes or until the squid is tender.

Cut the rest of the fish into good-size chunks, and add them to the pot with just enough water to cover. Bring the pot to a boil again, reduce the heat to low, and add the shrimp and the mussels. Cover the pot and continue cooking about 5 minutes or until the fish barely flakes, the

FISH:
½ pound small squid
½ pound mussels
½ pound medium shrimp
1 whiting
1 small red snapper or rosefish
½ halibut fillet
1 porgy, scup, or tautog

SOUP:
¼ cup olive oil
1 garlic clove
1 dried cayenne pepper pod, seeded
1 cup dry red wine
1 cup canned peeled plum tomatoes, cut in chunks
1 teaspoon tomato paste
2 to 3 teaspoons salt
Italian-style bread

mussels open, and the shrimp are cooked and coral colored. (Discard any mussels that did not open.) Taste for salt and add as needed.

Scoop out the fish with a slotted spoon, and serve in individual soup plates, giving each a little bit of everything. Pour a ladle or two of soup over the fish.

This may be served with a slice of fried or toasted bread in the bottom of each plate, but when in Rome, the real way is to dunk hot, crusty bread in the soup.

Yield: 6 portions

Adriatic Fish Soup

brodetto d'Ancona

This fish soup varies from its Roman cousin by using onion to flavor its base, vinegar instead of wine, and baby clams instead of mussels.

Clean the squid (page 16), cut the sacs in wide strips and the tentacles in half, and peel the shrimp. Have the rest of the fish scaled and cut in good-sized chunks. If possible, leave on the heads and tails for heightened flavor.

To make the soup, slice the onion in the thinnest possible slices. Add them to the garlic and olive oil in a big, heavy soup pot, and sauté over medium heat. When the garlic is golden, discard it. When the onion slices are translucent, add the cut-up squid and cook and stir until the color changes. Add the vinegar and when it has evaporated, add the tomatoes, fish chunks, clams, shrimp, and salt. Grind in a bit of fresh pepper. Add just enough water to cover fish. Bring to a boil, reduce the heat, and cook about 15 minutes or until the clams are open and the meatiest fish is cooked. (Discard any clams that remain closed, as well as any fish heads, if used.) Taste for salt and pepper, and adjust if necessary. Sprinkle with parsley, cook another minute, and serve with slices of hot, crusty Italian bread.

Yield: 6 to 8 portions

FISH:

2 or 3 small squid

½ pound large shrimp

3½ to 4 pounds fish from the following list: whiting, mullet, haddock, halibut, flounder, porgy, or scup

1 pound cherrystone clams, smallest possible

SOUP:

1 large onion

1 garlic clove

½ cup olive oil

½ cup red-wine vinegar

2 cups canned peeled plum tomatoes

2 to 3 teaspoons salt, or to taste

Freshly ground black pepper to taste

5 sprigs of fresh flat-leaf parsley, coarsely chopped

Italian-style bread

Sicilian Fish Soup

zuppa di pesce alla siciliana

1 or 2 porgies
1 whiting
1 cod fillet
½ pound medium shrimp
½ pound squid, cleaned (page 16),
    cut in rings, tentacles cut in half
1 pound mussels, scrubbed, "beards"
    removed
1 small onion
¼ cup chopped fresh flat-leaf parsley
¾ cup Sicilian or Greek olives,
    pitted
1 small garlic clove
4 peppercorns
Dash of Tabasco
1 bay leaf
½ cup olive oil
1½ teaspoons salt
1½ cups dry white wine
4 slices Italian-style bread

For a different method of making fish soup try this Sicilian way, where the fish is put in an earthenware casserole and baked in the oven. It is more a casserole than a soup, flavored with herbs and black olives, and it can use just about any fish in your market. For four people, we usually aim for five or six kinds of different-textured fish weighing in at about 4½ to 5½ pounds with heads, tails, or shells on. The fish listed is a suggestion of what will work well.

Preheat the oven to 350 degrees Fahrenheit.

Clean the fish, but leave on the heads and tails for flavor. Cut into chunks and put in the bottom of a 6-quart ovenproof casserole with a good cover. Put the unshelled shrimp on top of the fish. Distribute all the squid pieces over the shrimp. Put the mussels on top of everything.

Cut the onion in fine slivers and sprinkle them over the fish along with the chopped parsley and black olives. Add the garlic, peppercorns, and Tabasco, and sink the bay leaf in the middle of everything. Pour on the olive oil and tip the casserole gently back and forth to let the oil coat the fish. Sprinkle with salt and add the wine.

Cut a round of kraft paper or parchment paper just a little bit bigger than the casserole and place it between the cover and the casserole to seal in the steam while cooking. Bake for 30 minutes.

While the casserole bakes, deep-fry the bread slices in olive oil or toast them to a golden brown. Put the toast in the bottom of warmed soup plates, ladle the fish soup over them, and serve.

Yield: 4 to 6 portions

Tuscan Fish Soup

cacciucco

FISH:

3 small squid, cleaned (page 16)

½ pound medium shrimp

2 small fish such as mullet, porgy,
*   rosefish*

1 small sea bass

1 whole red snapper

½ halibut steak or 1 small haddock
*   fillet*

4 jumbo shrimp, uncooked, or
*   cooked meat of 1 small lobster*
*   (approximately 5 ounces)*

SOUP:

3 garlic cloves

1 dried cayenne pepper pod, seeded

⅓ cup olive oil

1 carrot, minced

1 celery rib, minced

3 or 4 sprigs of fresh flat-leaf
*   parsley, minced*

1 small onion, minced

1 cup dry red wine

The very name reminds us of the land of the ancient Medici and suggests the superior, even historic, food and high living of the Renaissance. But don't wait for another Renaissance to try this traditional soup, famous in the Tuscan port of Livorno for centuries.

This particular dish, unlike many of its cousins, uses red wine instead of white, which seems to make it more substantial.

Clean and cut up the squid. Clean and shell the shrimp, reserving the shells. Clean the small fish, but leave the heads on. Clean the larger fish as needed and cut off and reserve the heads; cut the bodies in chunks.

Put the garlic cloves and the pepper pod in the olive oil (see Note, page 167) and sauté until the garlic is golden and the pepper pod is dark brown, and then remove these two flavorings.

Add the carrot, celery, parsley, and onion, and sauté until limp. Add the wine and when it is almost evaporated, add the tomatoes, salt, and pepper. Bring the pot to a boil, lower the heat, and let the sauce simmer for about 10 minutes.

Add the shrimp shells, fish heads, and the small fish to the sauce plus the hot water. Bring the pot again to a boil, lower the heat to medium, and cook for about 20 minutes or until the small fish are really falling apart.

Turn off the heat, and with a wooden spoon stir and mash the fish, and then put the whole mixture through a sieve into a big top-of-the-stove casserole. Put in the chunks of the larger fish, the smaller shrimp, and the squid. Bring to a boil, and add the jumbo shrimp, if using them. The soup should be thick by this time, and should just barely cover the fish. If not, add a bit of boiling water to do so. Lower the heat to a simmer, and cook until the big fish flakes but is not overcooked (about 5 minutes). Cut the lobster, if using it, into bite-size pieces and add to the soup.

Rub the toasted bread with the clove of garlic and place a slice in each of four warmed soup plates. Place the fish in equal distribution over the bread and ladle in the soup. Serve immediately.

Yield: 6 to 8 portions

1 pound peeled plum tomatoes
    (fresh or canned), cut in chunks
1 teaspoon salt, or to taste
Freshly ground black pepper to taste
2 cups hot water
4 slices Italian-style bread, toasted
1 garlic clove

Quick Fish Soup

zuppetta

4 cups Basic Fish Stock I (page 166)

6 ounces monkfish or fresh cod fillet

8 small shrimp (approximately ¼ pound), shelled

1 dozen fresh mussels (approximately ½ pound) scrubbed, "beards" removed

½ pound squid, cleaned and cut up (page 16)

2 slices Italian-style bread, deep-fried in olive oil

1 tablespoon chopped fresh flat-leaf parsley, approximately

This is the sort of fish soup for which the basic broth was designed. Your fish may vary according to your market and palate, but the ease of making it shouldn't vary much. Frozen fish fillets, thawed in the refrigerator, work well for this, as does frozen squid, which can easily thaw under cold running water.

Heat the fish stock in a saucepan. Add the monkfish or cod, bring to a simmer, and cook about 2 minutes or until the fish is done. Add the shrimp, mussels, and squid, and cook another minute or until the shrimp has colored nicely and the mussels are open (discard any that do not open).

Place a slice of bread in each of two soup plates. Distribute the fish evenly over each slice, pour on the broth, sprinkle with parsley, and serve.

Yield: 4 portions

Salt Cod Soup, Italian Style

zuppa di baccalà all'italiana

Remove any skin and bones from the cod and cut it in 2-inch-square pieces.

Heat the olive oil in a large soup pot over medium heat, add the onions, and cook until limp. Add the wine, tomatoes, garlic, celery leaves, thyme, bay leaf, and parsley sprigs. Cook until the wine has almost evaporated. Add the potato slices and enough hot water to cover them well. Season with salt and pepper, bring to a boil, lower the heat, and simmer for about 15 minutes. Add the cod pieces and the chopped parsley, bring back to a boil, reduce the heat, and cook, covered, for about 10 minutes.

With a slotted spoon, remove the fish and potato slices to a heated, deep platter. Take out and discard the garlic cloves, the parsley sprigs, and the bay leaf. Taste for salt and pepper and adjust as desired. Pour the soup over the fish.

Put 2 slices of toasted bread in each plate and ladle soup and cod into each.

Yield: 6 portions

1 pound dried salt cod, soaked (page 17)
⅓ cup olive oil
2 medium onions, minced
½ cup dry white wine
4 canned plum tomatoes, peeled
2 garlic cloves, peeled
1 tablespoon minced celery leaves
¼ teaspoon dried thyme
1 bay leaf
5 sprigs plus 1 tablespoon chopped flat-leaf parsley
4 potatoes, peeled and cut in thick slices
Salt to taste
Freshly ground black pepper
12 slices Italian-style bread, toasted and rubbed with garlic, optional

Lobster Soup

zuppa del venerdi santo

1 cup loosely packed flat-leaf parsley

2 anchovy fillets

1 garlic clove

¼ cup olive oil

1 rounded teaspoon tomato paste

6 cups Basic Fish Stock I (page 166)

1½-pound lobster, or 6 to 7 ounces
cooked lobster meat

½ pound (approximately 1 dozen)
medium shrimp

Salt, optional

Dash of Tabasco, optional

4 slices Italian-style bread, deep-
fried in olive oil

This particular soup in Italy once carried the lovely name of Good Friday's Soup, and it is said to have been created for the Roman Catholic hierarchy centuries ago when the indulgence in a splendid soup in time of fasting was allowed for the tables of the Princes of the Church. Today it fills a special place for elegance alone, and we like it almost any day the lobster is available. Frozen fish broth on hand makes this sort of delicacy an everyday possibility.

Chop the parsley leaves, adding the anchovies and garlic as you chop. Place the flavorings in a soup pot with the olive oil. Sauté over moderate heat until the garlic bits are limp, the anchovies virtually melted.

Stir the tomato paste into ½ cup of the fish stock and then add it along with the rest of the stock to the soup pot. Bring to a boil, reduce the heat, and simmer 15 minutes.

Cook the whole lobster in abundant boiling salted water for 12 minutes. Remove the lobster from the water, and when it is cool enough to handle, shell it and cut into bite-size pieces.

Add the shrimp to the soup pot, raise the heat, and, when the soup boils, add the lobster and cook 1 minute or until the shrimp is nicely colored and cooked. Taste for seasonings and add salt and Tabasco if you wish. Stir.

Ladle onto fried bread in warmed soup plates.

Yield: 4 portions

Mussel Soup

zuppa di cozze

For heightened flavor as well as a bit of crunch to your soup, try putting a cup of celery slices into your olive oil pepper sauce or into the just-flavored oil after you remove the garlic and pepper pod. Stir and cook over medium heat about 3 minutes and then add the tomatoes and wine and proceed.

3 to 3½ pounds mussels
5 tablespoons olive oil
1 garlic clove
1 dried cayenne pepper pod, seeded
¾ cup canned peeled plum
    tomatoes, cubed
½ cup dry white wine
1 teaspoon salt
3 tablespoons chopped fresh flat-leaf
    parsley
Italian-style bread

Scrub the mussels clean and rinse carefully under running water.

Put the olive oil, garlic, and pepper (see Note, page 167) in a big soup pot and sauté over medium heat. Discard the garlic and pepper when golden and brown and add the tomatoes and wine. Cook for 4 minutes, raise the heat, and add the mussels. Stir them around a bit, add the salt, cover, and cook for about 5 minutes, or until all the shells have opened. If by any chance there are any unopened mussels, discard them. Add the parsley, stir, and serve in warmed soup plates with slices of hot Italian-style bread to dip in the soup. Or you may want to deep-fry the bread in olive oil and serve a slice at the bottom of each soup plate.

Yield: 4 portions

Cream of Mussel Soup

crema di cozze

2 pounds fresh mussels

Olive oil

1 cup milk

2 cups light cream

2 tablespoons unsalted butter

2 tablespoons unbleached all-
purpose flour

1 pound celery ribs, without leaves,
cut in ⅛-inch slices

½ cup mushrooms, chopped

3 tablespoons fresh or freeze-dried
chives, chopped

Salt to taste

Freshly ground white pepper to taste

Chopped fresh curly parsley for
garnish

Scrub the mussels clean, removing the "beards."

Put olive oil in a large sauté pan to cover the bottom. Heat the oil over medium heat.

Add the mussels, cover the pan, and cook, stirring once or twice, for about 2 to 3 minutes or until the mussels have opened. Remove the mussels from the pan and discard their shells and any mussels that did not open, letting the juice fall back into the pan.

Strain the pan liquid into the mussel bowl.

Heat the milk and cream together in a saucepan until simmering. In another saucepan, mix the butter and flour together over medium heat until well blended. Pour in the simmering cream-milk mixture, stir, and bring almost to a boil. Add the celery and cook and stir for about 2 minutes. Add the mushrooms and chives and continue cooking until celery and mushrooms are cooked but still a bit on the crisp side. Stir in the mussels and their juices.

Add salt and pepper, garnish with chopped fresh parsley, and serve immediately in warmed soup plates.

Yield: 4 portions

Cream of Baby Clam Soup

crema di vongole

Place the oil and the butter in a soup pot, add the minced onion, and cook until onion is limp, not browned.

Whisk in the flour and cook and whisk 1 minute.

Pour in the fish stock in a steady stream. Add the clam juice. Whisk and cook 4 minutes.

Add the potatoes to the pot and cook over medium heat until the potatoes are soft.

Add the cream and the clams.

Taste for salt and add as needed. Add a pinch of pepper to taste. Bring just to a boil, serve garnished with a bit of parsley, diced red pepper, or chives.

Yield: 4 to 6 portions

2 tablespoons olive oil
2 tablespoons unsalted butter
1 medium onion (5 to 6 ounces), minced
½ cup unbleached all-purpose flour
4 cups Basic Fish Stock I (page 166)
2 10-ounce cans baby clams, liquid reserved
3 large potatoes, cubed
2 cups light cream
Salt to taste
Freshly ground white pepper to taste
1½ to 2 tablespoons chopped fresh flat-leaf parsley, optional
½ red bell pepper, diced, optional
1 to 2 tablespoons finely minced fresh chives, optional

Shrimp Ravioli in Broth

ravioli di gamberi in brodo

FILLER AND BROTH:

2 shallots (about 3½ ounces)

5 sprigs of flat-leaf parsley

5 tablespoons olive oil

*Sprig of fresh rosemary, or 1
    teaspoon dried*

Sprig of thyme, or ½ teaspoon dried

*2 leaves fresh sage, or ½ teaspoon
    dried*

1 small celery rib

*1 cup canned peeled plum tomatoes,
    or 5 fresh plum tomatoes, peeled,
    seeded, and cubed*

1¾ to 2 pounds unshelled shrimp

1 teaspoon salt

*¼ teaspoon freshly ground pepper,
    preferably white*

1½ ounces brandy

¼ cup dry white wine

3 cups hot water

*4 crustless slices Italian-style bread,
    soaked in milk*

A recipe for shrimp ravioli belongs to those who love fresh pasta and seafood. It does require Homemade Pasta—but then any food lover ought not to mind making a batch of pasta from time to time, and when paired with a shrimp filler touched with herbs, the whole procedure is more than worthwhile.

Mince the shallots with the parsley and put them in a large sauté pan with the olive oil over medium heat. Cook until limp.

To the pan, add the remaining flavorings, the tomatoes, and the shrimp in their shells. Sprinkle with the salt and pepper and sauté over high heat for about 3 minutes.

Add the brandy, flame it, and when the flame dies, add the wine. When the wine has evaporated, add the water, bring to a boil, and then lower the heat to simmer for 30 minutes.

Remove the shrimp from the broth, shell them, and put the shells back in the pan. Leave the broth on to simmer. Devein the shrimp if necessary. Squeeze the bread dry, add to the shrimp, and mince finely. This can be done either with a food processor with the steel blade, or by putting the mixture through a meat grinder. Taste the shrimp mixture, adjusting the seasonings if necessary.

Make the pasta, roll it out, and then make the ravioli (as on page 112). If you prefer larger ravioli, cut the pasta

into 2-inch squares, place a bit of filling on one side and fold the pasta on the diagonal to form filled triangles.

Strain the broth into a clean pot, adding 1 cup of hot water if necessary. Taste for flavor and adjust salt and pepper.

Bring the broth to a boil, add the ravioli, and cook about 3 minutes or until they are done. Divide the ravioli into 4 hot soup bowls and ladle the broth over immediately. Garnish with chopped fresh parsley if you wish.

Yield: 4 to 6 portions, depending on appetite

PASTA:

*1 3-egg batch Homemade Pasta
   (page 110)*

GARNISH:

Chopped flat-leaf parsley, optional

Main Courses

Poached Bonito

Bonito in Parchment

Fresh Cod, Sicilian Style

Deep-fried Salt Cod, Roman Style

Salt Cod Baked with Potatoes

Salt Cod, Neapolitan Style

Salt Cod in Pizza-Maker's Sauce

Salt Cod with Peppers

Salt Cod in the Style of Ancona

Salt Cod, Roman Style

Salt Cod in the Style of Vicenza

Eels on Skewers

Marinated Eels

Venetian Eels and Peas

Flounder with Capers

Grouper with Tomato Sauce

Baked Grouper

Baked Haddock Fillet

Poached Hake with Green Sauce

Poached Lobster

Monkfish Skewers with Vegetables

Ocean Perch in the Style of Milan

Fried Pollock in the Style of Ancona

Grilled Porgy

Porgy in Parchment

Baked Red Snapper

Grilled or Broiled Salmon Steaks

Poached Salmon

Salmon Trout with Rice and Shrimp

Fried Scallops

Scallops, Florentine Style

Baked Sea Bass with Mussels

Black Sea Bass with Butter

Sea Bass, Marinated and Baked

Sea Bass in the Style of Genoa

Baked Sea Bass, Southern Italian Style

Black Sea Bass in Pastry

Grilled Striped Sea Bass

Shrimp Capri

Shrimp and Scallops in Brandy Sauce

Shrimp, Family Style

Golden-fried Sole

Sole Spirals

Fried Squid

Squid with Swiss Chard

Stuffed Squid

Squid in the Style of Genoa

Sturgeon with Herbed Tomato Sauce

Golden-fried Swordfish in the Style of Milan

Sautéed Swordfish

Swordfish Birds

Swordfish Skewers

Baked Swordfish in Savory Sauce

Baked Stuffed Tilefish

Trout Poached in Wine

Baked Trout with Sage

Trout Poached in Tomato Sauce

Fresh Tuna Steaks in Onion Sauce

Fresh Tuna, Sardinian Style

Broiled Turbot

Perch and Potato Cakes

Fresh Tuna Cakes

Fish Fillets, Broiled

Layered Fish Fillets in Pastry

Fish Steaks in Wine Sauce

Fish Steaks, Grilled or Broiled

Grilled Whole Fish with Green Sauce

Whole Fish Baked in White Sauce

Italian fish courses can trace their lineage to the early Roman Empire and to the hierarchy of the Roman Catholic Church during the Renaissance. The Roman emperors had lobster and red mullet sent to them from off the coast of Africa to large holding tanks in their gardens. It is said that the Roman legions whose men captured all of Gaul were also devoted to filling the imperial fish tanks with new, stranger, and more wonderful fish from abroad.

Most of those early fish holding tanks were destroyed by barbarians about the time that the Roman Catholic Church laid down the law for meatless days, 130 of them a year. This posed no problem for the rich as they had oysters for *antipasto* sent in from Corsica, crabs from Venice could be paired with rice for the first course, *primo piatto*, while great sturgeon from the Po River and trout from the northern lakes were sent down for the *secondo piatto* or main course. All were cherished, celebrated, and handled with care. Those for whom the transportation price was too high celebrated with local, inexpensive eel.

The tradition of celebration and fish for dinner swelled to a most important presentation on a most important day, the vigil of Christmas. Eel from outside of Venice held an important place at the dinner of the vigil. It was usually bought skinned, cut, and marinated in wine vinegar. Today, five hundred years later, Italian cooks do up their own eel and proudly proclaim it represents not only grand gastronomy but also economy. Bit by bit, we find families celebrating the Vigil of Christmas with more up-to-date choices such as smoked salmon from Scotland, sea bass, porgy, and American lobster. Thus, for the heart of the meal, the main course, we have selected both recent favorites as well as traditional, regional *secondi piatti*.

Bonito

A member of the tuna family, bonito is very like a small tuna with a nice firm white flesh that is perfect for poaching and equally good when baked in a parchment packet. Called *tonnetto*, baby tuna, in the Mediterranean, or *palamita*, it is found on both sides of the Atlantic and sometimes makes its way as far north as Cape Cod.

Poached Bonito

tonnetto in bianco

1 4-pound bonito, approximately,
    cleaned but with head and tail
    left on for extra flavor
Basic Fish Stock II (page 168)
1 cup Parsley Mayonnaise (page 41)
Juice of ½ lemon, or to taste
Extra parsley, cucumber, capers,
    lemon slices, if desired, for
    garnish

This is a summer party centerpiece that may be decorated fully or just simply, as you wish. Some cooks put wafer-thin slices of cucumbers between the fillets while others use a sprinkling of capers or chopped parsley.

Wrap the fish in cheesecloth and tie a knot at each end. Put together the fish stock, place the fish in the stock in a fish poacher, cover, and bring to a boil; lower the heat immediately and simmer for about 20 minutes (10 minutes per inch of fish measured at its thickest part) or until an "instant read" thermometer registers just under 140 degrees.

Lift out the fish, peel off the cheesecloth, and then skin the fish while it is still warm. Bone the fish and remove the head and tail and fins. Work carefully to maintain two large fillets.

Mix the parsley mayonnaise with the lemon juice.

Place 1 fillet on your serving platter. Cover it with garnish, such as parsley leaves or cucumber slices, as you please or add a bit of mayonnaise. Place the second fillet on top of the decorated one and spread with more mayonnaise. Dot with parsley leaves, or slices of lemon, or a sprinkling of capers. Serve with added lemon to taste.

Yield: 6 portions

Bonito in Parchment

tonnetto al cartoccio

When you are lucky enough to get a small tuna of about 3 pounds, we recommend this recipe. The enhancing flavors are included nicely in the parchment wrap and the bonito maintains its singularly delightful taste without losing texture. The opening of the packet is enticing to even those who have never tried bonito.

This treatment is good for any 2-pound fish such as bass, mullet, porgy, red snapper, or trout. And we also suggest you try it with fillets of halibut, swordfish, or salmon.

1 2 to 3 pound bonito, cleaned but with head and tail intact

1 teaspoon salt, or to taste

Freshly ground white pepper to taste

2 lemons

3 to 4 peeled plum tomatoes

2 tablespoons chopped fresh flat-leaf parsley

1½ dozen mussels (approximately ¾ pound)

4 tablespoons olive oil

Preheat the oven to 400 degrees Fahrenheit.

Sprinkle the cavity of the fish with salt and pepper.

Place the fish on a large piece of parchment and bring the edges up and around the fish. Squeeze one lemon and pour half the juice in the cavity and half over the fish. Add additional salt and pepper if desired.

Cut the second lemon in rounds and place them along the length of the fish.

Pass the tomatoes through a sieve or food mill and put a teaspoon of tomato (or thereabouts) on each lemon slice. Put any remaining tomato around the fish. Sprinkle with parsley. Place the mussels around the fish.

Dribble the olive oil over the entire fish. Seal the parchment so that none of the juices or the vapor can escape. Place the packet of fish in a shallow baking dish and bake for 30 minutes.

Place the fish in its packet on a serving platter. Open the packet at table, slice the fish along the spine, and remove first one fillet and then the other. Serve fillets with the sauce in the packet.

Yield: 4 portions

Cod

Cod is one of the most common and abundant family of fish. It swims the cold waters of the world, from the North Sea to the Georges Banks off New England, where cod fishing was essential to New England's early and flourishing economy, so much so that in 1784, in gratitude, a wooden carving of the "Sacred Cod" was hung—and still hangs—in the Boston House of Representatives.

Small members of the cod family reach the Mediterranean waters and are consumed fresh. It is considered a very delicate and nutritious fish and Italian mothers insist on poached fresh cod for growing children and delicate stomachs. Cod liver oil has been a blessing as well as a nightmare to generations of growing children everywhere. Otherwise, in Italy, the largest consumption of cod is in its salted and dried form, *baccalà*, which evades any regional connotation and becomes a truly national fish.

There are two principal methods to salting a cod. One is called "kench salting" in which layers of fish are alternated with layers of salt and stacked with the flesh side up. The salt pulls out the water and other liquids in the flesh which are allowed to drain off. This cure lasts about five days, after which the fish is pressed to eliminate any remaining fluid. There will be a bit of salt left, which requires that the dried cod be soaked before cooking. The second method is called pickle salting, in which dry salt is applied to the fish, which is then stored in crocks and the resulting pickle is not allowed to drain off. This salting lasts for about two days and produces a more lightly salted cod than does kench salting.

In the middle 1600s, ships out of Boston would deliver salt cod to Spain and Portugal and then sail on to West Africa where slaves would be taken aboard. The ships would sail to the West Indies to exchange the slave cargo for sugar and molasses to supply the distilleries of New England. Salt cod not only held the key to financing this Golden Triangle, but it was also was the staple food for the slaves.

Fresh Cod, Sicilian Style

merluzzo alla Siciliana

2 pounds fresh cod fillets
2 large eggs
½ cup unbleached all-purpose flour,
 approximately
1 cup unflavored breadcrumbs,
 approximately
12 anchovy fillets, with their oil
2 tablespoons olive oil
Vegetable oil for frying
3 tablespoons chopped fresh flat-leaf
 parsley
1½ lemons, cut in wedges

While a great many traditional recipes use dried salt cod, the islands around continental Italy, the boot, so to speak, honor fresh cod in a variety of ways. One of them is to fillet the fish, dip the fillets in egg and breadcrumbs, and pan-fry them. The fish is then served with anchovy-and-parsley sauce. Members of the cod family—hake, pollock, and haddock—are good alternatives as is the modest whiting.

If the fish fillets are unmanageably long (more than 7 inches), cut them in half.

Beat the eggs until light in color and foamy.

Put the flour on one plate and the breadcrumbs on another. Dredge the fillets in flour, pat them well to shake off any excess flour, dip them in the beaten eggs, and finally press them into the breadcrumbs, first one side and then the other, and pat well. Set aside.

Mince the anchovy fillets and their oil to a paste. Warm the olive oil in a small saucepan over low heat and stir in the anchovy paste. Cook, stirring constantly, until the anchovies have disintegrated. (Do not overheat, or the anchovy bits will just fry.) Once the mixture looks like a sauce, which usually occurs after about 4 minutes, set it aside in a warm place.

Heat the vegetable oil to 375 degrees Fahrenheit, or medium heat, in a big frying pan, and fry the fillets until

golden brown on both sides. (If the oil is not hot enough, the fillets will just absorb it and become soggy; if too hot, the oil tends to darken the breadcrumbs and egg coating too much before the inner fish is cooked.)

When the fillets are nicely browned on both sides, remove them and put them on absorbent paper to drain.

Once all the fish is cooked, place it on a warm serving platter. Add the parsley to the anchovy sauce, stir, and pour it over the fillets. Serve with lemon wedges.

Yield: 4 to 6 portions

Deep-fried Salt Cod, Roman Style

baccalà fritto alla romana

This is the dish that made Margaret fall in love with Roman food. It was early October and the warm temperature and the way the light painted the whole peninsula was a celebration. The fabulous squares and façades of Roman buildings glowed with a special tinge as if it were always sunset. Aromas, flowing from still-open kitchen doors and windows, were enough to make even the very well fed feel hungry for something more than just comforting, something different. It was time for a simple but glorious meal.

1 pound dried cod, soaked (page 17)
1 recipe Yeast Batter (page 29)*
Vegetable oil for frying
2 lemons, cut in wedges

Cut the cod in pieces about 4 inches long and 1½ inches wide. Pat dry with paper towels to absorb as much moisture as possible, and let rest at room temperature for 30 minutes or so. Mix the batter and let stand until puffed and bubbly, about 1 hour.

Bring a deep fryer or frying pan with vegetable oil to 375 degrees Fahrenheit.

Dip the pieces of cod into the batter, 3 or 4 at a time, and then place them in the hot oil. Fry to a crisp and remove to drain on paper towels.

When the whole bunch is fried, dip them back once more in the hot oil, remove, drain well, and serve with the lemon wedges.

Yield: 6 portions

* NOTE: You can use the Baking Powder Batter (page 28) when you are short of time, but it does not give the exact crispness that the twice-dipped yeast batter does.

Salt Cod Baked with Potatoes

baccalà al forno con patate

Growing up in the Midwest and in New England, codfish meant, for Margaret, salt cod served with a cream sauce and fluffy mashed potatoes. Depending on who was in the kitchen on any given Friday of the winter, the cod either came draped in a heavenly white sauce (neatly seasoned, brightened with a bit of paprika, Tabasco, and sometimes a few chives or parsley) or with a tepid and very heavy, rather tasteless blanket of a different white sauce. Groans went up at the latter, and cheers if the first version appeared.

In the following recipe chunks of cod fillets, layered with slivers of onions and potatoes, seasoned with parsley, rosemary, and a bit of plum tomato, make this a casserole for all seasons.

1½ to 2 pounds dried cod, soaked (page 17)

½ cup olive oil

3 large potatoes, peeled and cut in ½-inch-thick rounds

2 large onions, slivered

2 tablespoons minced fresh flat-leaf parsley

2 tablespoons fresh rosemary, or 1 tablespoon dried

Salt to taste

4 to 5 canned or very ripe fresh peeled plum tomatoes

Preheat the oven to 350 degrees Fahrenheit.

Cut the soaked cod into 2- by 3-inch pieces.

Put 2 tablespoons of the oil, or just enough to cover the bottom, in a deep baking dish. Put in a layer of potato rounds, then a layer of onion slivers. Sprinkle with some of the minced parsley and rosemary and a bit of salt (not too much, as the cod will have retained some of its salt), and dribble on a bit of olive oil. On top of this, make a layer of cod chunks. Mash up the tomatoes in a bowl or on a plate and distribute a few bits here and there over the cod.

Repeat the layering sequence until all the ingredients are in the casserole, aiming to make the last or top layer potato rounds. Garnish the top with the last of the parsley and rosemary, and a generous amount of olive oil. Bake for 45 minutes, or until the potatoes are cooked (a cake tester or thin skewer is ideal for testing).

Yield: 6 to 8 servings

Salt Cod, Neapolitan Style

baccalà alla napoletana

1 pound salt cod fillet, soaked (page 17)

Unbleached all-purpose flour

Vegetable oil for frying

3 tablespoons olive oil

2 garlic cloves

1 cayenne pepper pod, seeded, or ¼ teaspoon Tabasco

⅓ cup black Sicilian-style olives (packed in brine, not dried)

1 tablespoon capers

3 cups canned peeled plum tomatoes, chopped

Salt and freshly ground white pepper to taste

3 tablespoons chopped fresh flat-leaf parsley

When the cod has soaked and lost its saltiness, drain it well and cut it into pieces about 2 inches by 3 inches. Dredge the pieces in flour, patting both sides to get as much flour to stick as possible. In a 10-inch frying pan, bring the vegetable oil to a high heat and brown the cod thoroughly on both sides. Drain and cool on absorbent paper.

Put the olive oil in a wide saucepan or a deep frying pan big enough to hold the fried fish pieces in one layer if possible. Sauté the garlic and pepper in the olive oil until golden and brown and then discard them. (If using Tabasco, add it after the tomatoes.)

Drain and pit the olives and rinse the capers. Mince these two together and add with the tomatoes to the flavored olive oil, stir well, and return to a boil. Lower the

heat and simmer for 10 minutes. Add the fried cod and simmer, again for 10 minutes.

Taste for salt; it should not need any, but it might. Add freshly ground pepper to taste and continue to simmer for another 10 minutes. Sprinkle with parsley and serve.

Yield: 4 to 6 portions

Salt Cod in Pizza-Maker's Sauce

baccalà alla pizzaiola

Drain the cod on paper towels, pat dry, and cut into 2- by 3-inch or 3- by 4-inch pieces.

In a pan large enough to hold all the fish in one layer, sauté the garlic in the olive oil until golden and discard. Let the oil cool a moment. Cut the tomatoes into chunks and add to the frying pan along with the oregano and pepper. Stir, bring to a boil, and then simmer for 5 minutes.

Add the cod to the sauce and cook at a gentle boil covered for 10 minutes and uncovered for another 10 minutes, or until the cod flakes. Serve hot with Italian-style bread or mashed potatoes.

Yield: 4 to 6 portions

1 pound salt cod fillets, soaked (page 17)
2 garlic cloves
3 tablespoons olive oil
3 cups canned peeled plum tomatoes
1½ teaspoons dried oregano
Freshly ground black pepper
Italian-style bread, optional
Mashed potatoes, optional

Salt Cod with Peppers

baccalà in padella con peperoni

2 medium onions

½ cup olive oil

3 cups peeled plum tomatoes

Salt to taste

4 large green bell peppers

1 to 1½ pounds dried salt cod, soaked (page 17), or 2 to 3 pounds fresh fish

1 tablespoon chopped fresh flat-leaf parsley

This recipe was originally designed for salt cod, but pollock and hake may also benefit by the method as may turbot and halibut fillets.

Slice the onions into slivers and sauté them in the olive oil in a deep frying pan. When the onions are translucent, add the tomatoes and about 1 teaspoon salt.

Core the peppers and cut them in long, thin (¼-inch-wide) strips. Add them to the sauce. When the peppers are tender (after about 15 minutes), and the sauce has condensed, add the fish. Check for salt, adjust the seasonings, and cook for another 15 minutes, or until the fish flakes easily. If using fresh fish, it will reach this point after about 10 minutes, going by the Canadian timing method of 10 minutes per inch at the thickest part of the fish.

If using frozen fillets, wait until the sauce has become really thick before adding the fish, which should be defrosted and dried on paper towels before going into the pan.

When cooked, place the fish and its sauce on a platter. Sprinkle with parsley and serve.

Yield: 6 portions

Salt Cod in the Style of Ancona

baccalà all 'anconetana

Soak the cod as specified, changing the water from time to time. Cut the potatoes in thin rounds and put them in boiling water for 2 minutes. Drain the potatoes and let rest in cold water.

In a saucepan, sauté the garlic in the oil and discard when well browned. Add the onion, carrot, celery, tablespoon of minced parsley, marjoram, and rosemary, and let wilt over a low flame. Add the tomatoes, stir well, and cook for 10 minutes. Remove from heat.

Drain the soaked cod, cut in 3- to 4-inch squares, and pat dry with paper towels. Drain the potatoes.

Cover the bottom of a flameproof top-of-the-stove casserole with the parsley sprigs. Cover the parsley with a few tablespoons of the tomato sauce. Make a layer of cod squares and grind pepper over the fish. Cover the fish with more tablespoons of sauce. Continue to layer, alternating cod, sauce, and pepper. Finally, cover the casserole with a layer of potatoes, dot with butter, and pour the milk on top of everything. Swirl the casserole gently to distribute the liquids evenly. Cover the casserole (aluminum foil will do) and bring slowly to a boil. Let bubble slowly for about 30 to 40 minutes (or until the potatoes are cooked). Uncover and continue cooking for another 15 minutes.

1 pound dry salt cod, soaked (page 17)
1 pound potatoes, peeled
2 garlic cloves
3 tablespoons olive oil
1 medium onion, cut in thin slivers
1 small carrot, minced
1 celery rib, minced
1 tablespoon minced fresh flat-leaf parsley, plus 5 to 6 additional sprigs
1 teaspoon dried marjoram, or 2 teaspoons minced fresh marjoram
3 tablespoons fresh rosemary leaves
2 cups canned peeled plum tomatoes, chopped coarsely
Freshly ground black pepper
2 tablespoons unsalted butter
½ cup milk

Let rest about 15 minutes before serving—the liquids have worked into a stew sauce. This dish may be made ahead of time, and it tastes even better reheated.

Yield: 6 portions

Salt Cod, Roman Style

baccalà alla romana

1½ *pounds dried, boned salt cod, soaked (page 17)*

3 *medium red onions, cut in thin slivers*

1½ *tablespoons olive oil*

Salt

¼ *cup dry white wine*

3 *cups canned peeled plum tomatoes*

2 *tablespoons golden raisins, soaked in warm water*

1 *tablespoon pine nuts*

Freshly ground black pepper

3 *tablespoons minced fresh flat-leaf parsley*

Italian-style bread

Soak the cod as directed, changing the water frequently.

Sauté the onion slivers in the oil over medium heat. Sprinkle lightly with salt, and when the onions are limp, add the wine. Cook and stir until the wine has evaporated. Add the tomatoes, mashing them a bit with a fork. Raise the heat and let simmer briskly for about 10 minutes.

Drain the raisins, and add them to the sauce together with the pine nuts.

Drain the cod and pat dry on paper towels. Cut into 3-inch squares, approximately, and put in the sauce. Sprinkle with pepper—a few generous twists of the mill.

Bring the pan to a simmer and cook the cod in the sauce for 10 minutes, or until the cod is done and it flakes easily. Apportion on six warm plates and sprinkle with the minced parsley. Serve with thick slices of warm Italian bread.

Yield: 6 portions

Salt Cod in the Style of Vicenza

baccalà alla Vicentina

A poet from Vicenza has written: "This dish is a masterpiece, with a perfume of temptation: every mouthful a balm." It is baked very slowly, and is traditionally served with polenta.

Preheat the oven to 250 degrees Fahrenheit.

Having soaked the cod, skin and bone it if necessary and pat dry with paper towels. Cut it into pieces approximately 2½ inches square. Dredge the squares with the flour, pressing gently to let as much flour as possible adhere to the fish.

Chop the onions, garlic, anchovies, and parsley well and mix in the salt and pepper.

Use an ovenproof casserole (cast iron is fine but if you have an earthenware Italian casserole, that's better still). Pour into it enough oil just barely to cover the bottom. Put in a layer of floured fish squares. Sprinkle over the fish a bit of the mince, some of the Parmesan cheese, and a touch of the cinnamon. Finally, dribble over a little olive oil.

Repeat the layering until you have used all the fish and other ingredients. Pour the milk over the whole dish, tilt the casserole back and forth gently a couple of times to make sure the milk reaches all the layers.

2 pounds dried salt cod, soaked (page 17)
Unbleached all-purpose flour
2 large onions
1 garlic clove
4 anchovy fillets
⅓ cup chopped fresh flat-leaf parsley
½ teaspoon salt
Freshly ground white pepper to taste
½ cup olive oil
4 tablespoons grated Parmesan cheese
¼ teaspoon cinnamon
2 cups milk

Cover the casserole, and if the cover doesn't seal tightly, slip a round of brown paper between the pot and its cover, so that all the vapors are kept inside. Bake 2 or 3 hours or until the liquids are absorbed. Serve hot and, to be traditional, with polenta (page 158).

Yield: 6 to 8 portions

Eels

Eels, those fast moving, slippery snakes, bring soft cries of joy to a whole lot of diners. Eels have a nice texture, a delicate, light flavor, and are loved by Italian cooks. Eels come in fresh or salt-water versions. At one time, the marshes near Venice were renowned for their eels. When that supply ran low, the fishermen of Newburyport, Massachusetts, came to the rescue and had eels flown in live, in big batches, to fill the Venetian demand.

In many parts of the United States eels are rare creatures, but you can find them in many Italian-American communities dressed and ready to cook, especially at the Christmas season. If, however, you find yourself the proud possessor of live eels, you should know they are very alive. They are very slippery. It is not easy to kill an eel. And don't think you can just plain wring their necks. We once had three of them delivered to the door. They were taken in hand, around the neck, but that didn't help much. They slipped free and flipped and flopped all over the kitchen, hand to counter to floor, to door, to table, and off again, yards of them. After quick consultation, we got the scoop. Here are our modest guidelines:

Put the eels quickly in a deep, empty bucket. Add a cup or two of salt and cover completely with something heavy, almost anything that will fit. Shortly the eels will go to sleep and in fifteen to thirty minutes, they will have given up the ghost. With a rag or an old newspaper and some sand, rub the eels thoroughly. Or, put them under cold water and rub until the eels are no longer slippery. Make an incision on their belly up to the gills and clean them as you would any fish. If they are to be cooked with the skin on, cut off the head and tail. If they are to be skinned, make a partial incision around the head, leaving a small strip of skin intact. Lift an inch or so of skin from

the body near the head. Bend the head back (the backbone should snap) and hold the skinned portion with one hand. With the other hand, with the aid of pliers, pull down the skin resolutely toward the tail. The skin will strip off as easily as pulling off a sock.

Eels on Skewers

spiedini d' anguilla

If it is time for the outdoor grill or you have an indoor grill, you will find that this way of handling eels protects their delicate flavor quite wonderfully.

1 garlic clove, cut in half
¼ cup olive oil
Juice of 1 lemon
4 tablespoons red-wine vinegar
1¾ pounds eel, skin on, cut in
    2-inch pieces
1 tablespoon fresh rosemary leaves,
    or 1½ teaspoons dried
10 bay leaves
1 teaspoon salt, or to taste
Freshly ground black pepper to taste
1 dozen fresh mushrooms, cleaned
1 dozen cherry tomatoes
Italian-style bread

Rub a dish with the garlic clove and discard the clove. Mix the oil, lemon juice, and vinegar together, and put this mix in the dish. Arrange the eels in the dish and sprinkle them with the rosemary leaves, 2 bay leaves, crumbled, salt, and pepper. Marinate the eels for at least an hour, turning them over from time to time.

Arrange the eels on skewers alternately with the mushrooms, cherry tomatoes, and remaining bay leaves.

Once the skewers are filled, place them on the grill 4 to 5 inches above the coals. Grill about 8 minutes or until the flesh is soft and cooked. Baste the eels a few times as they cook, and turn the skewers over after each basting.

Serve on Italian bread, slices of which have been lightly moistened with the marinade and toasted.

Yield: 4 portions

Marinated Eels

anguille marinate

1½ to 2 pounds eels
½ cup olive oil
2 lemons
⅓ cup dry white wine
1 dozen fresh sage leaves (dried will
    not work)
1 teaspoon salt, approximately
Freshly ground black pepper
3 tablespoons unflavored
    breadcrumbs

Skin the eels (page 208), or have them skinned, and cut them in 3-inch pieces. Place the pieces in a dish that will hold them snugly.

Mix all but 3 tablespoons of the oil with the juice of 1 lemon and the wine, and pour over the eels.

Coarsely chop half the sage leaves and sprinkle them on the eels. Add salt and pepper. Turn and baste the eels, then let rest for at least an hour, turning occasionally.

Put the reserved oil in a skillet or sauté pan large enough to hold the eels in one layer. Add the remaining sage leaves, and sauté until they are limp.

Add the eels and sauté 2 minutes, turning frequently. Raise the heat, add the marinade, sprinkle in the breadcrumbs, and let the sauce thicken.

Place the eels on a serving plate and pour the sauce over them. Cut the remaining lemon into wedges and serve with the eels.

Yield: 4 portions

Venetian Eels and Peas

bisato e bisi

Cut the eels in 2- to 3-inch pieces and dredge them in flour.

Mince the parsley leaves and garlic together and sauté them briefly in oil.

Add the eels, brown them quickly on all sides, and add the tomatoes cut in chunks.

Add salt and pepper and bring to a boil; then lower the heat and simmer for 15 minutes, stirring occasionally and breaking up whatever tomato solids remain.

Remove the eels to a serving dish. Add the peas to the tomato sauce and cook at a low boil about 5 minutes or until the peas are tender. Pour sauce and peas over the eels. Serve with slices of hot Italian bread.

Yield: 4 portions

1¾ pounds eels, skinned (page 208)
Unbleached all-purpose flour for dredging
5 sprigs of fresh flat-leaf parsley
1 garlic clove, peeled
⅓ cup olive oil
1½ cups plum tomatoes, fresh or canned, peeled and seeded
Salt to taste
Freshly ground black pepper
10 ounces frozen peas or fresh peas, shelled
Italian-style bread

Flounder

When it comes to identifying flounder and sole, the confusion is so great that it is almost ridiculous. The term *sole* covers any number of flatfish in two families. "Dover sole," the common sole of Europe found from the Mediterranean to Denmark, is the name frequently attached to the Pacific flounder, which is found from California to Alaska. "English sole" is a common name for a small Pacific flounder, while "lemon sole" is the U.S. market name for a winter flounder of over three pounds that is found primarily from Long Island north to Block Island and the Georges Banks east of Massachusetts.

The American plaice (also known as Canadian plaice) is a deep-water boreal flounder found on both sides of the Atlantic from Cape Cod to the Grand Banks and in the eastern Atlantic from Greenland to Norway. It can reach twelve pounds, but the flounder you see in the market weighs in at two to three pounds. It is also marketed as dab, sanddab, long rough dab, and roughback.

While both flounder and sole are flat, the former are a bit rounder in general and the sole more elliptical. The largest of the flounder is the Atlantic halibut, which has a firm white meat and is sold whole or in fillet form, fresh or frozen.

Flounder with Capers

sogiolone al pompiere

2 tablespoons capers
2 pounds fresh flounder fillets
Unbleached all-purpose flour
3 tablespoons unsalted butter
3 tablespoons olive oil
3 tablespoons chopped fresh flat-leaf
   parsley
1½ lemons
2 tablespoons fine unflavored
   breadcrumbs

Rinse the capers in cold running water, and drain them well.

Dredge the fish fillets in flour, patting gently to get as much flour to adhere as possible.

Melt the butter in a large frying pan over low heat, and add the olive oil. Raise the heat and sauté the fish until golden brown on both sides; remove to a warm platter in a warm place.

Further chop the parsley with the capers, and stir into the melted butter and oil. Add the juice of ½ lemon, sauté 1 or 2 minutes, add the breadcrumbs, and stir again.

Spread the fillets with the parsley-caper-butter mixture. Serve with lemon wedges.

Yield: 6 portions

Grouper

Grouper is a lean, big fish, a member of a sprawling family, five types of which live in Mediterranean and eastern Atlantic waters. In Florida and the Gulf of Mexico the biggest of groupers, the jewfish, can weigh in at seven hundred pounds; it is excellent eating but is rarely found outside the area. The smaller Nassau grouper, especially in Florida and the Bahamas, is grand for fillets and steaks to be baked or grilled, or cubed and deep-fried.

Grouper with Tomato Sauce

cernia al pomodoro

Preheat the oven to 400 degrees Fahrenheit.

Cut the tomatoes in small chunks and put them in a baking dish with the olive oil, parsley, bay leaves, and marjoram.

Add the fish fillets to the dish, and turn them back and forth in the oil to coat them well.

Bake for 15 to 20 minutes, turning the fillets once. Remove from oven. Place fish on an ovenproof platter.

Pour the sauce from the baking dish through a food mill fitted with a large perforated disc, then into a sauté pan. Mash the butter with the flour and add it to the sauce; cook and stir 4 minutes. Taste for seasoning and adjust as you wish. Pour the sauce over the fish, and return the fish to the oven for 10 minutes. Serve immediately.

Yield: 4 portions

½ pound peeled plum tomatoes, fresh or canned

3 tablespoons olive oil

2 tablespoons chopped fresh flat-leaf parsley

2 bay leaves

¼ teaspoon dried marjoram

3 pounds grouper fillets, approximately

2 tablespoons unsalted butter

1 tablespoon unbleached all-purpose flour

Salt and freshly ground white pepper to taste

Baked Grouper

cernia al forno

1 whole grouper, (approximately 6
    pounds), or 4 pounds grouper
    fillets
5-inch sprig of fresh rosemary, or 1
    to 2 teaspoons dried
3 small bay leaves
2 garlic cloves
1½ teaspoons salt, or to taste
Freshly ground pepper, white if
    available
½ cup olive oil
1 teaspoon dried oregano
5 sprigs of fresh flat-leaf parsley
1 tablespoon red-wine vinegar
¼ cup tomato juice
2 dozen pitted Italian-style black
    olives, oil cured

*If you are lucky enough to find a whole grouper, this is
a nice way to put it to use. The recipe also works well
with sea bass or red snapper.*

If possible, buy a whole fish, cleaned, but with the head
and tail left on.

Preheat the oven to 400 degrees Fahrenheit.

Mince the rosemary, bay leaves, and garlic together,
and sprinkle the mince throughout the cavity (or over the
fillets, if a whole fish was not available). Add 1 teaspoon of
the salt and a generous sprinkling of pepper.

Put the oil in a dish just large enough to hold the fish.
Add the oregano to the oil. Put in the parsley, place the
fish on top of it, and sprinkle with the remaining ½ teaspoon of salt and a little more pepper.

Add the vinegar and tomato juice to the dish and
baste the fish 3 or 4 times.

Surround the fish with the olives.

Bake for approximately 45 minutes to 1 hour; cover
the fish with aluminum foil for the first 30 minutes, then
remove the foil and baste thoroughly and continue baking
another 15 to 30 minutes. Taste the now-reduced sauce
for salt and add more if desired.

Serve the fish with olives surrounding it and its sauce
poured over it.

Yield: 6 portions

Haddock

Haddock, in our New England markets, is a very popular fish, the second most important fish of the cod family. Although it closely resembles cod, haddock is much smaller, weighing about two to five pounds, and its flesh is softer. The tilefish, which used to haunt the shores of New England, and now can be found from Nova Scotia to Cape Hatteras, is an excellent substitute for haddock, being of approximately the same weight. While the flavors are somewhat different, either one stuffed is quite delicious and rather spectacular, especially if the head and tail are left on.

Baked Haddock Fillet

filetti di pesce al forno

You can use any solid, large, firm-fleshed fish for this recipe, such as fresh cod, haddock, halibut, hake, turbot, or whiting. Or try the recipe on page 267 for Baked Stuffed Tilefish, substituting haddock for the tilefish.

1½ to 2 pounds fish fillets or steaks
1 teaspoon salt, or to please
Freshly ground white pepper to please
3 tablespoons olive oil, approximately
15 sprigs of fresh flat-leaf parsley
1 slice day-old Italian-style bread, crust removed
1 garlic clove
2 anchovy fillets
1 rounded tablespoon capers, rinsed and drained
1 lemon, cut in wedges

Preheat the oven to 400 degrees Fahrenheit.

Sprinkle the fish with salt and pepper on both sides. Oil a baking dish just large enough to hold the fish comfortably. Cut off the stems of the parsley, reserving the leaves, and place the stems in the baking dish. Put the fish on top of the parsley stems.

Break the bread into small chunks and blend together in a food processor with the parsley leaves and all the remaining ingredients except the lemon. Or mince these flavorings by hand. Spread the mince on the fish. Dribble the remaining olive oil over all.

Bake for 15 minutes. Serve with lemon wedges.

Yield: 4 portions

Hake

Red hake and white hake, found in the western Atlantic, are used a lot in Mediterranean cuisines. They can get to be as big as sixty pounds, but the average weight of hake in most markets is two to three pounds. Striped bass, small cod, haddock, pollock, red snapper, rosefish, or sea bass may be substituted.

Poached Hake with Green Sauce

pesce bollito con salsa verde

Hake is a great choice for serving with green sauce; its flesh is sturdier than that of cod, and it has a more pronounced flavor that complements the sauce and vice versa.

Have the fish cleaned (or do it yourself), but leave the head and tail on for added flavor. Wrap it in kitchen cheesecloth so that it can be easily removed from its pan when cooked.

Put the fish in a fish poacher. Add the herbs, celery, onion, lemon, salt, peppercorns, and wine or vinegar. Add enough cold water just to cover the fish. Cover the pan, bring to a boil over medium heat, lower the heat, and simmer about 9 minutes to the pound, or until an instant-read thermometer registers just under 140 degrees Fahrenheit.

While the fish is poaching, make a batch of the green sauce.

When the fish is cooked, lift it out of its broth, skin it, bone it, and put the two fillets side by side or one on top of the other on a serving platter. Cover with green sauce and serve with the remaining sauce.

Yield: 6 portions

2 2-pound hakes or 1 large 4-pound hake
10 sprigs of fresh flat-leaf parsley
1 sprig of fresh rosemary
1 bay leaf
1 celery rib with leaves
1 medium onion, quartered
1 lemon, quartered
6 teaspoons salt, or to taste
10 peppercorns
3 cups dry white wine, or ¾ cup red-wine vinegar
1 recipe Green Sauce (page 38)

Lobster

The American lobster, with claws (one larger than the other), represents America's earliest abundance: the first settlers had so many lobsters they used them as fertilizer, and as short a time ago as the late 1800s fishermen used them for bait. Lobster is now considered precious, easy as anything to cook (mostly poached, and served hot or cold), and transported just about everywhere.

The other most commonly known lobster is the "spiny" lobster, which you find in Florida waters as well as in the Mediterranean. It has no claws but is appreciated quite as much as its cousin with claws.

Both these two lobsters can be found fresh, frozen, and canned. The tiny lobster, *langoustine* (lobsterette or scampo), is usually sold fresh in the Mid-Atlantic states, Florida, and the Caribbean. It is like a big shrimp with nicely sized claws, and most Italians serve it with the shell on whether it is broiled, skewered and grilled, or sautéed.

Poached Lobster

astice in bianco

It would be hard to calculate how many lobsters are flown in live, daily, from New England to Italy, where they are kept in tanks on view in posh restaurants and superlative fish markets. Nearly everybody loves a lobster, or so it seems.

Check page 18 for poaching and timing to fit the lobster you have on hand. This recipe is usually used for the large lobsters because it is a glorious party presentation. It can be prepared ahead of time, chilled thoroughly, and partially removed from its shell and served with special garnishes.

1 large lobster, about 4 pounds, or 2 2-pound lobsters
Abundant salted water in your largest pot
1 onion, peeled and quartered
1 large carrot, peeled
3 bay leaves
10 sprigs of fresh flat-leaf parsley
10 peppercorns
½ cup red-wine vinegar, or 1 cup dry white wine
Extra parsley, celery, hearts of lettuce, watercress, lemons, olives, capers, or hard-boiled eggs for decoration
1 cup mayonnaise mixed with the juice of 1 lemon, or virgin olive oil and lemon juice to please

For the best results, tie the lobster(s) to a sturdy wooden spoon(s) to keep the tail(s) straight during cooking.

Bring the water to a boil, add all the flavorings including the vinegar or wine, and when the water returns to a boil, let it simmer about 20 minutes.

Raise the heat and put in the lobster. Let cook according to the timing on page 18 or estimate 14 minutes for a 1½-pound lobster, adding 2 minutes per pound up to 5 pounds.

Remove the lobsters from the pot and, when cool enough to handle, remove the tail meat from its shell: with a very sharp scissors or knife, cut open the shell on the underside of the tail and extract the meat in one piece.

Cut the tail meat in ½-inch rounds.

Empty the body and discard the entrails but save any coral (roe).

Remove the claws and extract the meat from them. Leave the legs attached to the now empty body.

Place the body on a platter and surround it decoratively with parsley, celery leaves, or lettuce. Fill the body cavity with parsley or watercress.

Place the meat of the claws in position at the top of the body. Line the tail cavity with as many tail slices as will fit and put the others around the edge of the platter. Place the roe, if any, in little clumps on the extra tail slices.

Add olives or capers or hard-boiled eggs in wedges to complete the platter. Serve with mayonnaise to which you have added the juice of a lemon. Or serve with extra-virgin olive oil and lemon juice.

Yield: 6 to 8 portions, depending on how substantial the rest of the meal will be

Monkfish

What is commonly known as monkfish in many of our markets is also known as goosefish, frogfish, lotte, and anglerfish. It may well be the ugliest fish we eat, but, oh, what a simply grand flavor. At first glance, the monkfish is all head, with a huge mouth, the better to eat practically every fish we prize: flounder, skate, cod, and sea bass, not to mention lobsters, crabs, and squid. Even wooden buoys from lobster pots have been found in their stomachs.

Monkfish is usually found along the Atlantic Coast from the Grand Banks to North Carolina. It can grow to about four feet in length and some fifty pounds in weight. And it is versatile: it can be baked, broiled, poached, and sautéed as well as cut into strips, battered, and deep-fried.

Monkfish Skewers with Vegetables

spiedini di rana pescatrice

2 pounds monkfish, cut in ¾-inch
    slices
2 green bell peppers, cored, cut in
    1½-inch squares
½ pound large mushrooms, brushed
    clean, stems removed
18 cherry tomatoes, washed, stems
    removed
½ cup olive oil
½ cup dry white wine
2 tablespoons snipped fresh or freeze-
    dried chives
1 tablespoon chopped fresh flat-leaf
    parsley
1 teaspoon fresh rosemary leaves, or
    ½ teaspoon dried
½ teaspoon dried oregano
Freshly ground black pepper

When monkfish came to be popular a few years ago, we rejoiced: monkfish is an old friend and an easy fish to work with. It is a solid sort of fish; it can work wonderfully on skewers and it is a gentle but real contrast to almost anything you wish to serve with it—fresh tomatoes, carrots and mushrooms, a touch of onion, or brilliant greens.

Cut the fish into 1½-inch squares.

Place a piece of pepper at one end of a skewer. Add a mushroom, tomato, mushroom, piece of fish, tomato, mushroom, piece of pepper. Send another skewer up alongside the first to hold the pieces well.

Repeat on other skewers, aiming for 3 pieces of fish per skewer with a piece of pepper on each end to protect the more delicate pieces.

Place the skewers on a platter.

Put the oil, wine, herbs, and black pepper in a jar, shake well, and pour over the skewers. Let marinate for at least 30 minutes, basting from time to time.

Grill the skewers on an open grill or in a preheated broiler.

Turn the skewers over after about 3 minutes or when the fish is cooked on one side. Baste with any remaining

marinade and serve when both sides of the fish pieces are cooked. The tomatoes and the mushrooms will be barely cooked, the peppers still green and crisp.

Yield: about 8 9-inch skewers, enough for 4 portions

Ocean Perch

Ocean perch, a fish that resembles red snapper and may be substituted for it, goes by a number of names: redfish, red perch, and rosefish. It is a member of the rockfish family and can come as large as twelve pounds, but mostly you'll find them from one to four pounds. The meat or flesh is white, firm, and lean. Ocean perch is a big commercial item for American trawlers who land some 200 million pounds a year from Labrador to Maine. It is also known as Norway haddock in the eastern Atlantic.

Ocean Perch in the Style of Milan

persico alla milanese

2 pounds ocean perch fillets
¾ cup unbleached all-purpose flour
2 eggs
1 cup unflavored breadcrumbs
2 tablespoons unsalted butter
¼ cup vegetable oil
1 teaspoon salt
2 lemons, cut in wedges

Before Italian cuisine was so neatly dissected and labeled northern or southern, each and every region was recognized for its distinct sort of cookery, and each and every interesting town went so far as to either put its name to a dish or have the dishes themselves commemorated geographically. And so it was with Milan and the wonderfully golden-fried anything: fish, turkey, veal, thin pork chops, and fish fillets, dipped in flour, then in beaten egg, and finally rolled in breadcrumbs before being fried. So, call it Northern Italian cuisine if you like, or celebrate the grand city of Milano—but do try it.

If the season is right, sliced fresh garden salad tomatoes make a wonderful contrast in texture, color, and flavor when served as an accompanying vegetable.

Press the fillets into the flour, patting it on gently so that they absorb as much flour as possible, and shake off the excess. Beat the eggs until foamy and then dip the fillets in them. Finally, pat the fillets into the breadcrumbs, one side at a time.

Melt the butter with the oil in a heavy frying pan over medium heat and fry the fillets quickly until golden on both sides. Drain on paper towels, sprinkle with the salt, and serve with lemon wedges.

Yield: 6 portions

Pollock

Pollock, a member of the fabulous cod family, shows up on both sides of the Atlantic from Newfoundland south to Chesapeake Bay on the U.S. side and from the North Sea to the Bay of Biscay on the European side. Unlike its cousins the cod and the haddock, pollock swims in shallow waters and is taken by sports fishermen as well as commercial fishermen. It looks something like its cousin the cod but it has a more rounded body and a forked tail, in contrast to the squared-off tail of the cod. In the average market, one can find pollock weighing about four pounds, but they can reach a thirty-five-pound size, making them ideal for use in the making and marketing of commercial fish sticks.

Fried Pollock in the Style of Ancona

pesce all'anconetana

SAUCE:

3 cups canned peeled plum tomatoes

4 tablespoons olive oil

3 garlic cloves

3 tablespoons chopped fresh flat-leaf
   parsley

½ teaspoon salt

Freshly ground black pepper to taste

FISH:

2 to 2½ pounds pollock, fresh cod, or
   hake fillets

Unbleached all-purpose flour

Vegetable oil for frying

We feel rather secure in pairing the pollock to a culinary treatment from Ancona because the Anconetani are so knowledgeable about almost any kind of fish. The city is on the Adriatic sea, halfway down the Italian peninsula, just a few miles from the port of San Benedetto, with the biggest fish market of that eastern coast. Buyers and sellers there are renowned for knowing a great deal about fish, how to season, glorify, and present fish. The Anconetani celebrate all kinds of feasts with magnificent fish dinners in restaurants as well as homes.

Chop the tomatoes coarsely.

Put the olive oil and the garlic cloves in a saucepan. Cook over medium heat until the garlic is dark brown and then remove it. Add the tomatoes, parsley, salt, and pepper. Lower the heat and simmer the sauce for about 15 to 20 minutes or until reduced somewhat and darkened in color.

Meanwhile, cut the fish in pieces approximately 2 inches by 3 inches, dredge them in flour, wait 5 to 10 minutes, then dredge them again, patting on the flour well.

Put at least 1 inch of vegetable oil in a frying pan and

bring it to medium heat (about 375 degrees Fahrenheit). Fry the fish pieces a few at a time until all sides are golden brown. Let them drain on paper kitchen towels. Keep them in a warm place while reheating the sauce if that is necessary.

Put the fried fish on a serving dish, cover them with sauce, and serve.

Yield: 4 to 6 portions

Porgy

Porgies are another huge family, prized on both sides of the Atlantic. Family members show up under names such as red porgy, sheepshead, and dentex. In the U.S., porgy is called scup, taken from the Narragansett Indian word *mishcuppauog* and abbreviated to pauog or pogy which, in colonial times, meant fertilizer. Like the fabulous lobster, it was used for just that only a few centuries ago. Around the rest of the world, scup or porgy has a more reasonable name—sea bream—and at one time it could be chosen live, as carefully as lobsters, in fancy restaurants.

Grilled Porgy

dentice alla griglia

1 4-pound fish, including head and
   tail
1 garlic clove
5 sprigs of fresh rosemary
3 tablespoons fresh flat-leaf parsley
1½ teaspoons salt
Freshly ground black pepper to taste
⅓ cup olive oil
2 lemons

Any time you can purchase a whole small porgy (or any other medium-size fish such as red snapper, ocean perch, trout) grilling over open coals is ideal. It is virtually the same as grilling a steak, especially if you use a grilling basket. Broiling the fish on a preheated broiler pan is the indoor alternative we use when we must.

Light the outdoor grill or preheat the oven broiler.

Clean and scale the fish (if it is necessary, of course), but leave on the heads and tails. Mince the garlic, rosemary, and parsley together, add the salt and some pepper, and also a few drops of oil to turn the minced flavorings into a paste. Make 2 or 3 diagonal incisions on either side of the fish and spread some paste in the slits as well as in the cavity.

Mix ¼ cup of olive oil and the juice of ½ lemon and baste the fish with the mixture.

When the coals of the grill are ready, put the fish in an oiled grilling basket, and put the basket over but not too close to the heat source. If cooking inside under a broiler, place a piece of aluminum foil on the broiler pan, oil it lightly, place fish on it, and slide the pan under the broiler. When the fish is nicely browned, turn it, baste again with the oil and lemon mixture, and finish cooking. Place the fish on a platter, carefully cut off the head and tail, open up the underside from top to bottom, and remove the backbone. Serve with the remaining lemon cut in wedges.

Yield: 4 portions

Porgy in Parchment

dentice al cartoccio

Preheat the oven to 350 degrees Fahrenheit.

Clean the mushrooms as necessary, cut them in half, and sauté them in 1 to 2 tablespoons butter for 10 minutes.

Mince the leaves of the parsley, reserving the stems, and work them into a tablespoon of the butter. Place half of the parsley butter inside each fish. Place parsley stems on 2 pieces of parchment with a teaspoon of oil each. Put the fish on the parsley stems. Salt and pepper the fish.

Shake the remaining oil with the lemon juice and divide it between the fish. Surround each porgy with the mushrooms and shrimp and fold up the parchment and seal it.

Bake for about 20 minutes or until the parchment is puffed high. Serve from the parchment.

Yield: 2 portions

3 ounces mushrooms
2 to 3 tablespoons unsalted butter
5 sprigs of fresh flat-leaf parsley
2 small porgies, about 1 pound each, cleaned
2 to 3 tablespoons olive oil
Salt and freshly ground black pepper
Juice of 1 lemon
12 ounces small shrimp, approximately, shelled and deveined

Red Snapper

This superlative fish, available year-round, is found in the waters off North Carolina and all the way down to Brazil. The Gulf of Mexico provides the most numerous catches, and the fish itself is a prize, good any way you cook it: grilled, baked, poached, steamed, whole, or in fillets. Many knowledgeable cooks in the U.S. substitute small cod or grouper for red snapper, because of similarities in texture and flavor. In Italy, the treatment given the European sea bass (*branzino* or *spigola*), as well as sea bream (*dentice*) works well with red snapper.

Baked Red Snapper

pesce al forno

1 4-pound red snapper, cleaned but
    with the head and tail on, if
    possible, or 2 fillets,
    approximately 2 pounds each
4 tablespoons olive oil
½ teaspoon salt
Freshly ground white pepper
5 sprigs of fresh flat-leaf parsley
4 bay leaves
1 sprig of fresh rosemary
1 garlic clove
Juice of 1 lemon or ½ cup dry white
    wine
1 lemon for garnish
Parsley, radicchio, or Bibb lettuce
    for garnish

Preheat the oven to 400 degrees Fahrenheit.

Rinse the fish (or fillets) and pat dry with paper towels.

Put the olive oil in a baking dish large enough to hold the fish comfortably. Sprinkle a bit of salt and pepper on the oil. Place the parsley sprigs down the center of the dish.

Sprinkle the cavity of the fish (or the tops of the two fillets) with salt and pepper and place 2 of the bay leaves in the cavity or on one of the fillets. Put the remaining bay leaves in the pan. Mince the rosemary leaves with the garlic and put half the mince in the cavity or on top of the already seasoned fillet. Put remaining mince in the baking dish.

Put the whole fish (or the two fillets sandwiched over

the flavorings) on top of the parsley and place the dish in the oven.

Bake 10 minutes; then baste with the oil in the dish and the lemon juice or wine. Bake another 10 minutes and baste again. Bake a final 5 minutes or until the fish is cooked through. Remove the fish to a serving platter. Pour the baking liquids over the fish.

Garnish with the lemon, cut in wedges, butterflied, or sliced, and with sprigs of parsley, radicchio, or lettuce.

Yield: 4 portions

Salmon

Salmon is a national favorite in the U.S. and is being imported more and more by Italy. The Italian food magazines have gone to great lengths to explain the firm texture, how to smoke it to get that rare flavor, how to broil or grill it.

Depending on where we are, we are happy to have tried chum, king, pink, silver, sockeye, and Atlantic salmon. Driving through Utah, in search of America, we found the most impressive salmon display ever in a huge supermarket in St. George. At nine in the morning, we stood and watched with an ever-increasing appetite as the clerk arranged a display to show the various cuts to be bought for home smoking. The pink salmon, Margaret's childhood favorite, is the one used in about half the canning in the U.S.

Grilled or Broiled Salmon Steaks

salmone alla griglia

4 ½-pound, 1-inch-thick salmon
  steaks
1 recipe Parsley Butter (page 31)
Juice of 1½ lemons

This procedure works equally well with swordfish steaks.

Preheat the broiler, or start a grill going about 30 minutes before cooking time.

Make 2 cuts in the skin of each steak to prevent curling during cooking.

Make the parsley butter and put 1 tablespoon of it on each steak. Place the salmon on the hot grill or in the hot broiler and cook it for 7 minutes.

Remove the steaks to a serving platter and sprinkle them with lemon juice and serve.

Yield: 4 portions

Poached Salmon

salmone in bianco

Poached salmon is a Romagnoli family favorite which, even when in Italy, stars on our July 4th table as if we were in New England. Poached salmon is a beauty, to say the least. Poaching is easy and something we usually do early in the day so that the removal of skin and bone and the placement of the grand fish is arranged properly while still warm and before the kitchen is filled with family members asking when they can eat.

If by any chance there are any portions left, scrape the salmon clean of its mayonnaise and garnishes, place on a plate, cover with plastic wrap, and refrigerate.

Herbs and seasonings for Basic Fish Stock II (page 168)
1 4-pound salmon, cleaned, head and tail intact

Place all the herbs and seasonings listed as the ingredients for Basic Fish Stock II in a fish poacher large enough to hold the fish. Fill it with water up to about 1 inch from the top. Bring to a boil, lower the heat, cover the pan, and simmer for 15 minutes. Allow the stock to cool.

Wrap the fish in cheesecloth and tie it at each end with a simple knot. (If your poacher is just a bit too small, cut off the fish head but include it in the poaching process.) Place the wrapped salmon in the cooled stock, bring to a boil, and the minute it boils, lower the heat and cover the pan, but leave the lid just ever so slightly open and let cook at a very slow simmer—with hardly a ripple—for approx-

imately 20 minutes, or until the flesh of the salmon registers just under 140 degrees on an instant-read thermometer. Remove from heat and allow the fish to cool in the stock for about 20 minutes. Lift the fish out by pulling it up by the knots in the cheesecloth, place on a platter, uncover, and immediately peel off the skin and remove the head and tail. Gently remove the top fillet and place it on a serving platter. Lift off the salmon's backbone and fin bones. Turn over the fish, remove the skin and place this fillet either on top of the first fillet or alongside it.

The decorations may be according to your own artistic whim. If you have a pastry bag with a round tip, fill it with mayonnaise (page 40) and pipe artificial scales on the fish, or use cucumber rounds or lemon rounds for the same effect. Some cooks tuck curly-leafed salad greens under the edges of the fish while others use curly or flat-leaf parsley. Our warning is: Don't do too much, as the fish itself is a grand picture to behold.

Yield: 6 good portions

Salmon Trout

This is another of those fish with many look-alikes and cousins, all with a multitude of names. Salmon trout, also called brown trout, looks like salmon with its pink flesh, tastes like salmon, and cooks like salmon. Native to the Mediterranean area, this fish makes its way all the way to Norway and Siberia. Salmon trout was introduced to the U.S. in the 1800s and may be found in eastern U.S. markets weighing one and a half to two pounds, although they can grow much bigger, up to forty pounds.

Tracking down the salmon trout is a tricky business because there are fresh-water brown trout in Ireland known as gillaroo, the flesh of which is a good salmon color, while seagoing brown

trout can be a very pale pink indeed. In Italy, one can find salmon trout (sea-running brown trout) weighing about three and a half to four and a half pounds, while our local market in New England carries salmon trout (seagoing brown trout) when it is available on a rather irregular schedule.

Salmon Trout with Rice and Shrimp

trota salmonata con riso e gamberi

In poaching and presenting salmon trout with rice, you are making a one-course meal that is perfect for a party of six.

Place enough cold water in a large fish poacher to cover the fish plus about 2 cups extra. Add half the onion slivers, all of the carrot, parsley, bay leaves, and celery, one of the garlic cloves, the vinegar, salt, and peppercorns. Bring the pan to a boil, cover, lower the heat, and let simmer at least 30 minutes. Taste for salt and adjust if necessary.

Place the fish in the poacher, bring back to a boil, lower the heat until the water barely ripples, cover, and cook 10 minutes per inch of the fish at its widest girth.

When the fish has cooked about 10 minutes, mince the remaining onion and garlic together. Sauté in olive oil in a saucepan or in a pressure cooker. Add the rice and cook until it crackles.

Add to the rice 2 cups of the broth in which the fish is cooking and cover the pan. If using a normal saucepan, cook 14 minutes. If using a pressure cooker, bring the

4 to 5½-pound salmon trout, cleaned and wrapped in cheesecloth, or 2 smaller trout
1 onion, peeled and cut in thin slivers
1 large carrot, peeled and sliced
5 sprigs of fresh flat-leaf parsley
3 bay leaves
2 celery ribs with leaves
2 garlic cloves
¾ cup red-wine vinegar
2 to 3 tablespoons salt
10 peppercorns
4 tablespoons olive oil
2 cups American long-grain rice
2 pounds medium shrimp, peeled and deveined
4 tablespoons unsalted butter
Black olives
Extra-virgin olive oil
Juice of 2 lemons

pressure to 15 pounds, cook 8 minutes, bring the pressure down immediately, uncover, and stir the rice.

In another sauté pan, sauté the shrimp in the butter until bright coral colored, about 2 minutes. Add 3 table-spoons of the fish broth from the poacher, and cook another minute or so.

Place the cooked salmon trout on a work platter and open up its cheesecloth. Peel off the fish skin. If the fish has its head and tail, leave them on.

Center the trout on a serving platter, surround the fish with the rice, and decorate with the shrimp and olives. Serve with extra-virgin olive oil and lemon juice.

Yield: 8 portions

Scallops

Scallops, members of the mollusk family, come in many varieties to the U.S. market: bay scallops (from the Florida waters) and calico scallops (from the Atlantic) are the little ones about as big as the end of your thumb. They are often said to be the most exceptional in taste, having an almost sweet flavor. The bigger ones, the sea scallops, also from the Atlantic, are firmer in texture and, for most diners, equally appetizing. The large Mediterranean scallop, *conchiglie di San Giacomo*, is very like our sea scallop in size and the bay scallop in flavor. The edible part of the scallop is the big, plump, muscle inside the fan-shaped, rounded shells, which can be, according to type, as big as the spread of your hand.

In Italy, scallops are frequently combined with shrimp in pasta sauces and sautéed main courses, good partners in a number of dishes. Scallops are available all year frozen and found fresh in many coastal markets from early spring through the summer.

Fried Scallops

capesante fritte

The almost gentle flavor of scallops, either sea scallops or bay scallops, is quite wonderful when encased in a nice batter and deep-fried. There is something special about the crunchiness of the outside and the almost sweet, soft inside that pleases the palate no end.

Make the batter and let it rest for 30 minutes. Stir well before using.

Place the scallops in a dish in one layer and dress them with a mixture of the lemon juice, oil, salt, and pepper. Toss well and let rest for 30 minutes.

Bring a pan with at least 3 inches of vegetable oil to frying temperature (375 degrees Fahrenheit). Dip a few scallops at a time in the prepared batter, lift them out, and fry them until golden and crisp.

Drain on paper towels and place in a warm serving dish. Continue dipping, frying, and draining until all are ready. Garnish with parsley or watercress and lemon wedges.

Yield: 4 to 5 portions

1 recipe Egg Batter (page 29)
2¼ pounds sea scallops, cleaned and patted dry
2 tablespoons lemon juice
⅓ cup olive oil
Salt to taste
Freshly ground white pepper to taste
Vegetable oil for frying
2 tablespoons chopped flat-leaf parsley or watercress leaves
1½ lemons, cut in wedges

Scallops, Florentine Style

capesante alla fiorentina

This dish seems so rich yet evenly balanced that it puts on a very good show at any dinner table. Scallops carry a variety of names in Italian: capesante, pellegrine, conchiglie, *and* conchiglie di San Giacomo; *hence the dish name also appears in a variety of ways while the production remains the same.*

VEGETABLES:

1½ pounds fresh spinach

1 teaspoon salt

4 tablespoons unsalted butter

3½ cups freshly cooked mashed potatoes, made from about 6 or 7 medium potatoes

Freshly ground white pepper to taste

¼ to ½ teaspoon freshly grated nutmeg, approximately

1 tablespoon grated Parmesan cheese

1 cup milk, approximately

FISH AND SAUCE:

2 pounds sea scallops, cleaned and patted dry

2 tablespoons unsalted butter

1 tablespoon olive oil

2 tablespoons snipped fresh or freeze-dried chives

½ garlic clove, minced

1 tablespoon minced fresh flat-leaf parsley

½ cup dry white wine

Wash the fresh spinach well, discard the heaviest of the stems, and cook the remainder in the water that clings to the leaves. Add the salt and cook and stir until just tender. Drain and then squeeze dry.

Place cooked spinach in a saucepan with 2 tablespoons of the butter. Heat and stir until the butter has melted and coated the spinach.

Season the mashed potatoes with the pepper, nutmeg, remaining butter, and cheese. Add as much milk as necessary to the potatoes to make smooth whipped potatoes.

For the scallops, melt the butter in the olive oil in a sauté pan large enough to hold all the scallops in one layer. Add the chives, garlic, and parsley. Add the scallops. Raise the heat, cook for a minute or so, add the wine, ½ teaspoon of salt and ½ teaspoon of pepper. Bring to a boil, and when the wine has evaporated, cover, lower the heat, and cook 5 minutes.

Preheat the oven to 450 degrees Fahrenheit.

Divide the spinach equally into 6 ovenproof gratin dishes. Using a pastry bag with a wide nozzle, pipe the mashed potatoes around the spinach. (You may arrange the potatoes with a spoon or fork, but the pastry bag is better.)

Take the scallops from their pan, reserving the juices, and place them on the spinach.

Add flour to the sauté pan, mix with a whisk, add the milk and light cream, and bring to a boil slowly, whisking all the time. Taste for salt and pepper and correct to please. Cook at least 4 minutes.

Pour the sauce over the scallops in each dish. Sprinkle with Parmesan cheese.

Bake for 5 minutes or until slightly golden here and there.

Yield: 6 portions

Salt and freshly ground white pepper
2 tablespoons unbleached all-purpose flour
⅔ cup whole milk
½ cup light cream
6 tablespoons grated Parmesan cheese

Sea Bass

In Italian cuisine sea bass may mean *dentice, branzino*, or *spigola*. European sea bass (fish of the small seas) are very similar to the Atlantic sea bass or the Pacific white bass (fish of the big oceans). The European cousins tend to get lumped together and are also comparable to black sea bass, one of the finest-tasting and finest-textured fish in the markets. Striped sea bass, which is hard to find some years, is also a good substitute for the Mediterranean *branzino*. The sea bass we usually use weigh in at about 4 pounds. The Italian touch for any of this huge and varied family covers baking, grilling, broiling, marinating, poaching, and sautéeing.

Baked Sea Bass with Mussels

branzino alle cozze

1 4-pound sea bass, cleaned, head
    and tail intact

1 cup dry white wine

½ ounce brandy

2 tablespoons chopped fresh flat-leaf
    parsley

1 small onion (about 2 ounces),
    minced

1 garlic clove, minced

1½ teaspoons salt

½ teaspoon freshly ground white
    pepper

2 pounds mussels

2 tablespoons unsalted butter

1 lemon for garnish

Place the fish in a stainless-steel or ovenproof glass baking dish. Add the wine, brandy, parsley, onion, and garlic. Turn the fish over and over in the marinade. Add salt and pepper and let marinate 1 hour.

Preheat oven to 375 degrees Fahrenheit.

Clean the mussels and place them around the bass. Baste with the marinade. Dot the bass and border with the butter. Bake 10 minutes for every inch of the fish at its widest girth. Remove the fish and mussels to a hot platter (discarding any mussels that did not open) and keep warm for a minute or so while you strain the pan liquids into a small saucepan and reduce it a bit. Pour reduction over the fish, garnish with lemon wedges or slices, and serve.

Yield: 4 to 6 portions

Black Sea Bass with Butter

branzino al burro

Clean the fish and soak it in milk, turning it a couple of times. Shake off the milk, and dip the fish in flour while the butter melts in the pan. Fry the fish about 5 minutes to a side, turning it carefully. When cooked, remove, drain on absorbent paper, and sprinkle with salt.

Yield: 2 portions

1 small bass, approximately 2 pounds
Milk
Unbleached all-purpose flour
4 tablespoons unsalted butter, approximately
Salt

Sea Bass, Marinated and Baked

branzino marinato al forno

Preheat the oven to 350 degrees Fahrenheit.

Clean the bass but leave on the head and tail. Place the fish in a plastic bag with enough oil to baste it easily. Add the onion, bay leaf, thyme, and parsley. Marinate the fish in its bag, turning from time to time, for an hour. Remove the fish from the bag and place it and its marinade in a baking dish of suitable size. Add salt and pepper to your taste and bake for about 20 minutes, basting from time to time.

Yield: 4 portions

2 pounds whole sea bass
¼ cup olive oil
1 small onion (2 to 3 ounces), cut in rings
1 bay leaf
1 teaspoon fresh thyme, or ½ teaspoon dried
5 sprigs of fresh flat-leaf parsley
Salt and freshly ground black pepper

Sea Bass in the Style of Genoa

branzino alla genovese

2 2½-pound sea bass
1 carrot
1 celery rib
1 onion
½ garlic clove
3 to 4 sprigs of fresh flat-leaf parsley
1 anchovy fillet
2 dried porcini mushrooms, softened
   in warm water
1 tablespoon capers
Olive oil
Salt and pepper to taste

This recipe calls for porcini mushrooms, highly thought of by food lovers in central and northern Europe. Known for their very special flavor, porcini are placed alongside truffles for their different appeal. Prized by home and professional cooks alike, the porcini are gathered in the fall and dried for winter and export use. They may be found in many an Italian grocery store as well as in a number of specialty stores dealing in imported, packaged foods. To revive dried mushrooms, soak them in lukewarm water for about 15 minutes and then lift them out, leaving behind in the water any particles of dirt. Pat the mushrooms dry and continue with your recipe.

Clean the fish but leave on the head and tail. Mince the flavorings, including the mushrooms and capers.

Pour enough oil into the pan to cover the bottom generously. Add the minced flavorings and cook over moderate heat until limp but not browned.

Place the fish over the mince and lower the heat. Add salt and pepper halfway through the cooking step. Cover the pan and cook for about 30 minutes.

Yield: 4 portions

Baked Sea Bass, Southern Italian Style

branzino alla messinese

Preheat the oven to 350 degrees Fahrenheit.

In a baking dish large enough to hold the fish, place half the onion, tomatoes, mushrooms, pepper strips, garlic clove, and minced parsley.

Place the fish over the vegetables. Put the wine, oil, salt and pepper to your taste, and about ⅓ cup of water in a jar or 2-cup measure. Whisk or shake well. Pour the mixture over the fish, and tilt the dish back and forth to make sure the liquid is well distributed. Bake for about 30 minutes or 10 minutes per inch of the girth of the fish at its widest. Baste the fish a couple of times during baking.

Remove the fish from the baking dish. Cut off the head and tail and discard. Peel off the skin on the top side, and lift off the entire fillet to a hot serving plate.

Remove the backbone and transfer the second fillet to top the first. Remove the last of the skin and pour the baking juices over the recomposed fish. Arrange the vegetables around the sides of the fish and serve.

Yield: 4 portions

2½ pounds sea bass, approximately
1-pound onion, cut in rings
1 pound peeled plum tomatoes, fresh in season or canned
½ ounce dried porcini mushrooms, softened in warm water, or 6 to 8 ounces fresh mushrooms, sliced
2 bell peppers (preferably one yellow and one green or red), cut in julienne strips
1 garlic clove, peeled
2 tablespoons minced fresh flat-leaf parsley
1 cup dry white wine
⅓ cup olive oil
Salt
Freshly ground white pepper, optional

Black Sea Bass in Pastry

sfogliata di pesce

1 recipe Rough Puff Pastry (page
  304)

3 tablespoons unsalted butter

1 ½-pound onion, sliced

1 garlic clove, minced

¼ cup dry white wine

Unbleached all-purpose flour

1 cup Basic Fish Stock II (page 168)

1 chicken bouillon cube

2 ounces chopped fresh flat-leaf
  parsley

2 potatoes, boiled, peeled, and sliced
  thin

1¾ pounds striped or black sea bass,
  poached (page 21)

2 tablespoons unflavored
  breadcrumbs

1 egg, separated

Olive oil

Roll out the dough and cut it into two pieces, each the shape of a fish about 16 inches long, head to tail, and about 9 inches wide at the widest point.

Melt the butter and sauté the onion and garlic until soft. Add the wine and when it has evaporated sprinkle with 3 tablespoons of the flour, whisking the mixture constantly. Pour in the stock in a steady stream, continuing to whisk as you pour. Add about half the bouillon cube, crumbled, and continue to whisk and cook until a good sauce has been achieved, about 4 minutes. Stir in the chopped parsley.

Place the potato slices evenly lined up over the widest part of the dough fish. Top the potatoes with about half the sea bass, broken into pieces. (Be careful to check for bones.) Spoon about half the sauce over the fish. Distribute the last half of the fish over the entire shape. Cover with the last of the sauce. Finish with the sprinkling of the breadcrumbs.

With a pastry brush, paint the border of the exposed side of the second piece of dough with egg white and then oil the rest of that side and turn it over onto the layered fish on the first piece of dough. Press the edges together firmly.

Preheat the oven to 400 degrees Fahrenheit.

Roll out the remaining pieces of dough and cut them in approximately 80 to 90 disks about ½ to ¾ inch in diameter. (A small cookie cutter is good for this.)

Paint the fish with the remaining egg white and place the disks like scales on the pastry. Use a straight piece of dough for the mouth and a round ball of dough for the eye. Paint the decorations with the beaten egg yolk.

Bake the fish for 40 minutes. During the last 15 minutes, cover the fish with aluminum foil.

When the fish is baked, let it rest for 10 to 15 minutes before cutting.

Yield: 6 to 8 portions

Grilled Striped Sea Bass

branzino alla brace

Clean the fish, but leave on the head and tail.

Squeeze 1 lemon and mix the juice with the sherry and all the other ingredients in a bowl.

Put the fish in a deep dish or plastic bag large enough to hold it and pour the marinade over it. If using a bag, tie it shut. Marinate the fish for at least an hour, turning it over a few times to moisten every part.

While the fish marinates, start the grill. When the coals are ready, oil the grilling basket. Remove the fish from the marinade and place it in the basket (a fish-shaped one with folding supporters is perfect for this) and put the latched basket on the grill. Brush the fish with the marinade as it grills. When the fish skin blisters and crackles,

1 3-pound striped bass

2 lemons

½ cup dry sherry

*½ cup olive oil, plus additional for
  final touch*

*1 sprig fresh rosemary, or 2
  teaspoons dried*

½ teaspoon salt

*Dash of ground cayenne pepper, or
  3 or 4 drops of Tabasco*

Pinch of sugar

turn the basket; baste the fish with some more marinade and place it back on the grill.

When the fish is done, remove it to a platter, skin and bone it. Serve with the remaining lemon cut in wedges and a dribble of olive oil.

Yield: 4 portions

Shrimp

Shrimp is the second most popular seafood in America and the most ubiquitous. You find it in the freezer, at the refrigerated fish counter, cooked, with or without shells, mostly without a head, and in many sizes. If shrimp could talk, they'd talk in many tongues. And they'd all say "don't cook me too long." Italian cookery uses shrimp in *antipasti*, soup, with pasta and rice, in salads, as an entrée, in aspic. However, do not think for a moment that a shrimp (*gambero*) is a *langoustine* (*scampo*). In Italy, you won't find a dish called "shrimp *scampi*" but you will find *scampi*, similar to a dwarf lobster, and—like scampi—grilled or sautéed and flamed with a shot of brandy. It has a head, tail, and claws and is delicious.

Shrimp Capri

gamberi alla Capri

The name probably has little to do with the dish, but at least it brings to mind what may be the most honored little island off the coast of Italy, a sunny climate, a grand tolerance for visitors, and a welcome mat out year-round.

Flavor the olive oil by sautéeing the garlic in it until well browned. Discard the garlic and add the shrimp. Sauté over high heat for about 1½ minutes. Pour in the wine, raise the heat, and cook until the alcohol has evaporated. Sprinkle with lemon juice. Add the capers, olives, butter, salt, and pepper, and sauté for another 1½ minutes. Stir in the chopped parsley. Serve with the pan sauce and generous pieces of Italian bread.

Yield: 6 portions

Olive oil to cover the bottom of the
  sauté pan
2 garlic cloves
2 pounds medium shrimp, peeled
  and deveined
1 cup dry white wine,
  approximately
1 teaspoon lemon juice
1 tablespoon capers
2 dozen black olives, pitted and
  halved
4 tablespoons unsalted butter
Salt and freshly ground white
  pepper to taste
3 tablespoons chopped fresh flat-leaf
  parsley
Italian-style bread

Shrimp and Scallops in Brandy Sauce

capesante e gamberi al brandy

1 pound sea scallops
1 pound large shrimp
1 garlic clove, peeled and quartered
4 to 5 tablespoons olive oil
¾ teaspoon salt
Freshly ground white pepper to taste
1 rounded tablespoon capers, rinsed, drained, and chopped
Leaves of 5 to 6 sprigs of fresh flat-leaf parsley, chopped
2 to 3 dashes of Tabasco
3 tablespoons brandy
Juice of 1 lemon
Black olives, pitted and cut in halves or rings, for garnish

This might fit under the heading of fast food or elegant entrée. Either way, the two main stars complement each other nicely. If you are lucky enough to have prawns (langoustines *or* scampi) *at hand, they are a very fine substitute for the shrimp.*

Wash the scallops, and, if they are very large, cut them in half horizontally. Peel and clean the shrimp, reserving the shells.

Over medium heat, sauté the garlic and the shrimp shells in the olive oil until golden, then discard both. Let the oil cool a moment.

Add the scallops and shrimp, raise the heat, and sauté for about 2 minutes. Sprinkle with salt and pepper and continue to sauté.

Mix the capers and parsley together and add to the pan along with the Tabasco. Bring up the heat and sauté for 1 more minute.

Add the brandy and lemon juice. Cook and stir for 1 minute more. The shrimp should be bright coral and the scallops cooked but not dried out. Garnish with the black olives and serve.

Yield: 4 to 6 generous portions

Shrimp, Family Style

gamberi alla casalinga

If you ordered this dish in a small fishing port in Italy, the shrimp would arrive with their heads, tails, and peels on and you'd cope with the entire dish with your fingers. A bit messy but fun to eat.

1 garlic clove
4 tablespoons olive oil
2 pounds medium shrimp
2 tablespoons chopped fresh flat-leaf parsley
1 tablespoon capers
Juice of 1 lemon
1 teaspoon salt, or to taste

Sauté the garlic clove in olive oil over medium heat until golden and then discard it.

Cook the shrimp in the olive oil for about 2 minutes, stirring constantly, until they have turned a nice coral pink. Add the parsley and capers with the lemon juice. Stir, add salt, and taste. Adjust flavorings as needed. Cook another minute and remove from heat. Serve with finger bowls, if you have them.

Yield: 6 portions

Sole

While trying to figure out what kind of a sole we were buying in the U.S., it dawned on us that this was a case similar to the bass: there are lots of names, lots of soles, and some of them are really flounders. To be as definite and short as possible, the common sole of Europe, found from the Mediterranean to Denmark, is called the Dover sole. It is available, imported fresh or frozen, in some rather fancy restaurants. However, there are a number of flounders taken from both the Atlantic and the Pacific that are marketed under a variety of sole names: the "lemon sole," or winter flounder, is taken off Block Island and the Georges Bank; the "petral sole," or large Pacific flounder, is ranked first among the Pacific flatfish. Finally there is the "rex sole" or

small Pacific flounder that has a wonderfully delicate flavor and is small enough to use whole, and the "grey sole," or witch flounder, which has a delightful taste. All of these "soles" work well with practically any classic recipe.

Golden-fried Sole

sogliole fritte dorate

6 sole fillets
Unbleached all-purpose flour
2 eggs
¾ teaspoon salt
Olive oil
1½ lemons

When cooking sole, the crispness and the gentle flavor are the only things that count.

Gently press the fillets, one by one, into the flour, covering both sides. Beat the eggs lightly and add the salt. Dip the fish into the eggs, then fry in about ½ inch of olive oil.

When the fillets are golden on one side, turn them and fry the second side. Remove from the pan the minute both sides are nicely golden. Serve with lemon wedges.

Yield: 6 portions

Sole Spirals

spirali di sogliola

The delicate white and sweet flesh of the sole is made to stand out brilliantly with accents of bright green spinach. We tried this for its eye appeal and now it is a steady on our menu for its surprising combination of tastes.

4 sole fillets
Salt and freshly ground white
  pepper
2 tablespoons olive oil
6 to 7 ounces frozen spinach leaves,
  thawed
2 cups Basic Tomato Sauce (page
  43)

Spread the sole fillets out on the counter or cutting board. Salt and pepper them to your taste.

Place 1 tablespoon of the olive oil in a small sauté pan. Squeeze the thawed spinach leaves until as dry as possible. Chop the leaves finely and sauté them in the olive oil until tender and practically dry.

Spread the sole fillets with an even layer of spinach. Taking the narrowest end of a fillet, roll it up on itself, making a thick white-and-green spiral. Fix the spiral with a skewer.

Continue until all the fish is used.

Oil a piece of aluminum foil with the last of the olive oil. Place the spirals on the foil and enclose them in it; crimp the foil shut.

Put an inch or so of water in the bottom of a steamer or a pot with a colander insert and bring it to a boil. Slip in the steaming basket or the colander insert, place the aluminum foil packet in it, cover, and steam for 5 to 6 minutes.

While the sole cooks, heat the tomato sauce.

When the sole has cooked, remove the aluminum packet from the steamer, open carefully, and let the fillets cool. Remove the skewers. Then slice the spirals in rounds about 1 inch thick.

Place a pool of tomato sauce on each of four hot plates. Divide the sole spirals onto the plates and serve.

Yield: 4 portions

Squid

Squid is a crazy-looking little mollusk with a sacklike body, virtually no tail, ten arms, and a thin, pale purple skin. Sort of like a tiny octopus, it is used all over the world as a delicate seafood. Italy, in particular, capitalizes on squid in fish stews, deep-fried, in sauces, and stuffed. It is practically interchangeable with cuttlefish in cooking.

Like shrimp, squid should be cooked rapidly to maintain its texture. However, where squid is used to lend a gentle flavor to a fish soup, cooking over fifteen to twenty minutes leaves the texture as acceptable as the quick-cooking one-minute timing. If you've never tried squid, buy it cleaned for the first go-round. Once you taste it, you'll want to learn to peel off its thin skin, empty the sac, cut out the mouth and eyes (page 16), and you'll want to cook it frequently.

Fried Squid

Calamari fritti

If you have never tried squid in your life, then perhaps this is the way to start: you will find surprising crunch, light taste, and enough bite and flavor to the squid to satisfy any hungry diner. If the frying per se puts you off, think again: we have measured the oil that remains after frying a batch of squid, and, honestly, it showed that very little is absorbed in the frying.

1½ pounds fresh or frozen squid, cleaned (page 16)
Unbleached all-purpose flour
Vegetable oil for deep frying
Salt to taste
2 lemons, cut in wedges
Sprigs of fresh flat-leaf parsley or watercress for garnish

Cut the tentacles of the squid in half, the bodies in rings.

Put about ½ cup of flour and a handful of prepared squid in a heavy plastic or sturdy paper bag and shake the bag so that the squid is thoroughly floured. Repeat as necessary to flour all the squid.

Heat the oil to 375 degrees Fahrenheit and fry a handful or so of squid pieces at a time. Do not overcrowd the pan. Turn the squid with a slotted spoon as they become golden, no more than 30 seconds.

Remove and drain on absorbent paper. Sprinkle with salt. Serve right away with lemon wedges and parsley or watercress.

Yield: 4 portions

Squid with Swiss Chard

calamari in zimino

3 pounds small squid, fresh or
    frozen
1 medium onion
¾ cup chopped fresh flat-leaf parsley
1 celery rib
4 tablespoons olive oil
2 pounds Swiss chard, washed
    thoroughly
⅔ cup crushed canned plum
    tomatoes
1½ teaspoons salt, or to taste
Freshly ground black pepper
Italian-style bread

Clean the squid (page 16), and cut the tentacles in half lengthwise, the body in rings.

Chop the onion, parsley, and celery together, and sauté in the olive oil in a soup pot for 3 to 4 minutes or until golden green.

Discard the chard stems and cut the leaves into pieces; add pieces to the herb-flavored oil. Cook about 5 minutes, or until wilted.

Add the tomatoes, salt, and pepper. Stir, cover, and cook at a gentle boil for 15 minutes, until a loose sauce has formed. Uncover, add the squid, and cook about 1 minute or until the squid is tender. Taste for salt, and add some if desired. Serve with hot Italian-style bread.

Yield: 6 portions

Stuffed Squid

calamari ripieni

With a little patience, any cook can stuff a squid's body, which is then poached in sauce and served as a second course. If using the larger squid (7 to 8 inches long), plan on two to a portion.

12 large squid

1 small garlic clove

1 cup fresh flat-leaf parsley leaves

¼ teaspoon dried oregano

2 teaspoons salt

1 teaspoon freshly ground black pepper

3 or 4 slices Italian-style bread

4 tablespoons olive oil

½ cup dry white wine

6 very ripe fresh plum tomatoes, peeled, or canned plum tomatoes, optional

Clean the squid (page 16), and place to drain on paper towels. Put the garlic, parsley, oregano, salt, and pepper in the bowl of a food processor with its steel blade. Process until a good mince has formed. Add the tentacles and process on/off until they, too, are minced.

Shred the bread, discarding the crusts, into a bowl. Add the mince with tentacles, and mix well. Moisten with a bit of the olive oil to make a coarse paste. Fill the squid bodies with the paste until they are ½ to ¾ full. Don't stuff them too tightly or they will burst in cooking. Skewer the bodies shut with plain round wooden picks. Save any leftover stuffing.

Cover the bottom of a big frying pan with the rest of the olive oil and put in the stuffed squid in one layer. Brown gently over medium heat. Move the squid about a bit with a wooden spoon or spatula to prevent any possible sticking. When the squid are nicely browned, put in any remaining stuffing and cook for a moment or two. Add the wine, stir well, and continue to cook until the wine has evaporated.

At this point, if you are adding tomatoes, put them

through a food mill to crush them or use the food processor. Add the crushed tomatoes to the squid and pour in enough hot water to bring the sauce to cover the squid just barely. If you are not using tomatoes, add the water anyway, and continue to cook the squid at a simmer for about 20 minutes or until the squid is tender and the sauce has condensed. During the final cooking time, turn the squid occasionally to ensure even cooking.

Remove the squid to a platter, pour the sauce over them, and serve.

Yield: 6 portions

Squid in the Style of Genoa

calamari alla genovese

1 3-pound package frozen squid,
   cleaned if possible, thawed
4 tablespoons olive oil
2 garlic cloves
2 tablespoons chopped fresh flat-leaf
   parsley
2 teaspoons salt
½ teaspoon freshly ground white
   pepper
1 cup dry red wine
3 cups canned peeled plum tomatoes
1 10-ounce package frozen peas
Italian-style bread

This particular recipe is grand for the larger squid because of the generous sauce, suitable for a long simmering.

Clean the squid if necessary (page 16) and cut the bodies into squares or rings, the tentacles in half.

Heat the olive oil in a large frying pan, add the garlic, and cook until golden. Discard the garlic and add the squid, parsley, salt, and pepper. When the squid tentacles start to turn pink and lavender (after about 1 minute over medium heat), pour in the wine and cook until the alco-

hol has evaporated and the vapors no longer tingle the nose.

Add the tomatoes, mashing them with a wooden spoon against the side of the pan. Bring to a boil, lower the heat to the slowest simmer, and cook about 30 minutes or until the sauce has reduced a bit and the squid is tender. Add the peas and continue cooking about 5 minutes more or until the peas are cooked. Taste for salt, adding some if necessary. Serve hot with Italian-style bread.

Yield: 6 portions

Sturgeon

This is a big fish whose name immediately brings to mind caviar. While the caviar is truly wonderful, the sturgeon itself is also rather remarkable. Native to the North Temperate zone, it comes in both salt- and fresh-water flavors, is found in Pike Street Market in Seattle and in the Fulton Fish Market in New York, which has sturgeon from Georgia and South Carolina. The flesh is usually cut in steaks, but the smaller sturgeon may be baked whole.

Sturgeon with Herbed Tomato Sauce

storione in umido

1 medium onion

1 celery rib

1 bay leaf

2 to 2½ pounds sturgeon steaks, about 1 inch thick

1½ teaspoons salt, or to taste

Freshly ground white pepper

2 cups dry white wine, approximately

2 garlic cloves

3 tablespoons chopped fresh flat-leaf parsley

4 tablespoons olive oil

4 anchovy fillets

2 tablespoons tomato paste, diluted in ½ cup water, or 3 very ripe or canned peeled plum tomatoes, mashed

This is an elegant way to treat big fish steaks. It is also delicious for other large fish such as swordfish and fresh tuna.

Chop together very finely the onion, the celery, and bay leaf. Put this mixture into a deep platter or a plastic bag large enough to hold the sturgeon. Place the fish steaks over the herbs. Add salt and pepper and wine to cover. Tie the bag shut and turn it over a few times so that the marinade is well mixed and some of the herbs remain on top of the fish. Let stand for at least an hour, turning the steak a few times if using a platter—or turn the bag a few times.

Finely chop together the garlic and parsley. Put the oil in a saucepan large enough to hold the fish, add the garlic-parsley mixture and the anchovy fillets. Cook over low heat for 3 to 4 minutes, stirring slowly, until the anchovies have turned to bits.

Add the fish steaks and cook them on both sides until golden. Add enough of the marinade (strain it if you wish) to cover the fish. Cook for a moment or two. Add the diluted tomato paste or the mashed tomatoes. Continue cooking for about 10 minutes or until the fish flesh parts easily when pierced with a fork. Do not overcook. Taste

for seasoning during cooking and add more salt to taste as necessary.

Remove the fish to a serving platter and keep warm. Boil the sauce down slightly, pour it over the fish, and serve.

Yield: 6 portions

Swordfish

Swordfish is available year-round and from all over the globe. Because it is a big fish, like tuna and shark, weighing anywhere from two hundred to four hundred pounds, it is customary to think only of big steaks to be marinated, then grilled or broiled. But we must admit to being very partial to the golden, half-inch-thin slices of swordfish that are dipped in egg, breaded, and fried to crispness. Many times, a good fish dealer has stopped to cut these thin slices for us and sometimes we do it ourselves, cutting through a thick steak. The thicker swordfish steaks, on the other hand, are perfect cubed and assembled with a variety of vegetables on skewers.

Golden-fried Swordfish in the Style of Milan

pescespada fritto dorato

3 pounds swordfish
¾ cup unbleached all-purpose flour
½ to 1 teaspoon salt
2 large eggs
4 tablespoons olive oil,
    approximately
2 lemons, cut in wedges

Halibut steaks make a good alternate when swordfish is not available.

If you can't have the swordfish cut into ½-inch-thick slices on purchase, cut it yourself, carefully slicing through the steaks.

Mix the flour and salt on a big plate and dredge the slices in it, gently patting the flour on them so they absorb as much as possible.

Beat the eggs well and dip the floured fish in them.

Heat the olive oil in a heavy frying pan over medium heat and fry the fish slices to golden brown on each side. Drain on paper towels. Serve with lemon wedges.

Yield: 6 portions

Sautéed Swordfish

pescespada in padella

*To grill or broil swordfish steaks, follow the recipe for
Grilled or Broiled Salmon Steaks on page 232.*

3 to 4 tablespoons olive oil
2 sprigs fresh rosemary, or 2
    teaspoons dried
1 ¾-pound swordfish steak,
    approximately 1 inch thick
½ medium sweet onion, peeled and
    sliced in thin rounds
1½ teaspoons salt, or to taste
Freshly ground white pepper
Juice of 1½ to 2 lemons

Heat the olive oil over moderate heat in a pan large enough to hold the fish steak. Add half the rosemary. Add the fish. Put the onion rings on either side of the steak. Sprinkle with salt, add a generous amount of pepper and the juice of 1 of the lemons. Cook for 3 minutes, then turn the fish. Add a bit more salt, pepper, remaining rosemary, and as much additional lemon juice as you wish.

Continue cooking about 5 more minutes or until the fish, when cut, has lost its pink color and separates easily when pierced with a fork.

Remove from heat and serve.

Yield: 4 portions

Swordfish Birds

involtini di pescespada

Thin slices of swordfish, rolled around a delicate filling and sautéed, is the extended translation of these "birds." In southern Italy and on the islands off Sicily, there are several different ways for making and serving them. We recommend all three versions with American swordfish.

VERSION 1

1 pound swordfish steak cut very thin

1 tablespoon white-wine vinegar or juice of 1 lemon

1 tablespoon grated Parmesan cheese

1½ tablespoons unflavored breadcrumbs

⅓ cup olive oil, approximately

1 tablespoon minced fresh flat-leaf parsley

½ teaspoon salt

¼ teaspoon freshly ground white pepper

¼ cup dry white wine

Fresh basil leaves for garnish

The swordfish slices should be cut ¼ inch thick. If your market can't comply, this is how you do it yourself:

Buy the swordfish in the usual inch-thick steak. Cut the steak where the natural line divides it into two symmetrical parts. Set one of the pieces on a cutting board; put your hand flat on top of it, and, with a very sharp knife, cut through the steak parallel to your hand to get 3 to 4 slices. Repeat on the other half.

Put your thin slices between two layers of plastic wrap, and with the heel of your hand or a flat implement, gently pound the swordfish to flatten it out to ⅛-inch thickness, approximately. Should the fish tear, overlap the torn parts and pat them together. Trim the newer, thinner slices to about 3½- by 2½-inch rectangles, reserving the trimmings.

Put the trimmings in boiling, salted water to which you have added the white-wine vinegar or lemon juice and cook for 2 minutes. Drain and mince the cooked trims, and place them in a bowl with the cheese, breadcrumbs, 2 tablespoons of the olive oil, parsley, salt, and pepper. Mix to form a cohesive filling.

Spread each rectangle with some of the filling and then roll up and skewer with a round wooden toothpick and set aside.

Brush the bottom of a nonstick sauté pan with the remaining olive oil, and sauté the birds until golden. Squirt with the wine and move the birds around and about as the wine evaporates over medium heat. Place the fresh basil leaves on dinner plates with the birds on top of the basil. Divide the pan sauce equally among the servings.

Yield: 4 portions

To the filler in version 1, add the olives, capers, and 2 tablespoons of tomato sauce.

Proceed with the rolling and cooking as in version 1.

In a separate pan, heat the remaining tomato sauce with the Tabasco and, when both pans are ready, divide the sauce on the four plates, center the birds on the sauce, and serve.

Yield: 4 portions

To the filler in version 1, add the raisins and pine nuts together and mix with the swordfish trimmings, cheese, breadcrumbs, and parsley. Add salt and pepper and the wine to make the filler cohesive. Proceed and cook as in version 1.

Yield: 4 portions

VERSION 2

½ dozen Spanish green olives, pitted and chopped

1 tablespoon salted capers, rinsed and minced

1 cup (approximately) Basic Tomato Sauce (page 43)

2 to 3 dashes of Tabasco

VERSION 3

1 tablespoon golden raisins, soaked and drained

1 tablespoon pine nuts

2 tablespoons dry white wine

Swordfish Skewers

spiedini di pescespada

¼ *cup olive oil*

¼ *cup white wine*

Juice of ½ lemon

¼ *teaspoon dried oregano*

3 tablespoons chopped fresh or freeze-dried chives

1 generous sprig of fresh rosemary, or 1 teaspoon dried

8 large mushrooms, cleaned and stemmed

½ red bell pepper, cored and cut in 1-inch cubes to match the fish pieces

1 pound swordfish, cut in 1-inch cubes

½ green bell pepper, cut in 1-inch cubes

Salt and freshly ground black pepper to taste

In a small bowl, mix together the olive oil, wine, lemon juice, and herbs.

Fold a double sheet of aluminum foil to make a tray to contain four filled skewers. Slide a mushroom onto one of the skewers and follow it with a red pepper piece, a piece of fish, a green pepper, a piece of fish, a red pepper, a piece of fish, a green pepper, and finish with a second mushroom. Repeat the procedure until all four skewers are full.

Turn on the broiler.

Place the skewers in the aluminum foil tray, pour the marinade over the skewers, and rotate them until all pieces are generously covered. Salt and pepper the skewers and place them and their tray about 4 inches below the hot broiler.

Turn the skewers after about 10 minutes and baste them with more of the marinade.

Turn and baste again at the 20-minute mark and remove the skewers from the broiler at 25 minutes, approximately. The timing depends on the broiler and the fish more than on the written word. Serve immediately.

Yield: 2 portions

Baked Swordfish
in Savory Sauce

pescespada in salsa piccante

The use of swordfish, capers, and olives give this dish away as hailing from the Aeolian Islands, where these three ingredients are readily available and are frequently used to enhance the local cookery. Fresh tuna, halibut, or any other large, meaty fish (amberjack, grouper) can substitute for the swordfish with excellent results. Just adjust the cooking time.

Preheat the oven to 375 degrees Fahrenheit.

Chop together the onion, garlic, capers, olives, and anchovies. Mix in the parsley and put all in a saucepan with 3 tablespoons of the olive oil. Sauté over medium heat until the mince is barely limp. Add pepper with a few generous turns of the peppermill, and stir in ¼ cup of the wine and cook until the alcohol is almost all evaporated. Let the mince/sauce cool, and then spoon half of it into an ovenproof casserole. Roughly divide the fish in large pieces (ideally four) and put on top of the mince; spread the remaining mince on top of the fish, dribble the remaining oil over it, and add a few more grinds of the peppermill. Moisten all with the remaining wine and put in the oven for 15 to 20 minutes. Check once in a while and baste with its sauce, which at this stage, with the moisture added to it by the fish, should be reasonably liquid. Once the fish is cooked, scoop it out onto a serving

1 medium onion, approximately 5 to 6 ounces
1 garlic clove
1 tablespoon capers, rinsed and squeezed dry
8 Sicilian brine-packed green olives, pitted
2 anchovy fillets
4 tablespoons minced fresh flat-leaf parsley
4 tablespoons olive oil
Freshly ground black pepper
¾ cup dry white wine
1½ pounds swordfish
1 tablespoon unsalted butter
1 tablespoon unbleached all-purpose flour

platter and keep warm. Pour the sauce in the casserole into a saucepan; cream butter and flour together and stir it into the sauce. Simmer for a minute or so until sauce has a creamy consistency; spoon over the fish and serve.

Yield: 4 portions

Tilefish

Tilefish is a deep-water fish that used to haunt the shores of New England. Now it has been found anywhere from Nova Scotia to Cape Hatteras. It is a beautiful fish that has an aquamarine tint to its back, white to rose or pale lavender tints on its belly, and is dotted with yellow spots. The flesh is firm and some say its sweetness is similar to lobster, others say sea bass.

Baked Stuffed Tilefish

pesce ripiene al forno

Having seen a perfectly stunning tilefish in a New England market, we felt sure it would work as well as sea bass or haddock to stuff. And it did; the species responds nicely to the Italian touch.

Sea bass (loup de mer in France, spigola in Italy) is a good substitute for tilefish, as is striped bass, red snapper, small cod, and haddock.

1 whole 5- to 6-pound tilefish dressed and scaled, head and tail intact
1 teaspoon salt
4 tablespoons olive oil
4 slices day-old Italian-style bread, crustless, cut in ½-inch cubes
4 celery ribs, thinly sliced
½ pound fresh mushrooms, thinly sliced
Freshly ground white pepper
2 tablespoons coarsely chopped fresh flat-leaf parsley plus 5 to 6 additional sprigs
3 tablespoons fresh lemon juice
2 lemons for garnish

Preheat the oven to 425 degrees Fahrenheit.

With a very sharp knife and working from the inside of the fish, cut the flesh away from the spines on both sides of the backbone. Sever the bone just below the head and lift out the bone. This should remove most of the bones, but run your fingers over the flesh to find any that may have been missed. Open up the fish and sprinkle it with ½ teaspoon of the salt.

In a sauté pan, heat the olive oil over medium heat and brown the bread cubes, tossing frequently. Add the sliced celery and sauté 2 minutes. Add the sliced mushrooms and sauté until they give up their juices. Sprinkle with the remaining salt, add the pepper, and remove from heat. Add the chopped parsley, taste for seasonings, and adjust if necessary.

Mound the stuffing on one side of the fish and fold the other half over it. Secure with skewers and sew shut

with a strand of butcher's string (see Note). Remove the skewers.

Place a piece of aluminum foil in the bottom of a baking dish just large enough to hold the fish. Place the reserved parsley sprigs on the foil and center the fish on top.

Bake for about 25 minutes. Lower the heat to 375 degrees and continue baking another 15 minutes (about 8 minutes per pound) as the fish will cook in its own heat a minute or so after coming out of the oven.

With two spatulas, lift the fish onto a heated serving platter. Remove the strand of twine, and drizzle the lemon juice over the fish.

Cut the lemons in thin slices to surround the fish.

Yield: 8 portions

NOTE: When sewing up a fish, regular butcher's twine seems too coarse. Untwist it and use just one strand, or use regular heavy white cotton thread.

Trout

Trout is good for baking, braising, broiling, frying, grilling, and sautéing. You can sauce it or stuff it, and the flavor is delicate, the texture is light, the seasonings varied. While most of the trout you buy is farmed, there are, thank heavens, sport fishermen who still seek out the clean, clear streams where native trout thrive.

The list of trout available in the U.S. is even longer than that of bass but generally speaking you can find farm-raised brook and rainbow trout (one to two pounds) in the market. Anglers can land cutthroat and golden trout in the high mountain regions of western North America as well as lake trout of ten pounds or so.

Trout Poached in Wine

trotelle al vino

Clean the trout but leave the heads and tails intact. Rinse well in fresh water.

Finely chop together the onion, sage, garlic, rosemary, and lemon peel.

Put the olive oil in a big frying or saucepan large enough to hold the fish in one layer. Add the chopped herbs and sauté over medium heat until just barely golden. Remove from heat. Put the fish on top of the herbs. Add the vinegar, wine, and salt. Drain the raisins and add them. Finally, add enough water to cover the fish. Bring to a very gentle boil, cover the pan, and simmer about 5 minutes (more or less, depending on the size of the trout), or until the fish are cooked, but not falling apart.

Lift the fish from its broth and skin it while it is still warm. Then remove the heads and tails and bone the fish. Reassemble the fillets on a serving plate and keep warm.

Strain the poaching liquid into a small saucepan. Put the flour into a cup, and add enough of the cooled, strained broth to make a thin paste. Pour the paste into the remaining broth and bring it to a gentle boil, stirring constantly. Boil until the broth has turned into a creamy sauce. Pour on top of the trout and serve immediately.

3 to 4 pounds trout
1 small onion
4 fresh sage leaves
1 garlic clove
1 tablespoon dried rosemary, or 2
  fresh sprigs
Peel of ½ lemon
¼ cup olive oil
⅓ cup red-wine vinegar
⅓ cup dry white wine
1 teaspoon salt
¼ cup seedless golden raisins,
  plumped in ½ cup warm water
1 tablespoon unbleached all-purpose
  flour

Yield: 4 to 6 portions

Baked Trout with Sage

trotelle alla salvia

6 rainbow trout, about 1 pound
   each
Salt
18 fresh sage leaves
6 tablespoons unsalted butter
Freshly ground black pepper
1½ lemons, cut in wedges

Preheat the oven to 450 degrees Fahrenheit.

Clean the fish but leave on the head and tails. Salt the cavities lightly. Chop six of the sage leaves and sprinkle them inside the fish. Cut 1 tablespoon of the butter into 6 bits and place a bit in each fish.

Butter a baking dish just large enough to hold the fish. Distribute the remaining sage leaves along the bottom of the dish. Put in the fish; sprinkle it with salt and pepper. Melt the remaining butter and dribble it over the fish.

Bake for approximately 6 to 8 minutes, basting once during the baking. Garnish with more fresh sage leaves. Serve with lemon wedges.

Yield: 6 portions

Trout Poached in Tomato Sauce

trotelle all 'Abruzzese

If you wish, the sauce may be made early in the day, but don't cook the trout until just before serving time. Reheating doesn't do a thing for the fish except spoil them with overcooking.

4 small trout, about 1 pound each
2 garlic cloves
6 tablespoons olive oil
3 cups canned peeled plum tomatoes
5 tablespoons chopped fresh flat-leaf parsley
Pinch of oregano
1 teaspoon salt
Freshly ground black pepper to taste

Clean and wash the trout.

Sauté the garlic in the olive oil in a sauté pan large enough to hold the fish comfortably. When the garlic is golden, discard it and let the oil cool a bit.

Put the tomatoes through a sieve or food mill and add to the cooled oil. Cook over medium heat, stirring slowly, about 3 minutes, or until the oil and tomatoes have blended together. Add the parsley to the tomatoes. Add the oregano, salt, and pepper. Boil very gently for 10 to 15 minutes, or until the sauce has become thicker and has reduced a bit.

Add the trout to the sauce and simmer, covered, for 4 minutes. Uncover the pan, continue cooking at a gentle boil for 4 to 5 more minutes, or until the trout is cooked. Serve immediately.

Yield: 4 portions

Tuna

Canned tuna is ubiquitous in Italy, but it's in the southern regions that fresh tuna is king. Off the western tip of Sicily and the attending Aegadian Islands, the fishing of the yellowfin tuna has been carried on for centuries. In a practically unchanged fashion, the schools of tuna are funneled, through miles-long corridors of nets, into a final chamber where they are slaughtered and hauled into the surrounding barges. The huge fish—weighing up to twelve hundred pounds—are then brought to the tuna factory, where they are butchered and processed. The tuna has been compared to the pig: every part of its anatomy has a use and none is wasted. In accordance with this parsimony, the islanders have created a singular tuna gastronomy, which takes advantage of the less as well as the more valuable cuts of the fish.

Fresh Tuna Steaks in Onion Sauce

cipollata di tonno

In a classic dish of the Aegadian Islands, off the western coast of Sicily, fresh tuna steaks are pan-cooked, kept moist, and enriched by a sweet-sour onion sauce.

Cut the onions in thin slivers and sauté them in the olive oil and butter. Add salt and cook, stirring, until the slivers are limp. (This process can be speeded up by adding ¼ cup of warm water and letting it evaporate completely.) Stir in the vinegar and sugar and cook over low heat, stirring, until the vinegar has evaporated. Add the red pepper and the drained raisins, stir, and turn off the heat. The sauce should retain the texture of the slivers and have enough moisture to be spoonable. Cover the pan and keep the sauce warm.

To make the fish, put the olive oil, butter, and bay leaves in a large sauté pan. When warm, not hot, add the tuna steaks. Salt and pepper to taste and sauté 2 to 3 minutes per side, depending on thickness. Do not overcook: tuna tends to dry out. The steaks should be cooked outside but still moist inside. Raise the heat, add the wine, and cover the pan for a second or two, until the wine has stopped steaming.

SAUCE:

2 or 3 all-purpose onions, approximately ¾ pound

3 tablespoons olive oil

1 tablespoon unsalted butter

¼ teaspoon salt

¼ cup red-wine vinegar

1 teaspoon sugar

Dash of ground red pepper or Tabasco

1 tablespoon golden raisins, optional, plumped in warm water

FISH:

3 tablespoons olive oil

2 tablespoons unsalted butter

2 bay leaves

4 fresh tuna steaks, approximately 2 pounds

Salt and freshly ground black pepper to taste

¼ cup dry white wine

Uncover, cook a moment longer, and transfer the steaks with their pan sauce to warm serving plates. Spoon over them the warm onion sauce and serve.

Yield: 4 portions

Fresh Tuna, Sardinian Style

tonno alla sardegnola

2½ *pounds fresh tuna steaks*
½ *cup red-wine vinegar*
1 *medium onion*
1 *carrot*
1 *celery rib with leaves*
½ *teaspoon thyme*
2 *bay leaves*
3 *tablespoons olive oil*
½ *pound fresh mushrooms, sliced*
6 *flat anchovy fillets*
4 *canned peeled plum tomatoes and their juice*
¾ *teaspoon salt*
½ *teaspoon freshly ground black pepper*
2 *beef bouillon cubes, dissolved in ½ cup warm water*
1 *cup dry white wine*
Yolk of 1 large egg
3 *teaspoons lemon juice*

Thick slices of fresh tuna, flavored with herbs and seasoning vegetables, and poached in a sauce with sliced mushrooms, is a very different way of handling big fish. Since not all fish markets have fresh tuna, the same treatment may be used with the more easily found pollock, turbot, or swordfish, with absolutely beautiful results.

If using fresh tuna or swordfish, soak it in enough water to cover, including the wine vinegar. If using fresh turbot or pollock, proceed without the water-and-vinegar treatment.

Mince the flavoring vegetables and herbs together, and sauté until golden in the olive oil. When golden, add the mushrooms. Mash up the anchovy fillets with a fork and add them. Add the tomatoes, mashing them up a bit, and then add the salt, pepper, and the fish. Bring to a boil and then lower the heat and simmer for about 10

minutes. Add the bouillon solution to the sauce with the wine. Cook about 10 minutes or until the fish just flakes and the sauce has condensed a bit. Remove the fish to a warm platter. Beat the egg yolk, add the lemon juice to it, and then add the egg-lemon mixture to the sauce in the pan, stirring constantly. Cook for 1 or 2 minutes, or until smooth and slightly thickened. Pour over the fish and serve.

Yield: 6 portions

Turbot

This is a prize of a fish used a great deal in Europe and found increasingly in markets in America. It is big (about twenty-five pounds), wide, and flat; its size lets one choose very large fillets to be cut up and then grilled, sautéed, poached, or steamed. Its use goes back to Roman days (and before, no doubt) when an especially big pot was invented to steam the whole fish and not spoil it with boiling. Steamed turbot is wonderful with sauces of all sorts. The fish itself comes from the Black Sea and makes its way to the Mediterranean and then up the Atlantic to the Arctic.

The flavor is like the most perfect of Dover sole, which in Europe vies with turbot for a very special top rating in the flatfish category.

Broiled Turbot

rombo alla griglia

1 recipe Parsley Butter (page 31)
6 fresh basil leaves, chopped
2 1-pound turbot fillets
1 lemon
½ teaspoon salt, or to taste
Freshly ground white pepper to taste

Turbot usually shows up in our fish market in fillets large enough to serve two people each. It has a bit more character, shall we say, than sole, and it holds together well during and after broiling. Furthermore, like most fish, it lends itself nicely to herbs. However, if turbot isn't in the market, try this same method with fresh cod, hake, halibut, bluefish, flounder, salmon, or swordfish.

Preheat the broiler for 10 minutes.

Make the parsley butter and add the basil to it.

With a large piece of aluminum foil, shape a shallow boat to hold the two pieces of fish. Butter the foil lightly with about half the herbed butter. Place the fillets in the boat, dotting them with the remaining herbed butter; or if you wish, save just a small piece for when the fish is served.

Place the fish in its boat under the broiler for at least 7 minutes or until the fish is cooked through, the butter melted, and the herbs scattered.

Slide the fish onto a hot serving platter. Dot with any remaining butter.

Cut the lemon in half; sprinkle juice of one half over the fish, and cut the other half in wedges.

Sprinkle the fish with salt and pepper and serve immediately with the lemon wedges.

Yield: 4 portions

Fish Cakes

These little cakes, or fritters, follow in the long Italian tradition of using what is available and using it well. Codfish cakes are the most well known in our family, but perch cakes follow nicely and, for a special treat, we recommend tuna fritters from the Sicilian cuisine. Most recipes match fish with potatoes, or breadcrumbs, but for the real Southern Italian touch, golden raisins and pine nuts are added—a sweet-and-sour contrast that is a snap to make, a delight to eat.

Perch and Potato Cakes

crocchette di pesce

Peel the potatoes, wash and pat dry, and cut in the thinnest of julienne strips (matchsticks).

Beat the egg with ½ teaspoon of salt and then whisk in the flour until a smooth batter is developed. Mix in the julienned potatoes.

Cut the perch fillets lengthwise in about ¾-inch-wide strips and roll each up and pin it with a wooden pick. Dip the rolled fish fillets in the batter, making sure they are evenly coated and that the potatoes stick to the battered fish.

Heat the frying oil to 375 degrees Fahrenheit in a pan large and deep enough to fry 4 or 5 rolls at a time. Proceed

1¼ to 1½ pounds potatoes
1 large egg
Salt
½ cup unbleached all-purpose flour
1¼ to 1½ pounds perch fillets
Vegetable oil for frying
Lemon wedges

with the frying and when each roll is golden and crisp on the outside, remove it to drain on absorbent paper towels.

When all the fish is done, remove the picks, sprinkle with a little salt, if you wish, and serve with lemon wedges.

Yield: 4 portions

Fresh Tuna Cakes

polpette di tonno

10 to 12 fresh mint leaves
4 to 5 fresh basil leaves
4 to 5 fresh sage leaves
2 slices Italian-style bread, about 2
    ounces
½ cup milk
12 ounces fresh tuna
1 tablespoon capers
1 egg
½ teaspoon salt
¼ teaspoon freshly ground black
    pepper
1 tablespoon golden raisins
1 tablespoon pine nuts
1 cup unflavored breadcrumbs

This recipe, from the Aegadian Islands off the western tip of Sicily, is an appetizing way to demonstrate Italy's tasty frugality: trims from fresh tuna steaks are plumped up with local herbs, then breaded and fried.

Mince the herbs together and place in a mixing bowl. Remove the crusts from the bread and shred the slices into the milk to soak. With a sharp knife, chop the tuna fine (not a mince) and add to the herbs. Rinse and squeeze dry the capers, chop them coarsely and add to the tuna. Gently squeeze the bread, leaving it somewhat moist, and add it to the bowl. Add the egg, salt, pepper, raisins, and nuts, and mix everything together. Let rest for 30 minutes. At this point, if the mixture is too moist, add a tablespoon of the breadcrumbs.

Divide the mixture into eight equal parts, turn them

into balls, and roll in the breadcrumbs until well coated. Flatten the *polpette* so that they are about half as thick as they are wide.

Put the oil in a frying pan to a depth of at least half the thickness of the tuna cakes. Heat the oil to about 325 degrees Fahrenheit and fry the cakes until dark golden.

Serve with either one of the tomato sauces or with lemon slices.

Yield: 4 portions

Vegetable oil for frying
Basic Tomato Sauce (page 43) or
*   Tomato and Basil Sauce (page*
*   44), optional*
1 lemon, cut in slices, optional

Fish Fillets

A merica's markets invariably encourage the use of the frozen as well as the fresh fish fillets for sautéeing, baking, filling, deep frying, and poaching. Cod, flounder, hake, salmon, sole, and turbot are usually easy to find. Counter people in the big supermarkets are becoming more and more knowledgeable about sources, refrigeration dates, and cooking times and are usually helpful when customers have questions. In recent years, most fish are shipped from port to store without heads and tails, mainly for economic reasons: heads and tails mean added weight, which means added shipping costs. However, if you want the heads and tails, ask a day or so ahead: get to know your counter people, we were advised.

Fish Fillets, Broiled

filetti di pesce alla griglia

¾ to 1 pound fish fillets
2 tablespoons olive oil,
    approximately
2 garlic cloves
1½ tablespoons unsalted butter
2 tablespoons dry white wine
2 tablespoons lemon juice
4 large leaves fresh basil, cut in
    ribbons
2 slices lemon for garnish

This is a "catch of the day" formula that works well with Dover sole, salmon trout, flounder, and other easily filleted fish.

Rub both sides of the fish fillets generously with olive oil and place on the broiler pan. Peel and cut the garlic cloves into halves and place these pieces on the fillets. Put the pan in the broiler, about 4 inches from the heat.

While the fish cooks (about 3 minutes for the bigger fillets), put 2 teaspoons of the butter in a small sauté pan over medium heat. When the butter is melted, turn up the heat and add the wine and the lemon juice. When reduced slightly, add the rest of the butter, keeping the pan in motion until the butter is melted.

Remove the fish from the broiler. Discard the garlic, and place the fish on two warmed plates. Divide the basil ribbons and place on the fish. Cover with the lemon sauce. Garnish with the lemon slices and serve.

Yield: 2 portions

Layered Fish Fillets in Pastry

sfogliata di filetti di pesce

This particular recipe, in contrast to most of the others, is a real production, but it makes a beautiful dish in answer to its demands. It is suggested that the infrequent cook with book in hand might be well advised to use fresh or frozen puff pastry a few times as well as to try the fish mousse separately at another time before he or she gets down to the actual Layered Fish Fillets in Pastry.

2 sheets frozen puff pastry or 1 recipe Rough Puff Pastry (page 304)
1 recipe Basic Fish Mousse for layering (page 297)
2 flounder, salmon, sea bass, or sole fillets, fresh, approximately 1½ pounds total
1 egg, separated, white and yolk beaten lightly

Thaw the pastry as necessary, or make it. Make the fish mousse, but do not put it in a mold. Trim the fillets so that they are even on the edges and about the same length and width.

Roll the pastry out into two even rectangles about 2 to 3 inches longer than the fish and at least 2 inches wider.

Take one of the rectangles of pastry and put it on a floured cookie sheet. Center a fillet on it.

Spread the fillet with the mousse. Moisten the border of the dough with some of the egg white. Place the second fillet on top of the mousse and cover it with the remaining dough. Press the two borders together. With a pastry cutter, cut the two layers of dough in the shape of a fish, enclosing all of the fillets.

Place the pastry fish in the refrigerator for 15 minutes.

Preheat the oven to 425 degrees Fahrenheit.

With the round tube of a pastry bag, press scalelike patterns on the body of the fish. Cut a round for the eye, a line for the gills, and cut out a fin if you wish. With a sharp knife cut defining lines in the tail and fin.

Brush the whole creation with beaten egg yolk and place in the preheated oven for 15 minutes. Reduce the heat to 350 degrees.

The exact total timing of this depends on the exact thickness of the fish, filling, and pastry at its thickest. Figure 10 minutes per inch. For example, if your fillets are thin, your filling neither too high nor too low, you might have a 3½-inch measure, in which case, bake a total of 35 minutes. If the pastry gets too dark toward the end of cooking, cover with aluminum foil.

Yield: 4 to 6 portions

Fish Steaks

We doubt there are many people who do not rely on fish steaks when the season is right for outdoor grilling or when the time to cook has been squeezed between two other important happenings. Steaks work well on top of the stove or in the broiler, as well as on the outdoor grill. Steaks of one type of fish or another are generally in the market all year long, and the following recipes may be used with cod, halibut, pollock, swordfish, tuna, or turbot.

Fish Steaks in Wine Sauce

pesce 'mbriaco

'Mbriaco is dialect for someone who has imbibed too much wine. These fish steaks use less than a glass of wine, which in cooking is transformed into a delicate sauce. Fish most adapted to this treatment are halibut, swordfish, or tuna, cut in steaks.

1 medium onion
6 sprigs of fresh flat-leaf parsley
1 garlic clove
5 tablespoons olive oil
2 pounds fish steaks, cut no more than 1 inch thick
¾ cup dry red wine
1 tablespoon unbleached all-purpose flour dissolved in ¼ cup cold water
½ teaspoon salt, or to taste
Italian-style bread

Chop together finely the onion, parsley, and garlic. Sauté them in olive oil in a pan large enough to hold the fish steaks in one layer, if possible. When the chopped seasonings are limp and the parsley bits have darkened, add the fish steaks and sauté them a few minutes on each side.

Add the wine, raise the heat, and, as the wine evaporates, add the flour and water. Add the salt, and push the steaks back and forth to mix the sauce evenly. Cover the pan, lower the heat, and cook 10 minutes, or until the fish flesh breaks rather easily when pierced with a fork. Serve immediately with hot Italian-style bread.

Yield: 4 to 6 portions

Fish Steaks, Grilled or Broiled

trance di pesce alla griglia

⅓ cup olive oil

2 lemons

3 pounds thick fish steaks, such as
    halibut, cod, pollock, or turbot

1 garlic clove

1 6-inch sprig of fresh rosemary, or
    2 teaspoons dried

2 tablespoons chopped fresh flat-leaf
    parsley

1 teaspoon salt

⅛ teaspoon freshly ground white
    pepper, or to taste

While the grill is getting started or the broiler heating, mix the oil and juice of one of the lemons together. Brush both sides of the fish pieces with the mixture and place them on a platter.

Mince the garlic, rosemary, and parsley together. Add the salt and pepper to the mince and spread half of the paste on the top side of the fish steaks.

Place the fish, herbed side down, on the now ready grill or broiler. Sprinkle a bit of the remaining mince of herbs on the steaks. When the fish is well browned on the first side, turn it over. Sprinkle with the last of the herb mince and brush with the oil-lemon mixture. Cook until the second side is thoroughly browned, about 3 minutes.

Cut the second lemon in wedges and serve with the grilled fish.

Yield: 6 portions

Whole Fish

Fresh whole fish, ranging in weight from 2 to 5 pounds, work well over the barbecue. One of the contributing factors to grilling successfully is the fish-shaped grilling basket that allows you to turn the fish without damaging its shape or having to pry it from the grill itself. Whole fish seem to have a better flavor than filleted fish, thanks to the presence of the bones while cooking. Grilling is a particularly nice way to treat a gift of fish from a sports fisherman, as there is practically no preparation before putting the fish to the heat.

Grilled Whole Fish with Green Sauce

pesce alla griglia con salsa verde

You can use this recipe with ocean perch, porgy, rock-fish, red snapper, sea bass, trout, or any medium-size fish that grills well.

4 pounds whole fish
1 batch Green Sauce (page 38)
¼ cup olive oil, approximately

Start the grill or preheat the broiler (see Note, page 286).

Clean the fish but leave on the heads and tails.

Make the sauce and spread about a teaspoon of it in each fish cavity (enough to moisten the insides).

When the grill or broiler is ready, brush both sides of the fish with olive oil and put them in a grilling basket for the grill or on aluminum foil on the broiling pan. Turn

when the first sides are well browned and crackled with heat and grill or broil the second sides. Brush with olive oil as the fish cooks.

Serve with the remaining sauce.

Yield: 4 to 6 portions

NOTE: If using the broiler, be sure the fish sits on a rack so that the juices and oil aren't allowed to accumulate around the fish during the broiling, so that the fish doesn't become semi-poached instead of broiled.

Whole Fish Baked in White Sauce

pesce alla romagnola

1 2½ to 3½ pound whole fish
Salt to taste
4 tablespoons unsalted butter
3 tablespoons olive oil
1 cup dry white wine
½ recipe White Sauce (page 49)
½ cup unflavored breadcrumbs,
    approximately
Juice of ½ lemon

When you find a fish that weighs 2½ to 3½ pounds, it may be the perfect candidate for Fish Baked in White Sauce. This is from the Emilia-Romagna region of Italy, known for its fine treatment of all foods. The fish is cooked whole, with the bones in, and is thusly just a notch higher in flavor than fish fillets.

The secret in the following recipe is to barely cook the fish on top of the stove and then remove not only the skin but also the backbone. The latter is done by opening up the fish when it comes out of the pan, and, with the tip of a knife, lifting the backbone from its moor-

*ings at the top of the body and gently pulling it back
until you reach the tail end of the fish. Once the bone
has been removed, recompose the fish and proceed with
the cooking. Grouper, red snapper, black sea bass, and
white sea bass of the Pacific are four possible choices.*

Scale and clean the fish. Cut off the head and tail. Sprinkle
inside and outside lightly with salt.

Melt 3 tablespoons of the butter in a pan large enough
to hold the fish. Add the olive oil. Sauté the fish briefly on
both sides. Add the wine, lower the heat to simmer, cover
the pan, and cook for 10 minutes or until the fish is barely
done.

Lift the fish out of the pan and remove the skin and
backbone while it is still warm. Let the fish cool.

Preheat the oven to 375 degrees Fahrenheit.

While the fish is cooling, prepare the white sauce,
cooking it at least 4 minutes or until it is nice and thick
and no longer tastes of uncooked flour.

Lightly butter an ovenproof casserole, sprinkle with
about 2 tablespoons of the breadcrumbs, and put half the
white sauce in the bottom of the casserole. Reassemble
the fish on top of the white sauce.

Add the lemon juice to the pan liquid, stir, and boil it
down a bit. Pour a few spoonfuls over the fish just to
moisten it. Cover with the last of the white sauce. Sprinkle
with remaining breadcrumbs. Bake the casserole for
about 5 minutes, or until the butter has melted and the
breadcrumbs have toasted.

Yield: 4 portions

IX

Special Luncheons and Snacks

PASTRY DOUGHS

Rough Puff Pastry

Short Crust Pastry

Puff Pastry

Cream Puff Pastry

Quiche Dough

Lobster and Spinach Quiche

Smoked Salmon Quiche

Bay Scallop Quiche

Pizza Dough

Baby Clam Pizza

Shrimp Pizza

Tuna Pizza

Going back and forth from Italy to America, we have found preparing a special luncheon can be just perfect for sharing a meal with old friends with busy schedules. We also use the recipes in this chapter to greet a grandchild (pizza is always popular) and for Sunday-night suppers. Naturally, none of the dishes are to be nailed down to a predetermined occasion. Just like all food, they are part of a communications system that should work for any time, any day.

Aspic

Aspic is a shimmering, gleaming, wonderful-tasting (or tasteless, depending on the recipe) jell that may be used to cover, preserve, and enhance a chilled, pre-formed dish. The Italian, French, English, and American cuisines use aspic in many ways (from antipasto to dessert), and it is also made in many ways. It is a jelly that may be developed with a good fish or meat stock with bones and flavorings, or it may be made with artificial gelatin either sweet or plain. In its earliest days, it was made with an herb called spikenard or espic, which was put in the pot with the bones and other flavorings. The main purpose of aspic is to enhance and hold a decorative cold dish until your tablemates arrive. Aspic may be colored to please the eye and the ingredients of the dish; it may be flavored to accent the dish; it may also be layered with edible artistic and seasonal leaves and colorful cuts of vegetables. It is fun to experiment with and arrive at delightful innovations. Try it and play a bit. We think you'll like all the many aspects of aspic.

The following recipe, using a combination of chicken broth and beef broth, produces a very clear aspic.

Aspic

2 cups clarified chicken broth,
    defatted*
1 cup clarified beef broth, defatted
3 envelopes unflavored gelatin

Chill broths and skim off any solidified fat.

Dissolve the gelatin in ½ cup of mixed broths. Add the remaining broth and heat until all the gelatin crystals have dissolved. Pour the broth into a bowl, swirl it around, and set over ice in a much larger bowl or place it in the refrigerator until it cools to a syrupy stage, just beginning to thicken. It is now ready to build the aspic further: pour about half a cup into a chilled bowl, whirl and chill to make one layer of aspic. Repeat 2 or 3 times, swirling and chilling after each addition before adding another and then going on to the decorations you wish to use.

Aspic also may be poured in a single layer ⅛ to ¼ inch deep on a cookie sheet and then chilled and cut into a whole variety of shapes, using aspic cutters.

Yield: enough to line an 8- to 10-cup bowl, or a large fish mold

* NOTE: You may use commercially prepared broths provided they have been skimmed of any fat, or use your own broth, carefully clarified, of course. If you wish, the aspic may be made from one type of broth only.

Aspic with Sole, Crabmeat, and Shrimp

Aspic al sogliola, granchio e gamberi

Sauté the sole fillets in the butter, about 3 to 5 minutes, adding salt and pepper as they cook.

Drain the crabmeat and go over it to eliminate any possible bits of shell. Put the crabmeat, the sole, and the shrimp in the bowl of a food processor. Process on/off until a paste has been formed.

Add the mayonnaise, ketchup, and mustard, and process again on/off to mix.

Soften the gelatin in the cup of cold water in a small saucepan. Add 2 tablespoons of the cream and heat over low heat until the gelatin has dissolved completely. Add it to the fish mix.

Whip the remaining cream and fold it into the fish mix. Taste for salt and pepper and adjust as necessary. Place the mousse in a suitable mold and put it in the refrigerator for at least 6 hours.

When it is time to serve, put the mold in hot water for about 3 minutes, run a knife point around the edge of the mold to loosen well, and then place a serving plate over the mold and turn it all upside down, thus unmolding the aspic onto the serving plate. Decorate with curly endive (chicory), sprigs of dill, and olives as you wish.

2 to 4 sole fillets, depending on the size

1 tablespoon unsalted butter

Salt and freshly ground black pepper to taste

6 ounces canned crabmeat

5 ounces small shrimp, cooked and peeled, or 1 6-ounce can whole baby shrimp, drained

3 teaspoons mayonnaise

1 tablespoon tomato ketchup

½ teaspoon Dijon-style mustard

3 envelopes unflavored gelatin

1 cup cold water

1 cup heavy cream

1 heart curly endive

Sprigs of fresh dill and olives for garnish

Yield: 4 to 6 portions

Lobster in Aspic Cups

astice in gelatina

6 to 8 ounces frozen or canned
    lobster meat, or 1 1¼-pound fresh
    lobster, poached (see page 219)
    and shelled
1½ envelopes unflavored gelatin
2 cups clarified broth (chicken or
    chicken and beef)
1 red bell pepper, cored, cut in small
    rounds or thin julienne strips
Leaves of 2 or 3 sprigs of fresh flat-
    leaf parsley, washed and dried,
    plus 1 tablespoon minced
2 hard-boiled eggs
3 tablespoons mayonnaise
Salt and freshly ground white
    pepper to taste

When it comes to celebrations, it is frequently a great deal more fun and much easier to serve a group by offering a splendid buffet arrangement. The aspic of lobster, in individual custard cups, is made for such a happening. We have found the use of frozen, canned lobster from Canada is not only very easy but has a delicious result.

Thaw the lobster by placing it on the lowest shelf of the refrigerator overnight. Or, if poaching a fresh lobster, you may do so at this point.

Cut the tail(s) in 8 slices as near perfect as possible. With a food processor, purée the remaining pieces of lobster.

Chill 8 custard cups thoroughly.

Moisten the gelatin in 2 to 3 tablespoons of cold broth. Add the partially softened gelatin to the remaining broth and heat until completely dissolved. Place the broth in a bowl over ice in a larger bowl or in the refrigerator, and chill until it becomes slightly syrupy. Pour about half an inch of thickening broth into each custard cup. Dip the red pepper pieces and the parsley leaves in the syrupy broth and place some of each in a pleasant design in the 8 custard cups. Add a slice of tail meat to each cup. Add the cooked egg yolks to the lobster meat with the mayonnaise and process on/off until just mixed. Discard the egg

whites, or use for another recipe. Add the minced parsley and process on/off. Add the salt and pepper.

Using a pastry bag with a plain tip or 2 teaspoons, divide the lobster mixture into the custard cups. Pour the last of the broth around the edges of the lobster, to fill the cup completely. Chill in the refrigerator for at least 3 hours. To turn the cups out onto a serving platter, dip in hot water for about 2 minutes and turn them over onto the platter. Garnish as you please.

Yield: 8 portions

Cold Lobster Mold

sformato d'astice

Prepare a 1½-quart mold or soufflé dish: take a piece of foil just longer than the circumference of the dish. Fold it double so that by putting it around the rim it can extend the dish upward by at least 2 inches. Tie securely in place and staple at the top so that it won't buckle.

Remove the meat from the lobster shells, keeping the tails intact. Cut off the top and bottom of the tails so that you may cut the remaining meat into 6 to 8 nice-looking slices. Put the rest of the lobster meat (about 2 cups) in a food processor and process or blend in a blender until well minced.

Make a white sauce as follows: melt the butter in a 1-quart saucepan, whisk in the flour, and, after the combination has cooked a minute over medium heat, pour in 2 cups of the fish stock in a steady stream. Whisk continu-

2 1¼-pound lobsters, poached (page 219) and cooled
4 tablespoons unsalted butter
4 tablespoons unbleached all-purpose flour
5 cups clarified Basic Fish Stock II (page 168)
Salt to taste
Freshly ground white pepper to taste
1 teaspoon lemon juice
Dash of ground red pepper
¼ cup brandy
3 packets unflavored gelatin
½ cup cold water
1 cup heavy cream, whipped
Flat-leaf parsley for decoration

ously and cook for about 4 more minutes or until thick, smooth, and the flour has cooked. Add salt and pepper if needed. Let cool.

To the finely minced lobster meat, add 1 cup of white sauce, the lemon juice, ground red pepper, and brandy.

Moisten the gelatin in the water and then dissolve it in the remaining hot fish stock. Chill the clarified fish stock to which gelatin has been added. When the cooling aspic is beginning to jell, fold all but ½ cup of it into the lobster mixture.

Fold in the whipped cream and turn the entire mixture into the mold. Chill until solid.

Decorate the top of the mold with the tail slices and perhaps a bit of flat-leaf parsley if you wish. Coat with the last of the jelling fish stock and return to the refrigerator. Chill. Serve cold.

Yield: 8 portions

Basic Fish Mousse

spuma di pesce

If this is your first go-round with mousse, try this basic one that requires no fancy fish and uses easy seasonings. You should be home free. Do not, however, use previously frozen fish for mousse as the results are not very satisfactory.

The amount of egg white in a mousse is governed by the texture of the fish used, while the processing of the cream should last no longer than its incorporation. Too many egg whites make a rubbery mousse and too much mixing of the cream just whips the cream and does the mousse no benefit.

Fish mousse can be served with a sauce such as Green Sauce (page 38) or a light tomato sauce (Tomato and Basil Sauce, page 44) or a rather pourable Pesto (page 46): after turning out the mousse, make a nice puddle of sauce by pouring a reasonable amount around the base.

¾ *pound fresh halibut*
⅛ *teaspoon freshly ground white pepper*
Pinch of ground red pepper
⅛ *teaspoon freshly grated nutmeg*
1 large egg
¼ *to* ½ *teaspoon salt to taste*
1 cup heavy cream
1 egg white, at room temperature, optional
Sprigs of fresh dill or parsley, tomato roses (page 58), or lemon slices for decoration

To obtain the best results, make sure all your utensils and ingredients are well chilled.

Remove any skin and center bone from the fish. Cut the fish in pieces that can be easily worked in the food processor, about an inch square.

Purée the fish with the peppers and nutmeg in the food processor.

Add the egg and process on/off until the mixture begins to form a ball at the end of the blade.

Sprinkle in ¼ teaspoon salt and, with the motor running, add the cream in a slow, steady stream. Process about 30 seconds or until smooth.

Cook a teaspoonful of the mousse in simmering water for 2 to 3 minutes. Taste for seasonings and test the texture. Adjust the seasonings if necessary. If the mousse is too soft, beat the egg white (not chilled) until the soft-peak stage is reached and gently and quickly fold it into the mousse with a rubber spatula.

Preheat the oven to 350 degrees Fahrenheit. Butter a fish mold and place it and the mousse mixture in the refrigerator while the oven heats.

Gently scoop the mousse into the chilled, buttered mold. Place a piece of buttered parchment paper over the mousse and put the mold in a baking pan with enough water to come halfway up the sides of the mold.

Bake approximately 30 minutes or until the mousse is firm and set. Let stand about 15 minutes before unmolding. Remove the parchment paper and place a plate over the top of the mold. Invert the mold and plate in one quick turn. Decorate plate and/or mousse to please with sprigs of fresh dill, parsley, tomato roses, and/or lemon slices. Serve hot or warm.

Yield: 4 portions

Tuna Mousse

spuma di tonno

Drain the tuna thoroughly, and put it in the bowl of a food processor. Process on/off until well broken up, and then process until smooth.

Soften the gelatin in the cold water, then heat over a low flame until completely dissolved. Pour into the tuna, and process until absorbed.

Make a white sauce as follows: melt the butter over low heat, stir in the flour, and, finally, add the milk in a steady stream, stirring continually over the heat. Break the bouillon cube into bits, and add to the pan. Add the basil, salt, and pepper. Cook, stirring, over low heat for 4 minutes. Taste for seasonings and correct if necessary.

Add the white sauce to the tuna mixture, and process briefly until incorporated.

Grate the lemon and add the zest to the tuna; squeeze and pour the juice of the lemon through a sieve into the tuna mixture. Process on/off.

Pour the mixture into a fish mold (about 1½ quarts) and place it in the refrigerator for at least 2 hours or until very firm. It may stay in the refrigerator up to 24 hours.

To unmold the mousse, place the form in warm water for about 3 minutes and then turn it out on a serving platter. Make fish "scales" with the thinly sliced cucumber. Form tail, mouth, and eyes with bits of sweet red pepper. Serve with melba toast, toasted rounds of Italian-style bread, or crackers of your choice.

Yield: 10 portions or more

3 6½-ounce cans light tuna, packed in olive oil
2 envelopes unflavored gelatin
⅓ cup cold water
2½ tablespoons unsalted butter
3 tablespoons unbleached all-purpose flour
1 cup hot milk
1 chicken bouillon cube
1 teaspoon fresh basil, chopped, or 1½ teaspoon dried
¼ teaspoon salt
Freshly ground white pepper to taste
1 lemon
1 small cucumber, skin on, sliced very thin
½ red bell pepper
Melba toast, toasted Italian-style bread, or crackers

Tricolored Pike Mousse

luccio arlecchino

10 to 12 ounces pike (or trout) fillet
1 cup yogurt
2 egg whites
½ teaspoon salt
White pepper
1 rounded teaspoon tomato paste
7 ounces spinach leaves, cooked,
*   processed to a paste*
Butter for greasing the mold
4 to 6 ounces thinnest possible stalks
*   of asparagus, optional*
2 cups Tomato and Basil Sauce
*   (page 44)*
10 fresh basil leaves

Cut the pike (or trout) fillets in pieces and place in a blender or food processor. Blend or process until puréed.

Put the fish in a bowl and add the yogurt. Beat the egg whites to high, soft peaks, adding a pinch of the salt as you beat. Fold the egg whites into the fish paste as carefully as you can. Season with salt and white pepper.

Divide the fish/egg-white mixture into three parts. Let one part remain its natural color. Add the tomato paste to the second part and mix well. The third part gets the spinach, and then mix it well also.

Butter a rectangular mold (a very small bread pan is good for this) and make a layer of green mousse first, leveling it carefully. Follow with a layer of white mousse and finally the red mousse. The aim, of course, is to make a flag, each band of color equal to the other.

Heat the oven to 350 degrees Fahrenheit.

Put the mold in a baking pan large enough to hold it, and fill the pan with enough hot water to come halfway up the sides of the mold. Bake in the oven for 30 minutes. Let cool.

Break the ends of the asparagus where they snap easily, and then slice off the rough ends. Cook lying flat in boiling salted water (a sauté pan is good for this) for about 3 minutes or until just tender. Remove from the water and drain on paper towels.

Put the tomato sauce into the blender and blend to

make sure it is nicely puréed. Place over heat with the basil leaves and cook to reduce it slightly.

To serve the mousse, make a pool of tomato sauce on each plate. Turn the mousse out onto a serving plate, cut it in even slices, and place one slice on each pool of sauce. Decorate with the asparagus and serve.

Yield: 6 portions

Crêpes, Italian Style

crespelle

These versatile wrappings are served rolled or layered for a luncheon or as a first course in an elaborate meal. You can fill them with any fish and some sauce or with caviar and sour cream.

⅔ cup unbleached all-purpose flour
1 cup milk
¼ teaspoon salt
4 eggs
Vegetable oil for frying

Make a batter of the flour, milk, salt, and eggs, and mix well with a wire whisk until smooth. Lightly oil a 6- to 7-inch omelet or frying pan and bring it to medium heat. Spoon in enough batter to just cover the bottom of the pan, and cook as you would a pancake.

Add oil as needed to keep the pan lightly coated as you cook the rest of the batter into crêpes. This recipe should make about 24 little crêpes, about 4 per portion. Fill or layer as you wish.

Yield: 6 portions

Caviar Crêpes

crespelle al caviale

*1 recipe for Crêpes, Italian style
 (page 301)
1 cup sour cream, approximately
6 ounces salmon caviar or other
 caviar of your choice*

Spread each crêpe with a bit of sour cream and sprinkle on a few glistening roe. Crêpes may then be rolled individually or stacked, 2 to 3 per person, depending on the rest of the meal and the occasion.

Yield: 6 to 8 portions

Salmon Soufflé

soufflé di salmone

When a little fancy cooking began to creep into our everyday routine, soufflé was one of the first to attract our attention. Its anticipated high-rise and toasty top with its delicate, soft, almost spongelike inside was something extra special. We started with plain cheese soufflé and worked up to a few more complicated, depending on the enthusiasm of the diners. We readily admit it is not the sort of thing you whip up for a big family, but every now and then it is more than worth the minor production to achieve the palate pleasure of soufflé. As with so many other cooking delights, once you get the "hang" of it, full speed ahead.

Preheat the oven to 375 degrees Fahrenheit.

Melt the butter in a 1-quart saucepan over low heat, sprinkle in the flour, whisk and cook for 2 minutes over medium heat. Put the basil in the milk and add it all at once to the flour-butter mixture. Continue whisking and cooking for 3 to 4 minutes until the mixture is smooth and thick. Remove from heat and let cool about 5 minutes. Stir in pepper (two or three twists of the mill). Add the egg yolks one at a time and stir rapidly until each has been absorbed. Add the parsley.

Mince the salmon in a food processor or by hand with a sharp knife. Stir the salmon into the flour-egg mixture.

Beat the egg whites until they hold firm peaks, and fold them gently into the salmon mixture.

Place the mixture in a 1-quart buttered casserole or 2 14-ounce Pyrex ovenware dishes. With a knife, make a track all around the top of the soufflé about an inch in from the edge. Bake 35 minutes (if using the quart dish) or about 25 minutes if using the smaller dishes. When a soufflé is done, a cake tester or wooden pick comes out clean when inserted.

Yield: 2 portions

2 tablespoons unsalted butter plus additional for greasing the soufflé dish
2 tablespoons unbleached all-purpose flour
4 to 6 fresh basil leaves, chopped
¾ cup milk
Freshly ground white pepper
2 medium eggs, separated
1 teaspoon minced fresh flat-leaf parsley
3 ounces fresh salmon, poached in lightly salted water to cover, drained, skinned, and boned

Pastry Doughs

No matter how devoted one can be to the quick-and-easy, the defrost-and-serve, or the so-simple-it-is-plain, there comes a day when a bit of extravagant pastry to enhance a dish is just the ticket.

Like practitioners of many other cuisines, Italians use puff pastry for appetizers as well as

dessert. A variety of small seafood in cream sauce, ensconced in crisp patty shells, can change the whole tone of a meal.

For starters, you may wish to practice with the Rough Puff Pastry, which makes a smaller amount of dough, uses less butter, and contains no alcohol—while regular puff pastry takes longer to roll out, is a bigger recipe and, in the long run, is just a bit flakier.

Rough Puff Pastry

pasta sfogliata semplice

1 cup unbleached all-purpose flour
¼ teaspoon salt
8 tablespoons unsalted butter, cut
    in ¼-inch pieces
3 to 4 tablespoons ice water

This recipe makes half a pound of pastry dough, enough for 4 to 6 patty shells or tartlets.

Place the flour, salt, and butter in the bowl of a food processor with the steel blade. Process on/off until the mixture looks like coarse crumbs. Do not overprocess. Slowly add 3 tablespoons of ice water as you process again. Add about ½ the last tablespoon of water, process on/off twice. Open up the bowl, press a bit of the dough together with your fingers and, if it sticks nicely, do not add any more water. Turn the dough out onto a floured surface and form it into a thick oval. Flatten the oval a bit and push it into a fat rectangle, then wrap in plastic wrap and chill for at least an hour.

To roll out, place the dough on a floured surface, bang it with your rolling pin to flatten it more, and then roll it out into a rectangle about 12 inches by 6 inches. Fold the two ends to meet in the middle of the pastry.

Fold again to have the fold edges meet. With the rolling pin at right angles to the fold marks, roll the dough out to a rectangle again.

Fold a second time, wrap in plastic wrap, and place in the freezer for 15 or 20 minutes.

Roll the dough out at least two times if not three before using, placing it in the freezer between rollings. Keep in the refrigerator until you wish to use it.

This is the dough you will find helpful when making puff pastries for Seafood in Puff Pastry (page 77). The puff pastry cutter in the shape of a fish is useful for this recipe. You may also enjoy using the Rough Puff Pastry as a free-form shell.

Yield: ½ pound pastry, enough for 4 patty shells

Short Crust Pastry

pasta sfogliata 2

Using the preceding recipe but only half the amount of butter, you will achieve a standby for tarts and quiche that will yield 8 3-inch tart crusts or 1 large tart crust.

Puff Pastry

pasta sfogliata

4 cups chilled unbleached all-
    purpose flour
4 sticks chilled unsalted butter
1 teaspoon salt
⅞ cup ice water
2 tablespoons aquavit, *vodka, or*
    strained lemon juice

This can be made any day you want, and it is wonder-
ful to freeze in pieces of ½ pound each, which is what
you would need to turn out four puff pastry fish forms
or four classic puff pastries for shellfish in a sauce, or
one tart crust.

Following tradition, in Italy one would add 2 ta-
blespoons of acquavite or vodka to the dough. In En-
gland and America, there are many who use lemon
juice.

Before you start, chill materials involved: measur-
ing cups, rolling pin (one lady we know has a glass one
that holds ice cubes in its cylinder), even the flour in its
container. During the first rolling, if any butter breaks
through, do not despair: repair the hole with a bit of
dough, dampened and placed over the escaping butter.

This recipe makes about 3 pounds of dough, which
we recommend for those who have the freezer space, the
inclination, and the happy reason to keep their own
dough on hand.

If you freeze puff pastry, label packages by weight
and date, and after thawing (on the least cold shelf of
the refrigerator), plan to give the dough two turns
before cutting it.

Fit your food-processor bowl with its steel cutting blade
and put in 3½ cups of the chilled flour. Add 4½ tablespoons of the chilled butter cut into ¼-inch cubes. Add

salt and process until the butter is thoroughly cut into the flour. Add the *aquavit*, vodka, or lemon juice and continue to process until a ball of soft dough forms at one end of the blade. Remove the dough and knead it briefly on a floured, chilled pastry board until it is smooth. Wrap in plastic or wax paper and chill for half an hour. This is your flour mixture.

Cut the remaining butter into ¼-inch cubes and place them in the food processor bowl. Sprinkle in the last of the flour. Process on/off until the mixture is cut into tiny beads and will stick together readily when pinched.

Turn the mixture out onto plastic wrap on the pastry board and work it with your fingers until it is pressed into a 3- by 8- by 1½-inch rectangle. Wrap in plastic wrap and chill 20 minutes. This is your butter mixture.

When both mixtures are chilled and of the same firmness, roll out the flour mixture to approximately 10 × 18 inches. Place the butter mixture in the center of the upper two-thirds of flour mixture. Bring up the lower (uncovered) third of the flour mixture and cover half the butter mixture. Fold the upper third of the flour mixture and its butter mixture down over the already folded lower third. Seal the two ends with a good pinch. You now have a packet of dough with three layers of flour mixture separated by two layers of butter mixture.

Turn the packet with the seam side facing right, with a narrow end toward you. Bang the dough lightly with a rolling pin up and down the length of the packet. Then roll the dough away from you until it is about ½-inch thick and approximately its original length and width.

Fold the ends to meet in the middle and then fold the

new ends to meet each other. You now have a book of four layers of dough. Wrap and chill for half an hour.

Remove the dough from the refrigerator and again put it on a chilled, lightly floured pastry board. Roll out to 10 by 18 inches, fold the ends to the middle, and fold again. Roll again, fold again, and chill half an hour.

Roll out as above, fold and roll, and fold again. Chill at least 2 hours. Overnight is even better.

Roll the dough out twice more before cutting and then chill after cutting and before baking for best results.

Yield: about 3 pounds, which can be frozen in ½-pound pieces for 1 tart crust, or 4 to 6 tartlets per piece

Cream Puff Pastry

bigné

1¼ cups water
5 tablespoons unsalted butter
¾ cup unbleached all-purpose flour
4 eggs
½ teaspoon grated lemon rind
1½ tablespoons cognac
Vegetable oil for frying

Bring the water and butter to a boil in a saucepan over high heat. When the water boils, take the pan off the heat, and add the flour all at once. Stir immediately with a wooden spoon, putting the pan back over the heat. The mixture turns into a paste right away and must be stirred continuously until it forms a ball and no longer clings to the sides of the pan. Keep on stirring a little more until the paste sounds as if it were frying. Remove from the heat, and cool.

Add the eggs, one at a time, stirring each in com-

pletely before adding the next. Stir in the lemon rind and cognac. Keep on stirring until the dough is perfectly amalgamated, smooth, and rather like cookie dough. Cover and let stand 15 minutes in a cool place.

Heat vegetable oil to 300 degrees Fahrenheit, drop in the dough a tablespoon at a time, and fry 4 or 5 at a time. As the dough fries and one side becomes browned, the puffs will turn themselves over, and the temperature of the oil will rise to 350 or so degrees. Since puffs must start cooking at a lower-than-frying heat, turn down the heat after each group has cooked, so that the second and the third installments start, like the first, at about 300 degrees and finish cooking at 350 degrees. Starting with oil that is too hot will overcook the puffs on the outside and leave the inside undercooked.

Yield: 16 bigné *or 8 portions*

Quiche Dough

pasta per flan

Quiche *is a grand word of French origin that means an open-faced tart. It is in use all over the English-speaking world. Italians call it* flan, *as do diners in the British Isles but there seems to be an inclination to expand the use of the word* quiche *internationally. In the beginning quiche was made with bread dough, but*

1½ *cups unbleached all-purpose flour, plus additional for dusting the counter*
8 *tablespoons unsalted butter, chilled, plus additional for greasing the tart pan*
Pinch of salt
½ *cup ice water*

nowadays it is usually made with a butter-and-flour dough that is called pâte brisée *in French. The fillings have always been made with a custardlike base and a variety of morsels such as mushrooms, shrimp, and ham. The titles of the recipes usually include the main ingredient.*

This is a basic dough, sturdier than Rough Puff Pastry, and enough for a 10- to 11-inch tart pan.

Place the flour in the bowl of a food processor with its steel knife. Cut the butter into ½-inch bits and add it with the salt to the flour. Turn the processor on/off briefly until the butter is broken down a bit and yet you can still see little pieces of it, a matter of seconds. Pour in the ice water slowly and process until just barely mixed, again a matter of seconds. The dough is now practically a ball at one end of the steel knife. With floured hands, remove the dough and place on a sheet of plastic wrap. Form it into a thick disk, fold up inside the plastic, and chill for an hour at least. (A good test of the mixing process: once wrapped, you can still see little pieces of butter here and there—which means your crust should turn out to be flaky.)

Butter the tart pan.

Preheat the oven to 400 degrees Fahrenheit.

Once chilled, roll out the dough until it is 1 inch wider than the tart pan, including the rim. Lift up the dough by wrapping it over the rolling pin, and place it in the tart pan. Cut off the edge smoothly after you have measured for the 1-inch-extra width. Fold that extra piece of dough back into the tart pan and press it against the rim, but do not let any go down onto the bottom of the pan.

Cover the dough with aluminum foil, and add pastry

weights (aluminum or real beans). Bake about 15 minutes or until the crust begins to brown. Remove from oven and remove the weights and aluminum wrap. Place the pan back in the oven for about 5 more minutes. (If there is a slight puff to the bottom, it should disappear as the dough cools.) It is now ready for filling, or wrap it up for later use (up to 3 days).

Yield: 1 quiche shell

Lobster and Spinach Quiche

flan d'astice e spinaci

Place the olive oil in a small skillet or sauté pan. Add the sliced celery and scallion. Stir and cook until beginning to soften. Chop the spinach coarsely, add it to the pan, stir, cook a few seconds, and remove from heat.

Preheat the oven to 400 degrees Fahrenheit.

Spread the lobster bits over the quiche shell. Sprinkle with half the cheese. Remove the spinach-celery mixture from the pan with a slotted spoon and press with a second spoon to allow the cooking liquids to fall back in the pan. Spread the vegetables over the lobster and cheese.

Beat the eggs, cream, and remaining cheese together well. Add the salt and pepper and pour over the vegetables. Bake for 20 minutes or until lightly toasted, and the

2 tablespoons olive oil, approximately
3 celery ribs (about 6 ounces), trimmed and sliced thin
1 scallion, white part only, sliced thin
3½ ounces fresh spinach leaves, blanched and squeezed dry
1 cup bite-size cooked lobster, approximately 3½ to 3¾ ounces
1 quiche shell (page 309), baked
3 ounces Muenster, Emmenthal, or Parmesan cheese, grated
3 eggs
½ cup light cream
Pinch of salt
Freshly ground white pepper to taste

egg-cream cheese mixture has become like a cooked custard. Serve at once or let cool and reheat for serving later if necessary.

Yield: 4 to 6 portions

Smoked Salmon Quiche

flan di salmone affumicato

2 tablespoons olive oil

6 ounces (3 to 4 stalks) white part of leeks, washed and chopped

3½ ounces fresh spinach, blanched and squeezed dry

3½ ounces smoked salmon in thin slices

1 quiche shell (page 309), baked

3 ounces fresh mozzarella or Emmenthal, shredded

3 eggs

½ cup milk or light cream

Salt and freshly ground white pepper

Preheat the oven to 400 degrees Fahrenheit.

Place the olive oil in a sauté pan; add the chopped leeks and sauté until limp. Chop the blanched spinach coarsely and add it to the pan. Stir briefly and remove from heat.

Place the slices of smoked salmon (with the exception of 1 slice) on the bottom of the baked quiche dough. Sprinkle with half the cheese. Remove the vegetables from their pan with a slotted spoon, and press down on the vegetables with a second spoon, letting the juices fall back into the pan.

Spread the spinach and leeks over the cheese. Beat the eggs with the milk or cream, and add the remaining cheese and the salt and pepper. Pour over the now-layered quiche. Cut the last slice of smoked salmon in thin strips and sprinkle them around, poking them slightly under the egg mixture.

Bake for 20 minutes or until the eggs are firm and the dough has taken on a final really toasted look.

Yield: 4 to 6 portions

Bay Scallop Quiche

flan di capesante

Preheat the oven to 400 degrees Fahrenheit.

Roll out the dough on a floured surface until it is about 1 inch larger than a 10-inch tart pan. Place the dough on the pan. Fold back the overhanging dough and pinch it into the border to double its thickness. Spread the scallops on the dough, and sprinkle with the cheese.

Beat the eggs and mix with the milk or cream. Add the salt and pepper and pour over the scallops and cheese.

Bake for 35 to 45 minutes or until the dough is crisp and the filling is puffed and cooked through.

Yield: 6 portions

1 recipe Quiche Dough (page 309)
½ pound bay scallops, patted dry
   and dusted with flour
¼ pound grated Parmesan cheese
3 eggs
2 cups milk or light cream
1 teaspoon salt
⅛ teaspoon cayenne pepper

Pizza Dough

pasta per pizza

6 cups unbleached all-purpose flour,
    plus additional for dusting
    counter and hands
2 packets (2 tablespoons) "rapid
    rise" yeast
1 teaspoon sugar
2 cups warm water (120–130
    degrees for "rapid rise")
2 tablespoons olive oil
1 teaspoon salt

This recipe makes four 10-inch pizzas, but there is no telling how appetites respond or demand. The dough itself can also be used to make two baguettes, or six to 8 pizzette, or two dozen plump, old-fashioned breadsticks. It goes together in about 10 minutes, rises to almost triple its size in an hour, may be frozen, and may be kept in the refrigerator for up to three days.

Put the flour, yeast, and sugar in the bowl of a food processor with its steel blade in place and process on/off to mix.

With the processor on, pour in the water in a steady stream. Keep on processing until dough forms a ball and clumps together at one end of the blade. Turn the motor off, and remove the dough to a floured flat surface. The dough is now rather moist and sticky.

With floured hands, knead rapidly for 5 to 7 minutes or until the dough is elastic, soft, and no longer sticks to your hands. Let rest for about 5 minutes.

Put the olive oil in a big (4-quart) bowl. Put the ball of dough in the bowl and twirl it around to coat both bowl and dough with oil. Cover the bowl with a strip of plastic, leaving an opening on each side of the strip, or, if using an even larger bowl, you may put a clean, dampened dish towel across the top, and put the bowl in a warm place for about 45 minutes or until almost tripled in size.

Remove the towel and turn out the dough onto a floured surface. Flour your hands, punch the dough down, and then flatten it into a fat oval. Sprinkle each side of the oval with the salt and then knead it in briefly.

Divide the dough into four even pieces and roll each piece into a flat disk about 10 inches in diameter. If not baking right away, wrap each pizza in plastic and place in the refrigerator.

If you wish to freeze any of the pizzas, place them individually on a flat surface in the freezer. Pizza dough freezes or thaws in about 15 minutes.

Preheat the oven to 450 degrees Fahrenheit. Place the pizza rounds on heavy metal cookie sheets or pizza tiles. Press the rims of the pizzas up a bit to make a small border. Press your fingers down here and there on the flat of the dough to make a series of small dimples. Let the pizzas sit while the oven heats and you start assembling the toppings.

Yield: 4 10-inch pizzas, ready to be topped

Baby Clam Pizza

pizza alle vongole

1 recipe Pizza Dough (page 314)

2 tablespoons olive oil, approximately

3 to 4 plum tomatoes, peeled and seeded, or 1 cup Basic Tomato Sauce (page 43)

½ dozen black olives, pitted and broken into pieces

4 rounded tablespoons (approximately 2 ounces) grated mozzarella

2 teaspoons (approximately 6 sprigs) chopped fresh flat-leaf parsley

⅛ teaspoon dried oregano

2 anchovy fillets, cut into small bits

Freshly ground white pepper

3 ounces canned baby clams, drained well*

2 tablespoons (approximately ½ ounce) chopped onion

This recipe makes enough topping for one 10-inch pizza. It is easily multiplied for more.

Preheat the oven to 450 degrees Fahrenheit.

When the Pizza Dough has been shaped, paint it with 1 tablespoon of the olive oil, reserving what is left for the final touch.

Break the tomatoes into small pieces and place them over the oiled pizza, or use the tomato sauce. Add the olives, half the cheese, half the parsley, the oregano, and the anchovy bits.

Bake for 10 minutes. Remove the pizza momentarily and pepper it lightly.

Mix the drained clams with onion and the last of the parsley. Sprinkle the mix over the pizza and finish with the remaining cheese. Dribble the last of the olive oil over all, brushing the rim lightly again.

Bake another 5 minutes or until the cheese has melted and the clams are hot.

Yield: 1 pizza

*NOTE: The 10-ounce can of whole baby clams yields 6 ounces of clams (enough for 2 pizzas) and 4 ounces clam juice.

Shrimp Pizza

pizza ai gamberetti

Preheat the oven to 450 degrees Fahrenheit.

Paint the shaped dough with 1 tablespoon of the oil. Break the tomatoes into small pieces and distribute them evenly or place spoonfuls of tomato sauce over the pizza. Add the basil and half the mozzarella.

Bake for 10 minutes.

Bring the water to a boil, add the salt, cider vinegar and frozen shrimp. Leave over heat until the water comes back to a boil and the shrimp are coral colored (about 1 minute). Drain and pat dry. If using the canned baby shrimp, drain well.

Remove the pizza from the oven, sprinkle with the shrimp, the last of the cheese, the capers, and the pepper. Dribble the last of the olive oil over the shrimp, using a bit to paint the rim. Bake for 5 more minutes and serve.

Yield: 1 pizza

*NOTE: Canned whole baby shrimp usually come in a 6-ounce size with a yield of 5 ounces of shrimp, enough for two pizzas.

1 recipe Pizza Dough (page 314)

2 tablespoons olive oil

3 or 4 canned plum tomatoes, peeled and seeded, or 1 cup Basic Tomato Sauce (page 43)

¼ teaspoon dried basil or 3 leaves fresh, chopped (if using canned plum tomatoes)

4 rounded tablespoons grated mozzarella

3 cups water

1 teaspoon salt

1 tablespoon cider vinegar

2 ounces small, peeled, frozen shrimp, or canned whole baby shrimp*

½ dozen fat capers or 1 dozen small ones, drained

Freshly ground white pepper

Tuna Pizza

pizza al tonno

1 recipe Pizza Dough (page 314)
3½ ounces olive oil–packed light
   tuna, olive oil reserved
3 or 4 plum tomatoes, peeled and
   seeded, or 1 cup Basic Tomato
   Sauce (page 43)
4 tablespoons (approximately 2
   ounces) grated mozzarella
1 dozen anchovy-stuffed green olives
Freshly ground white pepper to taste

In our trio of toppings, this is the easiest of all and, like the others, doubles or quadruples easily.

Preheat the oven to 450 degrees Fahrenheit.

Paint the Pizza Dough with 1 tablespoon of the reserved tuna oil. Spread with the tomatoes or tomato sauce. Sprinkle with half the cheese.

Bake for 10 minutes. Remove from the oven; spread with tuna and the last of the cheese. Cut the stuffed olives in half and place them here and there around the pizza. Dribble with one more tablespoon of the reserved oil. Add a bit of freshly ground pepper.

Bake 5 minutes more and serve.

Yield: 1 pizza

Index